ROUTLEDGE LIBRARY EDITIONS: SOCRATES

Volume 3

SOCRATES, THE MAN AND HIS MISSION

SOCRATES, THE MAN AND HIS MISSION

R. NICOL CROSS

LONDON AND NEW YORK

First published in 1914 by Methuen & Co. Ltd.

This edition first published in 2019
by Routledge
2 Park Square, Milton Park, Abingdon, Oxon OX14 4RN

and by Routledge
711 Third Avenue, New York, NY 10017

Routledge is an imprint of the Taylor & Francis Group, an informa business

All rights reserved. No part of this book may be reprinted or reproduced or utilised in any form or by any electronic, mechanical, or other means, now known or hereafter invented, including photocopying and recording, or in any information storage or retrieval system, without permission in writing from the publishers.

Trademark notice: Product or corporate names may be trademarks or registered trademarks, and are used only for identification and explanation without intent to infringe.

British Library Cataloguing in Publication Data
A catalogue record for this book is available from the British Library

ISBN: 978-1-138-61842-8 (Set)
ISBN: 978-0-429-45011-2 (Set) (ebk)
ISBN: 978-1-138-62394-1 (Volume 3) (hbk)
ISBN: 978-1-138-62395-8 (Volume 3) (pbk)
ISBN: 978-0-429-46106-4 (Volume 3) (ebk)

Publisher's Note
The publisher has gone to great lengths to ensure the quality of this reprint but points out that some imperfections in the original copies may be apparent.

Disclaimer
The publisher has made every effort to trace copyright holders and would welcome correspondence from those they have been unable to trace.

SOCRATES
THE MAN AND HIS MISSION

BY

R. NICOL CROSS, M.A.

METHUEN & CO. LTD.
36 ESSEX STREET W.C.
LONDON

First Published in 1914

TO

MY MOTHER

PREFACE

THE present study of Socrates and his mission has been done in the leisure gathered from other avocations, and was undertaken as the result of a profound personal reverence for Athens' saint and sage. It records the impression made on the writer by the ancient authorities. It has not been written for experts and scholars, but in order to tempt the average Englishman of culture to hold company for a little while with one of earth's most elect spirits and leaders. Accordingly discussion of disputed matters has been reduced to a minimum, though it could not be quite eliminated. The class of readers for whom the book is intended will also account for the introduction of material connected with life and ideas contemporary with Socrates, superfluous for the Greek student, but, one hopes, not uninteresting to the general reader, nor without relevance and use in giving him the needed background of light and shade in order to a just appreciation of the man's character and work. I only hope it will be the means of sending some to more authoritative and better sources, for to know Socrates is to love him and to reverence human nature. I have been helped by the various modern authorities to whom references are given, and have to thank Professors Phillimore and Latta of Glasgow University for initial guidance to the literature, and also Professor Taylor of St. Andrews for discussing one or two points with me. I am also obliged to Messrs. Macmillan & Co., and to the Clarendon Press, Oxford, for permission to quote from Dakyns' transation of Xenophon, and Jowett's translation of Plato, respectively.

R. N. C.

CONTENTS

CHAP.		PAGE
I. INTRODUCTORY	. . . . .	1
II. BOYHOOD AND EDUCATION, YOUTH	. .	5
(a) THE AUTHORITIES	. . .	5
(b) PARENTAGE AND HOME	. . .	9
(c) SCHOOL LIFE	. . . .	14
(d) ADVANCED EDUCATION	. . .	17
III. THE MAN	. . . . . .	36
(a) HIS APPEARANCE	. . . .	36
(b) HIS CHARACTER	. . . .	41
(c) SOCRATES AND ASCETICISM	. .	49
IV. DOMESTIC LIFE	. . . . .	59
(a) THE ATHENIAN HOME AND LIVING: HIS POVERTY	. . . . .	59
(b) THE ATHENIAN WIFE: XANTHIPPE	.	69
(c) ATHENIAN MARRIAGE: XANTHIPPE	.	71
(d) POSITION OF WOMAN: XANTHIPPE	.	73
(e) HIS VIEW OF THE FAMILY	. .	80
V. PUBLIC LIFE	. . . . . .	82
(a) SOCRATES AS FRIEND	. . .	82
(b) SOCRATES AS CITIZEN	. . .	102
(c) HIS MISSION	. . . .	110
VI. HIS TEACHING: ON WORK	. . .	142
VII. ,, ,, TREATMENT OF ENEMIES	.	150
VIII. ,, ,, THE STATE AND THE INDIVIDUAL	. . . . .	162

CHAP.		PAGE
IX. HIS TEACHING: HIS ETHICS		173
(a) HIS METHOD		173
(b) KNOWLEDGE AND VIRTUE		179
(c) THE GOOD		194
X. HIS RELIGION		208
(a) THE WORLD AND MIND		208
(b) GOD AND GODS		213
(c) SOCRATES ON PIETY		231
(d) SOCRATES ON SACRIFICE		234
(e) SOCRATES ON PRAYER		238
(f) THE DIVINE VOICE		243
(g) THE SOUL AND THE HEREAFTER		266
XI. THE "CLOUDS" OF ARISTOPHANES		272
XII. THE TRIAL: ITS CAUSES		289
XIII. THE TRIAL		298
XIV. (a) THE LAST SCENES		319
(b) TRIBUTES TO SOCRATES		333
INDEX		339

SOCRATES
THE MAN AND HIS MISSION

SOCRATES, THE MAN AND HIS MISSION

CHAPTER I

INTRODUCTORY

"He that meditateth in the law of the Most High will seek out the wisdom of all the ancients."—The Book of Ecclesiasticus.

"UNIVERSAL History," said Thomas Carlyle, "the history of what man has accomplished in this world, is at bottom the History of the Great Men who have worked here." And Goethe has written that what is called the spirit of the age is the spirit of the man in whom the age is mirrored. Socrates was one of those historic personalities who reflect and summarise an epoch. He gathered into his own experience the profoundest movements of the mind of Greece in his time, a time when authority in religion, morality, and society had broken down or was breaking down, and thought wandered between two worlds, the dying world of tradition and convention and the world that now travailed to be born, the world of reason and freedom. It was a transition period in the history of Greek civilisation and therefore of world-civilisation, and Socrates looms out of it the figure of one who in the midst of the flux of nationalism in thought, sentiment, and outlook stood steady and secure, building a bridge between the old and the new, between that which had been and that which was to be. He is of those few select spirits who have drawn and fascinated men with the spell of masters. Schools rose to carry on his work, to own him master, to propagate his fertile impulse, but they had the usual defect of incapacity to develop the spirit that gave them birth, either wholly, justly, or symmetrically. It is the fate of schools to be confined to an aspect.

Socrates, however, not only made disciples and lovers among his contemporaries, but he has made pupils and lovers ever since. He was an inspiring personality as well as a penetrating thinker, and his character has, by its strong, simple, manly charm, won the reverence and affection of those of other climes and faiths who have come to know him. Erasmus, the great humanist and reformer, the flower of Christian scholarship in the sixteenth century, one not apt to fall into romantic admirations, gave him in his own heart a place among the saints of religion: " Sancte Socrates, ora pro nobis."

It is the combination of a masculine Greek sainthood, in which the merely low and selfish were completely submerged, with extraordinary intellectual power, which commands our enthusiastic regard and puts Socrates among those who, by reason of their spiritual magnitude, should be familiar to all who seek to take a great view of man and of life, companions of all who desire to use life nobly and well. He overlooks the horizons that bound the world of common men, and speaks to the mind and heart of all ages.

The last scenes of all in his life sets the seal to that quality in his character which moves the human soul everywhere and attests an irrefragable place among the elect of the earth.

It was 399 B.C., on a day of late May or of June. Just as the sun was near its setting over the modest

INTRODUCTORY

houses and stately temples of the wonderful little city of Athens, and the long shadows were stretching across the ground, you might have seen a group of men in one of the rooms of an Athenian gaol. They were looking sad, and could with difficulty keep the tears from welling up in their eyes, as they looked now and then into the face of one old rugged-looking fellow, who moved about with good cheer on his countenance and a genial playfulness on his lips. Never before had that rough and homely face, on which rested the peaceful afterglow of the light of high-thinking, seemed to them to reveal so much of mingled dignity and pathos,—never before had the sense of how poor and empty life would be to them without his great manly words, searching questions, and cheering company been so strong; they were heavy at heart, for Socrates was about to die at the hands of the people for whose good he had always sought to live.

Within the cool shadow of the prison walls their movements and their words were muffled in the quiet which wraps all deep sorrow, and which was hardly broken when an official entered and stood by Socrates to tell him that now his hour had arrived and he must go out to meet death. Even the hardened official could not go about his duty in the usual way; his voice faltered as he spoke to the condemned man: " Socrates, I have known you all the time as the noblest and gentlest and best of all who have ever come here. I know you do not blame me, you have no hard feeling against me. I only do what I must. Try to bear your lot as easily as you can "—and the tears burst into his eyes as he turned and went away. Socrates looked up and said, " Good-bye, we shall bear it."

It was the recompense of a true and good life, thus at the end to have about him the friends for whom he had made life a thing grand enough to be worth living, thus to witness the reverence and affection even of the man who was to carry out upon him the stern sentence of death. Socrates' career had been a triumph of character all the way through; it was a triumph of character at the end.

But who was this man and what had he done, that he should be so hated and so loved at the same time? How could he be worthy of all honour in the opinion of some, and of death in that of others?

It is the purpose of this book to set forth his character, aims, and work in such a way as to bring out for the ordinary modern reader something of that grandeur of Socrates as a man and a thinker which has made him one of the most haunting and influential figures of history.

CHAPTER II

BOYHOOD AND EDUCATION

"Desired to gain one prize
In place of many,—the secret of the world,
Of man, and man's true purpose, path, and fate."
—BROWNING'S "Paracelsus."

(a) THE AUTHORITIES

IT may seem strange that we know so little about the early years of the world's greatest men. Moses, Buddha, Jesus, they have introduced fresh epochs in the life and thought of peoples, but we know practically nothing of their boyhood and youth. In the case of the Founder of Christianity a few stories of a mythical kind, the result not of contemporary observation but of pious imagination, which works in the haze of subsequent glory, have to suffice.[1]

Such knowledge of the life as we have is derived from the Gospels of the New Testament, the earliest of which, viz. Mark, dates from a period at least three decades after Christ's death, and gives no information about him prior to his public ministry. Matthew and Luke, which were written any time between 70 or 80 A.D. and the close of the first century,[2] though incorporating earlier material, do give stories about his miraculous birth and his infancy; these, however, do not represent duly ascertained facts; they rather

[1] Cp. Bousset's "Jesus" in "Die Religion des Neuen Testaments."
[2] See, *e.g.*, Jülicher's Introduction to New Testament, pp. 308, 324, 337.

elucidate the beliefs which had grown up in the Christian Church subsequent to his death ?[1]

As Professor Bousset puts it : " It is very little that we know of Jesus. . . . The beginnings lie in darkness. . . . Everywhere almost we are confined to uncertainties and hypotheses. We shall do well to give up all attempt at a ' Life ' or ' History ' of Jesus."[2]

These statements apply in a measure to Socrates, the fact being that biography in the sense in which we know it is a form of literature which unfortunately did not arise in Greece till the Christian era, and to this comparatively late date belong the so-called " Lives of Homer," and, of course, such works as the Lives by Plutarch (50–120 A.D.) and those of Diogenes Laertius (about 200–250 A.D.).

Not only is comparatively little recorded, and that referring chiefly to the later part of Socrates' career, but in the case of one of our two chief authorities, Xenophon (about 440 or 431–354 B.C.), we have to remember that the " Reminiscences " were very probably not written in their present form till after 387 B.C.,[3] an interval which permits a considerable number of slips and modifications in the details of any reminiscences of a man's words, though not sufficient to efface the impression of the spirit and purport of his habitual character and conversations.[4]

Those were not the days when, through the plenti-

---

[1] See J. Estlin Carpenter, First Three Gospels, ch. iii.

[2] Bousset, *op. cit.*, p. 10. Cp. Burkitt, Gospel History and Transmission, p. 20.

[3] Dakyns' Xenophon, Vol. I. p. cxxx. Cp. Vol. III. p. xl. See Discussion in Joël's " Sokrates," I. Einleitung, pp. 21–24.

[4] " Socrates is seen through a vista of years. The young man's memoranda, however faithfully preserved, represent also the mature reflections of one who has himself gone through many experiences, since, as a youth, he sat in some saddler's shop and imbibed words of wisdom,"—Dakyns, *op. cit.*, p. xl.

fulness of good paper and especially through the art of printing, it was easy to give fixed and unvarying form to floating recollections and stories about an impressive personality. Notebooks, such as they were, must have been awkward, clumsy furniture. The material used might be papyrus roll, made of the pith of papyrus reed cut in long vertical strips, which were laid side by side in parallels and transversely, pressed into a flat surface, then dried in the sun so as to make long rolls. The ink was got either from cuttle-fish or from oak-galls, the pen being either reed or bird quill. From as early as the fifth century in Greece tablets of wood were also commonly used. They were coated over with a smooth surface of wax, a metal stylus being used for writing on them. The ends of the tablets might be joined together by rings, thus forming a rude, cumbersome sort of book.[1] Everything then had to be written or imprinted by hand on such tablets, and it is therefore easy to understand why so few authorities for the life and teaching of Socrates have come down to us. We have to rely on the Socratic writings of Xenophon, which pass "from matter-of-fact, shorthand-note narrative at one point to pure artistic dramatisation at another,"[2] and on the Dialogues of Plato, some of which antedate Xenophon's recollections, but which make no profession of being more than dramatic portraiture of Socrates, and the historical value of which accordingly varies considerably, and is at the present day a subject of renewed debate. In addition to these two authorities, we have a few notices by Aristotle on the philosophy of Socrates. Aristotle, whether dependent on Plato or not for his statements, as Professors Döring and A. E. Taylor have argued, was at any rate much nearer

[1] On all this see Whibley, Companion to Greek Studies: or Schools of Hellas, p. 85 ff., by Freeman.
[2] Dakyns, *op. cit.*, III. xli.

the available sources than we are, besides being a systematic historian of previous Greek philosophy, and a highly-trained investigator and original thinker. So far as his evidence goes, therefore, it is of paramount value.

It is not our purpose to place before readers of this book the variations of view held by modern writers as to the relative value of these three chief sources, to which should be added a fourth, of which Professor Taylor has made great use and whose significance he has, we venture to think, very much overrated—that is, the Comedy of Aristophanes called " The Clouds," first produced at Athens in the year 424 B.C., but subjected to revision later. The divergence which exists on the part of scholars as to the historical worth of the portraiture of each of these ancient sources can hardly be exaggerated, and the student has to fall back largely on his own judgment in using the extant material. Any later authorities, such as Diogenes Laertius, have no independent value, and must be used only on insignificant points. At present the state of discussion is more confused than ever, and, to find a parallel, we should have to go to the Higher Criticism of the Gospels of the New Testament. Nevertheless, certain broad and prominent features emerge both in the character and teaching of the master, which stand out bold and secure amid the troubled waves and conflicting currents of modern opinion. And certain parts of his life are not exposed to any serious doubt, because they are attested by Xenophon and Plato alike.

From this brief reference to the chief authorities we now turn to the life itself.

(b) Parentage and Home

Socrates was born about 470 B.C.[1] in the parish of Alopece,[2] close to Athens. His father was Sophroniscus,[3] a worker in stone,[4] and a man highly spoken of. Lysimaches, in Plato's "Laches," refers to him as one of the best of men,[5] and one whose friendship he had enjoyed till death without a break or a difference.[6] Very little is known of his mother. Her name was Phænareté,[7] and according to her son's description in the Theætetus, she was a person of formidable appearance but of sterling quality. "Brave and burly,"[8] is the description her son gives of her, from which we should judge that Socrates rather took after his mother in the matter of his physical characteristics, while with regard to the moral he was perhaps a most happy blend of both parents, combining the geniality of his father with the honest naturalness of his mother. He tells us she was in the habit of acting as a midwife.[9]

The latter circumstance would seem to point to the conclusion that the home was a poor one. It should, however, be remembered that the domestic straits, which presumably accounted for Phænareté's practice of midwifery, may only have pressed upon the family at a fairly late period, as a result of the calamities following upon the Peloponnesian War, which broke out between Athens and Sparta in 431 B.C. Many

---

[1] At his trial in 399 B.C. he speaks of himself as over seventy (Plato, Apology, 17 d).
[2] Diogenes Laertius, ii. 5, § 18.
[3] 1st Alcibiades, 131 E; Laches, 180 D; Hellenica, i. 7, § 15.
[4] Diogenes Laertius, *loc. cit.*
[5] 181 A. [6] 180 E.
[7] Theætetus, 149 A; 1st Alcibiades, 131 E; Diogenes Laertius, ii. 5, § 18. [8] Theætetus, *loc. cit.*
[9] Theætetus, *loc. cit.* Cp. Diogenes Laertius, *loc. cit.*

Athenians, but especially the country people living round about, lost their property and were reduced to destitution[1] or poverty by the calamities of that notorious war, which was destined to be the beginning of the end of the imperial greatness of the city of Athena. The policy of Pericles, the leading statesman, had been to withdraw the Attic population into Athens, leaving the land to be ravaged by the Peloponnesians, while he fortified the city and attacked the enemy on the sea.[2] The immediate consequences of this plan can, of course, be conceived. The country people and those Athenian citizens who had estates on the land became concentrated in Athens, with their wives, families, and furniture.[3] The ordinary resources of the city were not great or elastic enough to meet such an influx. Some found lodgings, others received the hospitality of friends, but the bulk of them had to be accommodated in the temples.[4] Altogether the situation was harrowing. The land of Attica was ravaged by the enemy,[5] prices in the city naturally rose high, while many had been deprived of their means of livelihood and ruined.[6] On the back of this plague broke out in the overcrowded city, and men gave themselves up to practise the philosophy of "Eat and drink, for to-morrow we die."[7] The terrible straits to which the common Greek population involved were reduced is described by the powerful pen of Aristophanes in his Comedy "The Acharnians" produced in 425 B.C.[8] The farcical character of the piece, designed

---

[1] Thucydides, ii. ch. 65.
[2] Thucydides, ii. ch. 13.
[3] Thucydides, ii. ch. 14.   [4] *Ibid.*, ch. 17.
[5] Thucydides, ii. ch. 47.
[6] Xenophon, Mem., ii. ch. 8, and Banquet, ch. 4.
[7] *Ibid.*, ch. 52, 53.
[8] See, *e.g.*, Rogers' edition of Acharnians, with English translation.

for pretty loud laughter, cannot suffice to drown the pathos of the bitter conditions it seeks to indicate.

May it not then have been that Sophroniscus's in any case modest competence foundered in the general debacle, and that Phænareté, with her strong practical sense and vigorous personality, came to the rescue by deciding to go out as a nurse? Suppose her to have married at eighteen, which is by no means early for a Greek girl,[1] and Socrates to have been born two years later, that would make Phænareté about sixty years of age in 430 B.C., when Socrates was just over forty. So that chronology does not necessarily exclude our hypothesis.

In any case it is not likely that Sophroniscus was, even previous to the Peloponnesian War, more fortunate than to belong to the class of honest respectable artisans (whose means were generally very limited) in ancient Greece, and whose wages, as well as their standards of living, in various ways, were much lower than in our modern civilisation.

Such then is the home, as regards wealth, in which we must conceive the future master to have been brought up. In default of all information, we may be permitted to picture him as a sturdy little fellow, full of fun and good spirits, playing, as the boys of Athens did, with hoop and top,[2] but also at times very serious, and prone to ask questions about things, which his mother could not answer to his satisfaction, and which at times perhaps rather annoyed her.[3] Again we

---

[1] Aristotle, De. Rep., vii. 16, p. 1335, thinks eighteen a good age for girls to marry. In Xenophon's Œconomicus the young wife is not yet fifteen years (Œc., ch. 7, § 4). Plato suggests twenty for girl's age (Republic, 460 E).

[2] Becker's Charicles, p. 223.

[3] In fact, judging by his mature life, he must have been one of those gifted infants of George MacDonald's enthusiastic imagination, of whom he says: " I believe that even the new-born infant

imagine him playing among the marble chips that fall from his father's chisel, and sitting looking up at him as he slowly shaped the rough block into some image. It would only be in accordance with the common practice, as described to us by Plato, that his father should instruct him in worthy principles of conduct, no doubt bidding him be diligent and some day he might rise to be a famous sculptor. His mother too would teach him the usual moral lessons and stories, and instruct him in the way that he should go. It is true he would miss the Shorter Catechism, but in other respects his moral and religious training would be as assiduously seen to as if he had been born among the " Auld Lichts " of Scotland. Plato in the " Protagoras " gives us a glimpse of parental responsibility at work in these matters. " As soon as ever the child can understand what is said to him, his nurse, his mother, his attendant, nay, his father himself, begin to vie in efforts for his improvement. Every word and act is an occasion for instruction by precept and example ; he is taught that so-and-so is just or unjust, fair or ugly, right or wrong. He must do this and not do that. If he is disobedient, like a piece of wood getting warped and crooked, then he is scolded and whipped."[1] The instrument of torture was usually a slipper or sandal.[2] It is rather a pity that the metaphor of " wood " should have got attached to children in the grown-up mind which has to deal with them. It shows an undue lack of respect, and may lead to a rather constant

is, in some of his moods, already grappling with the deepest metaphysical problems, in forms infinitely too rudimental for the understanding of the grown philosopher—as far in fact removed from his ken on the one side, that of intelligential beginning, the germinal subjective, as his abstrusest speculations are from the final solution of absolute entity on the other."—Robert Falconer, ch. 14.

[1] Protagoras, 325 c, d. Cp. Republic, 377 ff.
[2] Becker's Charicles, p. 224 (Eng. trans.).

bending of the twig so that the tree may be inclined like other trees. But at any rate there is no excuse for thinking that little Greek children were left entirely to the devices of the Evil One who haunted the outer darkness of an immoral Paganism, or that they were brought up without God or religious hope in the world.

Socrates would be taught according to the lights then available, that the gods must be revered and their good-will secured; that they would brook no human insolence, no transgression of the law of respect and modesty; that indeed the mighty they cast down, and exalted them of reverent mien.[1]

Regularly he would see the family worship, in which his father was priest; worship the same in spirit, though with different beliefs and rites, as that described so simply and finely by Burns in his " Cottar's Saturday Night." The Athenians were, as a rule, great sticklers for the pieties; they were even superstitiously afraid of their gods, those higher powers on whose knees lay the disposal of the human lot, and on whose good graces depended the general security and prosperity of national and individual life. He would be brought up in the nurture and admonition of Homer and Hesiod, with their tales of gods and heroes. There was some scepticism among a few thinkers in the age, but it was not an age of universal or of popular scepticism that built the temples of the Acropolis.

> " Not from a low or shallow thought
> His awful Jove young Phidias wrought."

Even interpreted as a means of humouring the people, rather than of honouring the traditional gods, on the

[1] The pious doctrine of the prosperity of the good and adversity of the evil did not stand the test of experience in Greece any more than in Israel. See, *e.g.*, Aristophanes, Plutus, 26 ff.

part of Pericles and his circle, they would still stand as a monument of current popular sentiment in the matter of religion and religious rites. Religion entered closely and at all points [1] into the private and public life of the Greeks so that amid the seen and temporal they were ever being reminded of the unseen and eternal. It invested all life with a higher meaning and deeper dignity. All this was bound to have its influence on the mind of the young Socrates, and surely through the profound piety of the man we may rightly trace some effect of the training of the child.

(c) School Life

Of the school life of Socrates we only know what is to be inferred from the course of education general among Athenian boys. The customary age for beginning school was about six. The schools were not provided by the city authority, but were private institutions,[2] the profession, as far as elementary education is concerned, being but poorly esteemed and as poorly paid.[3] It is also noteworthy that such educational provision existed for boys alone. We nowhere read of institutions for girls,[4] though Plato later desiderated their establishment,[5] so that women could share the interests of men. The home-training was, however, generally regarded as enough to equip girls for all the duties they would be expected or allowed to undertake in after-life. The elementary school education was compulsory for boys.[6]

[1] Fustel De Coulanges, La Cité antique, chs. iv. and vi.
[2] Schools of Hellas, p. 61. Cp. Becker, *op. cit.*, p. 228.
[3] Plato later advocated inspectors and a Minister of Education (Laws, vi. 755).
[4] Becker, *op. cit.*, p. 236. [5] Laws, vi. 764; vii. 805.
[6] Cp. Plato, Laws, vii. 804. Fustel de Coulanges, La Cité antique, p. 267.

BOYHOOD AND EDUCATION

Socrates then would be dragged out of bed before sunrise, for, by a law of Solon, the schools were open by dawn,[1] then he would get the sleep washed from his eyes, and partake of a slight vegetarian breakfast, very light, after which he must trot off to where the young and sleepy idea would be taught to shoot. Scions of richer sires were accompanied by a "pedagogue," one of the household slaves, but in all probability comparative poverty would give little Socrates the privilege of trotting along by the side of his father,[2] who would carry the necessary paraphernalia, the wax tablet and stylus, which took the place of the modern slate and pencil, and also the lead ruler and the sponge for erasing the impressions on the wax, the lyre, etc.[3]

We do not know what sort of fees would have to be paid, but in the less well-equipped schools, at any rate, they must have been extremely low, and occasionally very poor boys might pay their way by doing menial duties like preparing the ink, washing the benches,[4] and sweeping the rooms.[5] The standard of life generally was, of course, far lower and the cost of living cheaper than in our modern civilisation.[6]

At school Socrates would spend all the day till sundown, with a break for midday meal; he would have no weekly holiday on Sundays, its place, however, being taken by the many religious festivals in the Athenian calendar. The subjects of elementary instruction which occupied the years from six to fourteen were (a) reading, writing, arithmetic, with the addition, sometimes, of

[1] Cp. Thucydides, vii. 29. Becker, *op. cit.*, p. 231.
[2] See, for such a case, Demosthenes, De Corona, p. 313.
[3] Cp. Lucian (A.D. 125–180, app.), Loves, 44, on the schoolboy.
[4] For equipment of the schools in the way of furniture, maps, etc., see Freeman, Schools of Hellas, p. 84.
[5] As Æschines did (Demosthenes, De Corona, p. 313).
[6] See, *e.g.*, Zimmern, Greek Commonwealth, *ad loc.*

drawing and painting. (b) Learning to play the lyre and sing to it. (c) Gymnastic exercises.

The literature read comprised extracts from the great Homer and Hesiod, who together constituted the Greek Bible. The greatest importance attached to this instruction, which was designed not only to educate the mind but to awaken and form the soul, and educe all the higher loyalties of life. Indeed, so clearly was the importance of the moral aspect of education recognised that the government appointed inspectors to supervise this particular branch, and the recognition of its supreme place in the hierarchy of pedagogic ends emerges beyond all doubt in the work of the great philosophers and educationalists, Plato and Aristotle.[1] Every branch was considered by them in relation to its effect upon the soul and character of the pupils, the aim of all education being to fit its recipient for the highest, fullest exercise of all the faculties in a life which is good.

Literature and music was varied by physical exercises and games, and Socrates no doubt learned like the rest of boys to play " with hoops and tops, stones and dice."[2] The "Lysis" of Plato gives us a pleasing little glimpse into school life as it was lived at Athens, and we notice that religious rites were not neglected. The master was a friend of Socrates, and when the latter visited the school he found that " the boys had just finished sacrifice and the offerings were nearly over, and they were all in their best playing knucklebones. Most of the games were outside in the courtyard, but some were in a corner of the vestibule playing at odd and even with knuckle-bones, which they took

---

[1] See, e.g., Plato, Republic, §§ 378 ff. Aristotle, Politics, bk. vii. 17 and bk. viii. 1–7. Burnet's Aristotle on Education, pp. 102 ff. Grote's Plato, iv. pp. 23–5. Nettleship Lectures on Plato's Republic, ch. v.   [2] Schools of Hellas, p. 83.

out of baskets, while others stood and watched." We are indebted to the august philosopher for these delightful *mises en scène,* which bring the past so near and make even grey philosophy so fresh and human. The type of boy that was turned out by these methods has been described by the inimitable pen of Aristophanes in "The Clouds,"[1] and hinted in fine touches of realism by Plato.[2] Grace of form and movement, modesty of mien, piety of soul, and reverence of disposition, were its chief and its normal results.

(d) Advanced Education

About fourteen years of age, what we should call the secondary curriculum was entered upon by boys whose circumstances were such that it could be afforded. It was carried on by a class of trained teachers known as Sophists, who were specialists in their own particular subjects, which included language, literature, history, laws of Athens, rhetoric, and various branches of science, the aim being to fit the youthful Athenians for the public life they would have to enter, and also to render them capable of a dignified and suitable use of their leisure, in the higher occupations of intellectual and political activity, which distinguish the true and liberal human life. The physical department of the earlier training was also pursued, for the freeman had not only to discharge political and judicial functions[3] as a citizen of his city, but also military functions as its guardian. The sound mind in the sound body was therefore a desideratum of life for every citizen. Theirs was the very ideal of education that Herbert Spencer has expounded for us.[4] Not only so, but the more

---

[1] Clouds, ll. 961 ff.   [2] Plato, Lysis, 207 a, b.
[3] See, *e.g.*, Fustel de Coulanges, La Cité antique, p. 267.
[4] Principles of Education, ch. i.

reflective minds at any rate recognised a close relationship between body and mind, so that their harmonious development was a condition of even distinctively mental excellence, a point in which they were ahead of our modern state schools.[1] The more is the pity. Ian Maclaren once said: "No one can estimate how much Germany has gained from Luther's genial and robust nature or Scotland lost through Calvin being a chronic invalid and Knox being a broken man." It is certain that if Carlyle had not had to "swallow whole hogsheads of castor oil," as he pathetically and hyperbolically put it, he would not have been quite so "ill to get on wi'," nor so pessimistic and bitter in his tone of thought. There would have been less Avernus and more azure in his philosophy. It is also certain that the abounding health which training developed out of the constitution of a horse in Socrates gave his "sainthood" that full, solid, red-blooded, and blue-eyed virtue it possessed and enjoyed to its own advantage.

The education in music was also continued, no small part of the reason being its effect upon moral character. Both Plato and Aristotle lay the greatest stress upon its value as an instrument for developing spirit, and accustoming the soul to a love of harmony and beauty, which would tend to subdue the passions to their proper place as the obedient ministers of the higher spiritual powers in man.[2] Indeed the whole artistic side of the curriculum is with a view to develop that delicate and just æsthetic taste which to a Greek was never separable from moral sensibility and right ethical judgment. It is to bring gracefulness into the whole character, to make "the eye keen for all defects, whether in the

---

[1] See, e.g., Plato's Republic, bk. iii. §§ 403 ff., but especially § 410.
[2] Plato's Republic, bk. iii. §§ 398 ff., especially § 401.

BOYHOOD AND EDUCATION

failures of art or the misgrowths of nature," so that a man "will gladly receive beautiful objects into his soul, feed upon them, and grow noble and good."[1] It did not fail of this in Socrates. In another respect it must have played its part in producing that profound patriotism which we shall see exemplified in the life of Socrates, for it concerned itself, in earlier and later stages, with the heroic literature of Greece which, amid much that was open to the grave censure of philosophers and sceptical poets, held up before its readers high examples of romantic and chivalrous sacrifice for one's country. It was a literature of heroes which fostered that national and civic piety which was part of the deepest religion of the members of Greek cities. Indeed, "the real religion of the fifth century," says Professor Gilbert Murray, " was a devotion to the city itself."[2]

Advanced education included rhetoric, ethics, and science, and Socrates by some means was able to obtain considerable expert instruction in these matters. How it was made possible to him is not a matter of certainty. We are told that he was taken from school and apprenticed to his father's occupation of sculpture.[3] Not only so, but he must have wrought at it for years, and acquired high skill, for what was said to be a piece of his work—Hermes and the Graces, robed—was to be found at the entrance to the Acropolis,[4] the highest eminence and the fortified centre of the city, as late as the time of Pausanias in the latter half of the second century A.D.[5]

---

[1] Plato, *loc. cit.*
[2] Four Stages of Greek Religion, p. 96; also p. 91.
[3] Diogenes, ii. 5, 19.
[4] Acropolis, art. "Athens," in Encyclopædia Britannica, or any Dictionary of Classical Antiquities, like Smith's.
[5] Pausanias, i. 22, 8 and ix. 35, 7. Diogenes Laertius, ii. ch. 5, § 19.

There is ample reason, then, to believe that when Socrates had to leave school, he determined that it should not be the end of his education. The fire that cannot be quenched was in his bones, the burning desire for knowledge, which time and again in history has turned the heart-beats of poor lads into the throb of an incarnate Fate, and propelled them on through every disadvantage and difficulty toward their goal. Knowledge is said to be the child of wonder, and Socrates had the capacity for wonder in a saving degree. The spark was in him that disturbs the clods. As he wrought the hard stubborn marble into shape, he was busy also trying to bring order out of chaos in his inner world, struggling to give form to the formless feelings and ideas and inklings which flitted about in his soul. As he thought about the universe it came to him as a superlative wonder, a riddle, a secret, the inscrutable Sphinx, fascinating and unescapable.

If you had seen this raw-boned, rough-featured lad you would not have been struck by his appearance, unless it were by the circumstance that he was uglier than usual. He came from the common people and he looked it, with ponderous skull, that might have been "a storehouse of lead," a nose that lacked any sense of dignity or eminence, eyes that seemed to turn away ashamed of it and to be conscious of trying to remedy the defect: altogether a country bumpkin look about him. But below that exterior was a mind and soul, like a royalty travelling incognito, and destined yet to prove itself one of the finest, biggest, and strongest in all Greece and all history. He was one of those who have to take their kingdom by force, and in whom the might is the basis of the right. Diogenes Laertius[1] relates, on the authority of Demetrius the Byzantine, that

---

[1] Diogenes Laertius, ii. 5, 20.

Crito took him from the workshop and had him educated, being charmed by his mental accomplishment, his " grace of soul." What ground in fact there was for this story we cannot say. It might be true, and it might be a myth spun out of the circumstance that in the latter part of Socrates' career Crito was ready to offer any help which might preserve the precious services of Socrates to the world. But there is no doubt at all about Socrates' youthful insatiable interest in science. He had a passion to know everything knowable. " When young I had a prodigious zeal for that branch of knowledge which is called Natural Philosophy." So Plato makes him say in the " Phædo."[1] His invincible enthusiasm for knowledge seems to have led him to make himself conversant with the previous speculations of the Greek philosophers, and, in time, to have won for him the acquaintance of the great contemporary teachers who were drawn to Athens as the metropolis of culture in Greece at that period. We have the statement of Plato that while Socrates was still very young he had listened to the great thinker, Parmenides, who was then a very old man.[2] In the dialogue " Parmenides " it is stated that at the time Parmenides must have been about sixty-five years of age at the outside, a figure of refined and gentlemanly bearing.[3] In his company was Zeno, then about forty, tall and elegant in build,[4] noted for the dialectical ability with which he defended the absolute monism of Parmenides, showing that on any pluralistic hypothesis motion was as paradoxical as on the Parmenidean principles.[5]

Socrates, on hearing of their arrival outside Athens,

---

[1] Phædo, § 96.
[2] Theætetus, 183 E ; Parmenides, 127 b ; cp. Sophistes, 217 d.
[3] For Parmenides' philosophy, see Burnet, pp. 183 ff.
[4] Plato's Parmenides, § 127.
[5] Burnet, *op. cit.*, p. 331 ; Plutarch, Life of Pericles, ch. iv.

along with a great many others sets off with eagerness to listen to Zeno's discourses. It is emphasized that he was very young at this time, when already speculation had won him as an ardent disciple. Xenophon also alludes to this search for knowledge, which was a permanent characteristic of Socrates.[1] "I go about hunting up, along with my friends, all the treasures that the ancient sages have left in writing in their books, and if I find anything good, I profit by it."[2] "Of all the men I have ever known," says Xenophon,[3] speaking of a later period of the master's life, "he was the most anxious to ascertain in what any of those about him was really versed." And the youth was father of the man. He ultimately attained what in those days would be equivalent to what is now called encyclopædic knowledge. Xenophon does not omit to mention that when Socrates later turned from natural science as his central interest it was not because he was ignorant of its higher developments. Alike of geometry[4] and astronomy,[5] he had acquired knowledge, and had heard lectures in them.[6]

Diogenes Laertius[7] calls Archelaos, the pupil of Anaxagoras of Clazomenæ, his teacher, and, on the authority of Ion of Chios, relates that he once was away from Athens in company with Archelaos. He also became familiar with the physical speculations[8] of Anaxagoras by his own reading.[9]

He further enjoyed the friendship of Damon, who, according to Plutarch, while ostensibly professing to be only a teacher of music, was really a very accom-

---

[1] Cp. Laches, 180 C.
[2] Quoted Fouillée, La Philosophie de Socrate, i. p. 6.
[3] Mem., iv. 7.   [4] Mem., iv. 7, 3.   [5] Mem., iv. 7, 5.
[6] Mem., ii. 4, 16.   [7] Diogenes, ii. 5, 23.
[8] For these, see Burnet, *op. cit.*, ch. vi.
[9] Plato, Phædo, 97 C. Xen., Mem., iv. 7, 6.

plished and cultured man,[1] from whom Pericles received tuition[2] in the arts of the politician,[3] and who was banished as a Sophist by the Athenians. It was quite a common thing for these "professors" to disguise in this way the real nature of their teaching, owing to the odium it roused among the public.[4]

Damon professed to teach music, and Socrates discussed its principles with him; but the master whom he mentions as giving him musical lessons on the lyre till well on in life is Connus, the son of Metrobius.[5] The boys who also took lessons from Connus, Socrates good-humouredly tells us, used to laugh at himself and call their master the old man's teacher.[6]

As showing how Socrates from humble beginnings had penetrated to the highest circles of society in Athens, we have his allusion—about which plays the humour that was a constant feature of his conversation as Plato delineates it—the allusion which he makes to Aspasia as his instructor in rhetoric.[7] Aspasia was the "new-woman" who became the companion and all but wife of Pericles, the greatest statesman and politician of the age, and who by reason of her brilliant gifts and conversation, formed the centre and cynosure of the coterie of intellectuals and heretics who adorned the Periclean circle and added éclat to the salons of his paramour.

This phase of Socrates' career, the example it affords of how great gifts, and tireless industry in their cultivation, can overcome the obstacles of social position and comparative poverty, and give a man entrance to the highest aristocracies of life and literature, reminds

---

[1] Cp. Laches, 180 D.   [2] Menexenus, 235 E.
[3] Plutarch, Life of Pericles, ch. iv.
[4] Plato, Protagoras, § 316.
[5] Euthydemus, 272 C; Menexenus, 236 A.
[6] Euthydemus, 272 C.   [7] Menexenus, 236 A.

one of the similar elevation of Robert Burns from the plough-handle to the most highly cultured and literary circles of Edinburgh in its great days, though, of course, in Athens of the fifth century the social contrasts were not so marked, and even famous politicians lived in very humble state. Socrates and Burns, widely contrasted as they were in some features of character, seem to have had the same intellectual precocity, and, one might add, the same moral perspicacity, which made upon the most distinguished men who met them an impression of extraordinary native endowment and rare mental force.

Plato gives artistic expression to what must have been the general feeling created in those capable of intellectual and moral appreciation with regard to the destiny which Socrates' adroitness of ethical judgments and dexterity of logical analysis marked out for him. They were qualities which gave him that air of inevitability which is the evident claim of genius on the future. Protagoras, the greatest of contemporary humanists, says of the ardent young philosopher: "I for my part, Socrates, applaud your enthusiasm and resource in argument. I am not, on the whole, a bad man, and least of all am I given to jealousy, for I have said to many regarding you that of any I come across I admire you far and away above all, especially among those of your own age, and I say that I should not be surprised if you achieve a place among men renowned for wisdom."[1]

Prodicus of Ceos was another of the most noted of the travelling teachers of that time, called "Sophists," and Socrates had relations with him,[2] even attending a short course of his lectures, which cost a drachma, in default of being able to afford the larger 50-drachma

---

[1] Protagoras, 361 E.   [2] Meno, 96 d; Charmides, 163 d.

BOYHOOD AND EDUCATION

course, which, according to Prodicus, was a complete education in language and grammar.[1] Prodicus professed philology, the meaning of words, composition, and moral instruction, and the famous apologue, "The Choice of Heracles," often repeated by Socrates as a fine piece of moral allegory, was his work. One gathers from Plato that Socrates regarded him with considerable respect,[2] and, as has been suggested by one writer, Prodicus's work in the exact definition of words may have contributed something to Socrates' rage for the exact definition of ideas and ethical standards.

In Socrates, then, we have a youth impelled by an encyclopædic interest, and an unbounded curiosity, one who, by reason of his irrepressible zeal and conspicuous mental acumen, wins from poverty an access to the best sources of contemporary culture, in addition to plumbing the shoals and deeps of the thought of the past.

But it all fails to satisfy him. The philosophical or cosmological theories of the great pioneers in speculation are but husks to this youth's hunger for an intelligible explanation of the universe. Plato in the "Phædo" has put into Socrates' mouth a graphic confession of his state of mind during these *wanderjahre* of the soul, when it was achieving its struggling exodus from the bricks-without-straw materialisms of previous Greek thought to the promised land, flowing with peace and happiness, of his own spiritual philosophy, to him a land of freedom and expansion which offered fields to be explored and tracts to be subdued beyond the measure of one life.

"Listen, then, when I tell you, Cebes, that in my youth I walked in wonder [3]—the thrill for that wisdom

---

[1] Cratylus, 384 b.
[2] Protagoras, 341 A.
[3] Phædo, 96. For his sense of the mystery of common things, cp. Xen.; Banquet, ch. vii.; Dakyns, iii. 335, 336.

which they call the study of nature. Life's excelling glory seemed to me to be to know the causes of things —*rerum cognoscere causas*—to be in their secret, why they come to be and cease to be, why they are. Many a time and oft was I tossed hither and thither, now lifted up, now cast down, as I brooded on that question whether living things take form, from the hot and the cold, when touched by corruption; whether it is the blood by which we think, or air, or fire, or whether it is none of these, but the brain that is the cause of our faculties of perception, whether from these perceptions spring memory and opinion, and whether from these in the same way, when they settle, springs knowledge. Brooding on the problem of the decay of these faculties, too, and on the phenomena of heaven and earth with their vicissitudes, I at last came to despair of my capacity for such things; all was vanity and futility. The knowledge I had that seemed so clear to myself and to others became mere darkness to me as a result of this thinking; I was gradually losing what I thought I had known, on many subjects," and so on he goes, telling us how he broke into the world, and found it mystery and the dark.[1] The whole story is so fascinating, so modern, so real, of this youth away back in Athens looking for the first time at things with his own eyes and his own mind, instead of through the eyes and mind of others, looking like a child on a strange heaven and a strange earth, dark, mysterious, unfathomable, knowing one thing only—that he knows nothing! There he stands naked and alone, at the mouth of the cave of shadows.

It was his "Baphometic fire-baptism," the rite by which the gods confer selfhood and its privileges upon us, if we have been built in moulds worthy to receive them. It was the experience which plunges a man

[1] See Phædo, §§ 96, 97.

into unutterable solitude and voiceless wilderness, that he may learn to know himself and God. "I paused in my wild wanderings and sat me down to wait and consider; for it was as if the hour of change drew nigh. I seemed to surrender, to renounce utterly, and say: 'Fly, then, false shadows of Hope; I will chase you no more, I will believe you no more. And ye too, haggard spectres of Fear, I care not for you; ye too are all shadows and a lie. Let me rest here for I am way-weary and life-weary; I will rest here."[1]

Every thinker must go along his via dolorosa, and be content to drink his cup of *welt-schmerz,* without which there is no initiation into the great brotherhood of Thought: it is the lowest cash price of original greatness.

> "Mother of this unfathomable world!
> Favour my solemn song, for I have loved
> Thee ever, and thee only; I have watched
> Thy shadow, and the darkness of thy steps,
> And my heart ever gazes on the depth
> Of thy deep mysteries. I have made my bed
> In charnels and on coffins, where black death
> Keeps record of the trophies won from thee,
> Hoping to still these obstinate questionings
> Of thee and thine, by forcing some lone ghost,
> Thy messenger, to render up the tale
> Of what we are. In low and silent hours,
> When night makes a weird sound of its own stillness,
> Like an inspired and desperate alchymist
> Staking his very life on some dark hope."

Justice will not be done, nor due homage paid to Socrates and his achievements, until we vividly realise what his quest of truth must have cost him. We are apt to treat those men of olden time and other clime as a sort of lay figures, forgetting that they were real flesh and blood like ourselves, and subject to the same

---

[1] Sartor Resartus. ch. viii.

laws of inner experience. The night of the soul could be as dark for those bygone seekers of the day as for us moderns.

The subjects of Socrates' earlier absorption, we gather from the passage in the "Phædo" just quoted, were biology, psychology, and natural science. Previous solutions of these world-problems were of a materialistic or semi-materialistic and mechanical kind.

Thales,[1] recognised as the founder of Greek philosophy, a remarkable man of the beginning of the sixth century B.C., who had been astronomer, geometrician, engineer, and statesman, but who is more famous for having fallen into a well than for more solid and important achievements, declared water to be the first principle from which all things came.

Anaximander, the next name, "taught that there was one eternal, indestructible substance out of which everything arises and into which everything once more returns; a boundless stock of matter from which the waste of existence is continually being made good."[2] The "boundless" of Anaximander is just infinite mass or matter. Our world has emerged from this by the separating out of the opposites, moist and dry, warm and cold.[3] Man has ascended from the lower species, fish, all living things being originally derived from the moisture as it was evaporated by the sun.[4]

Anaximenes (flourished about middle of sixth century B.C.) identified the infinite substance with air, which becomes fire when rarefied, and water or earth when condensed. Air is the source and substratum of all things.

---

[1] For these names, see Burnet's Early Greek Philosophy, or the cheaper and available Benn's Ancient Philosophy, in the "History of Science" Series (1s. each).
[2] Burnet, *op. cit.*, p. 50.   [3] Burnet, *op. cit.*, p. 62.
[4] *Op. cit.*, p. 73.

Xenophanes of Colophon, in Asia Minor, regarded earth as the primordial base of things, while Heraclitus of Ephesus (about end of sixth century) gave fire his suffrage. "This universe the same for all, was not made by any god or any man, but was and is and ever shall be, an ever-living fire, kindled and quenched by measure." The soul of man also he considered to be just a form of fire.

Parmenides of Elea launched the view that reality simply *is;* the universe is uncreated, indestructible, immovable, complete. Change and motion are illusion, they are not-being, and not-being simply is not. In his cosmology, Parmenides adopted the theory that everything is composed from the warm and the cold element, and man also takes his rise from these.

Empedocles of Acragas, in Sicily, who adopted the Pythagorean doctrine of re-incarnation, and otherwise seems to have had a touch of the mythologising temperament, took for his basis of explanation of the world all the four elements already alluded to, water, air, earth, fire. The process of things consists in the separation and union of these elements under the influence of what he calls Strife and Love, but Strife and Love are principles as corporeal as the elements themselves. The truth of the matter is that the distinction between material and spiritual, corporeal and incorporeal, had not yet been clearly evolved in Greek philosophy. And these speculators were dealing with inadequate categories. This criticism applies also to the views of Leucippus and Democritus, who held that the cosmos is evolved from atoms, *i.e.* particles of matter too small for sense to perceive, differing only in size, form, and position, and subject to motion in the void, a motion which leads to all sorts of combinations of the atoms and so gives rise to the heterogeneity of the world we know.

These theories were open to the same objections as are modern scientific theories when set forth as complete and satisfying explanations of the world, and Socrates was deep-skulled enough to be conscious of their inadequacy. For example, we are told that stones fall because of the law of the gravitation. But the law of gravitation is a mere general summary of the facts as we experience them, and leaves the facts themselves as far from elucidation as ever. That masses should attract each other with a force proportionate to the mass and inversely proportionate to the square of their distance apart is by no means a self-evident axiom, especially since in certain states they repel each other, as, for example, when charged with like electricities. No more does the world become transparent by being reduced to its simplest elements. Atoms and motion account for atoms and motion, that alone.

Socrates then was in a state of disillusionment and discontent. Like Faust, after poring over the lore of the ancients, he felt the door still barred and himself on the wrong side of it.

> "Habe nun, ach, Philosophie
> Juristerei und Medicin,
> Und leider, auch Theologie
> Durchaus studirt, mit heissem Bemühn.
> Da steh' ich nun, ich armer Tor,
> Und bin so klug als wie zuvor."[1]

One day,[2] however, he "heard some one reading from a book by a certain Anaxagoras saying that *Mind* is

---

[1] "I've studied now Philosophy,
And Jurisprudence, Medicine,—
And even, alas! Theology,—
From end to end with labour keen;
And here, poor fool! with all my lore
I stand no wiser than before."
Bayard Taylor's Trans.

[2] Phædo, 97 C.

the disposer and cause of all things." The words fell like flashes of light from the upper air on the eyes of a man groping in some dark mine. They seemed to light up the obscurity.

> "Before him shone a glorious world,
> Fresh as a banner bright unfurled
> To music suddenly."

Hope was rekindled in his heart, and seizing the books, as a drowning man clutches at a raft, he plunged through them as fast as he could. But, alas! he was doomed to disappointment. He had expected that anyone who took the principle of Mind seriously in his theory of the world would work it out in detail, and show how, as mind is the source of the order in things, *that* order is the best in all particulars.[1]

As mind always seeks the best, the idea of what is best and most excellent will be the clue to all facts; it will explain why they are where they are and what they are. That is inherently true of all the operations of mind; wherever you have intelligence, you find that action is with a view to what is better.[2] I do certain things because I shall then be more satisfied: I act for the best—as a modern idealist would say, from the idea of the Good. Thus a world that is a rational world must be one in which all is well ordered, and on the best lines.

> Mind's on its throne,
> All's right with the world.

Moreover, a universe whose Principle is intelligent must also be intelligible, that is to say, one whose ways are man's ways and its thoughts man's thoughts, for man is intelligent. Community of nature is the source of sympathy and understanding. And so the mind of

[1] Phædo, 97 C. [2] Phædo, 97 E and 98 A.

man is the key to the Mind of the World, and the Ethical is the Real. The cosmos must be directed by reasonable motives, therefore, not by blind mechanical laws.

Socrates is in prison, his position there is to be accounted for not by the fact that he is composed of bones and flesh and sinews, but because the Athenians condemned him, and he regards it as better and more right to remain and undergo his punishment than to flee.[1] Rational explanation demands teleology. The *reason* behind all things is the cause of all things.

Anaxagoras, however, did not attempt to work out his principle, but fell back like the others on ether and water and such like altogether inappropriate and irrelevant causes.[2] To put the position in more modern terms, the explanation of the world does not lie in atoms or molecules or electrons. These do not tell why things are, but only *what* they probably are. The reason for this book is not to be found in pen and ink and paper, but in the aim and motive of the writer. The former are mere conditions for the carrying out of the latter, which is at once the final and the efficient cause. It was one of Socrates' great discoveries that materialistic and mechanical principles give only the conditions but not the causes or reasons of phenomena.[3]

The world is really a living organism like our own body, it is a rational being like ourselves; and we shall only understand its phenomena and their inter-relations by penetrating to the innermost reality of our own being and discovering the principles of our own action.

The world is slowly moving to some goal; it is controlled by ends on the analogy and likeness of human conduct. To be able to say what kind of world it is

---

[1] Phædo, 98 C–E. [2] Ibid., 98 C.
[3] Ibid., 99 A.

therefore, we must know what sort of ends it is aiming at. Is its inner impulse to evil or to good, to ugliness or to beauty? To get light on that we shall have to find by analysis of our own being, and from knowledge of *it*, just what sort of end all rational seeking and desiring involves. To know the world, then, is to know ourselves. Man—man, that is, as rational will—is the measure of all things. And thus it is that for Socrates metaphysics is closely bound up with psychology and ethics.

The two great principles which had crystallised in his mind from the experiences of his "Sturm und Drang" period are now before us; (1) *the knowledge of our own ignorance*, which alone can set the mind off in an original quest for the true knowledge, alone make that quest a real thing, *the* real thing, of life, that without which, in fact, life is neither tolerable nor possible: "Know that thou dost not know"; and (2) this quest for true knowledge must be pursued through the knowledge of ourselves: "Know thyself." Self-knowledge, then, becomes Socrates' one lifelong discipline and pursuit; and as the nature of the self is rational, and the nature of the rational is the ethical, ethics becomes for him the basis and starting-point and goal of metaphysics. And at this period of his life, at all events, we may class him as a Humanist or a Pragmatist, though we shall see that, as in the case of his great successor, Plato, it was a Humanism which was never to be content with anything less than Absolutism. Socrates was no pluralist or relativist.

Thus it was, then, that he turned from his first absorptions in science and nature-study to inquiry into man and the principles of his moral nature. It was in these latter alone that the Riddle of the Universe was going to find its solution. In this phase of his thought he represented and symbolised one of the characteristic movements of his age, the Humanistic movement, which found expression in some of the great Sophists of Greece, particularly in Protagoras, exercised a decided influence in literature, and came into conflict with the established faiths and customs of the various states or cities where it got a footing. We note this in passing simply to indicate, what we shall later enlarge upon, that the life of Socrates had not merely an individual but a national significance. He was more than a man; he was a historical movement. And so far from illustrating that form of originality which is isolated from, and independent of, one's social environment, a form of originality more technically described as insanity, Socrates was rather the beam of light from which one can analyse out the many-coloured spectrum of the age. His centralising interest, after his "conversion" that day when Anaxagoras kindled the light in his soul, was man. And it was out among men that he was likely to find "man," not in a laboratory or study, where

> "Statt der lebendigen Natur,
> Da Gott die Menschen schuf hinein,
> Umgiebt in Rauch und Moder nur
> Dich Tiergeripp' und Totenbein."

The sculpture trade was neglected, given up, probably. The first and foremost thing in Socrates' estimate was not the making of statues, but the making up of his own mind. The first article in his short Catechism was: Man's chief end is to achieve the end of man. We must be ourselves first, and anything else after that. It is certainly an awkward and difficult view of life to take seriously, but for Socrates it was the only real, the only possible, view. He couldn't live on bread alone, he must have the Word of Truth. To him it was no hobby, but a necessity, to be a seeker of Truth. The world could do, and must do, without his statues; he could not do, and would not do, without its secret. It was a bold thing for him to follow out this inner call. It exposed him, no doubt, to misunderstanding and criticism on the part of his practical and common-sense friends and relations. Such incidental inconveniences, however, must not be abjured, but endured, by him who is in earnest about ideas. He gave himself up to questioning everybody he came across who was likely to be of help to him in his purpose, and his career to the very end was a patient, indefatigable, unwearyable search for true knowledge by the interrogation of others. He was always animated by the same spirit as Newton, who felt that he was but a child gathering pebbles on the beach, while the undiscovered oceans rolled beyond his feet. He never ceased to be a learner. He never let an opportunity slip.

Indeed, his expertness in picking other people's brains amounted to a fine art, and his importunity was such as to be a severe irritant to those less fanatical for truth. He stands a remarkable prototype of Browning's Grammarian :

> " He knew the signal, and stepped on with pride
>   Over men's pity ;
> Left play for work, and grappled with the world
>   Bent on escaping.
>
> Oh, such a life as he resolved to live
>   When he had learned it.
> Imagine the whole, then execute the parts—
>   Fancy the fabric
> Quite, ere you build, ere steel strike fire from quartz,
>   Ere mortar dab brick.
>
> Still before living, he'd learn how to live—
>   No end to learning.
> Earn the means first, God surely will contrive
>   Use for our earning."[1]

---

[1] Grammarian's Funeral.

CHAPTER III

THE MAN

"La vie dévote est une vie douce, heureuse, et aimable."—
Saint Francois de Sales.

(a) His Appearance

IT is only gradually we can unfold the features of Socrates' spiritual and intellectual greatness. We turn now to ask what manner of man he was in looks. He had a wonderful gift of attracting the generous-souled youth to himself; but it was no grace or comeliness of the outward form for which they desired him. It must be confessed that Socrates was ugly in appearance. But he is by no means the only ugly man in history who has exercised a magnetic spell over others. There is a type of face, ordinarily unpleasing, which, when lit up by the spiritual emotion within, and kindling with the soul's rapt intensity, becomes strangely fascinating. Savonarola, the great Florentine priest and preacher, had a face like that. George Eliot, in her "Romola," one of the greatest and most eloquent of modern novels, with the spirit of Æschylus in it, indicates what it was like. "There was nothing transcendent in Savonarola's face. It was not beautiful. It was strong featured and owed all its refinement to habits of mind and rigid discipline of body, . . . with a gaze in which simple human fellowship expressed itself as a strongly felt bond. Such a glance is half the vocation of the priest or spiritual guide of men."[1] We can well believe that the spirit within must often

[1] Romola, ch. 40.

THE MAN

have flooded the repellent physiognomy of Socrates with the rapt fire of an unearthly enthusiasm and the subduing grace of an intense human interest. Plato's prayer was: "Give me beauty in the inward soul, and may the outward and the inward man be one," and under the transforming touch of a mingled spiritual and intellectual ardour, we imagine the repellent traits of feature being lost to sight in Socrates, and the inner majesty of a seeing soul unfolding itself before the eyes of eager onlookers.

But at ordinary times what was he like? We get details from various sources—the "Symposium" and "Apology" of Plato as well as other dialogues, Aristophanes, and the "Banquet" ascribed to Xenophon.[1] In the last named Socrates is staged as a jolly, good-natured fellow, singing the praises of his own homely features among his boon companions. Square, squat, strong built; rough-hewn from the rock; face-bones thick set, and not too much flesh to soften their angularities; in spite of abstemious habits amounting to austerity, stout and corpulent in body;[2] protruding eyes[3] that seemed to want to see round the back of his head; snub nose,[4] with wide nostrils; thick lips, straight wiry hair, and irregular beard—about the last man in Athens to be taken for its Alastor and intellectual prophet. He must, we think, have had some resemblance to Macaulay, who was described in a contemporary number of *Blackwood*, as a "little, splay-footed, ugly, dumpling of a fellow, with a mouth from ear to ear."

In his bovine eyes slept fires, which at times were belched out as from the eyes of a bull.[5] Withal in his

[1] There are grave doubts as to its authenticity, and the picture of Socrates may be a bit over-coloured.
[2] Xen., Banquet, ch. iv. For other features, ch. vi.
[3] Cp. Theætetus, 209.   [4] Cp. Theætetus, 209.
[5] See Phædo, 117 b: "He looked like a bull at the man, as was his wont."

mien there was a haughtiness, which might even become majesty, as he walked, with head tossed high in the air, sphering his eyes about. "Why do you carry your head so high, and do the haughty?" asks one character of another in a comedy of Callias.[1] "I have a good right," is the reply, "I'm only following Socrates' example."

In Aristophanes' "Clouds,"[2] the chorus of Clouds thus address their high priest, Socrates: "You hold your nose high in the streets, and merely wheel your eyes on folk. Barefooted, you put up with many ills; a high solemnity is on your face, because of us."

A strange figure he must have cut as he marched along, with his shabby old cloak and his bare feet, and yet with the tread of an Olympian, bestriding the world like a Colossus. We surmise it must have made gods as well as men laugh, this insignificant plebeian figure, that might have been the sausage seller, stepped out from Aristophanes' "Knights," yet with all the bearing of the veriest aristocrat; an air which condescends to accept the universe and tolerate mankind, Aristotle's "great-minded man" come to life, "one who claims much because he deserves it," . . . who "utterly despises honour from ordinary men, for that is not what he deserves, who likewise makes light of dishonour, for he will never merit it, . . . who never looks down on others without justice, . . . whose nature it is not to receive benefits, but to confer them, dignified to equals, affable to inferiors, . . . who cares not that men should praise him, nor lowers himself to blame others, . . . not doing many things, but what he does, great and notable, . . . his gait slow, his voice deep, his speech measured, not likely to be in a hurry when there are few things in which he is deeply in-

[1] fr. 12. Quoted Couat, Aristophane, p. 283.
[2] ll. 362, 363.

THE MAN

terested, never excited, as one who holds nothing to be of very great importance."[1] We can believe that his old cloak swung about him in lordly fashion.[2]

Such, then, the exterior of the philosopher seen by the poor outsider of the markets, the view reproduced for us by Plutarch when he says of the great Roman, Marcus Cato: "He was cheerful and harsh all at once, pleasant and yet severe as a companion, fond of jokes but morose at the same time, just as Plato tells us that Socrates, if judged merely from his outside, appeared to be only a silly man with a face like a satyr, who was rude to all he met, though his inner nature was earnest and full of thoughts that moved his hearers to tears and touched their hearts."[3] However formidable and majestic, Socrates, with all his eccentricity, may have appeared to the man in the street, yet, in congenial company at least, he could coin a joke at himself. We have referred to Macaulay. It is related of him that, after seeing his portrait as painted by Hayter for a picture of the House of Commons, the great litterateur good-humouredly quoted Charles the Second's comment on seeing his own portrait, "Odds fish, if I'm like this, I am an ugly fellow." Socrates, we are given to understand, was wont to take an equally genial view of his unprepossessing features. He forgave Nature for taking a very utilitarian view of beauty in the hour of deciding upon him, a view with which in more serious moments and in regard to more impersonal matters, he had himself unfeigned sympathy. The fifth chapter of Xenophon's "Banquet" is an apology by Socrates for his face in detail, carried out with a raillery and fun which clamour to be taken

---

[1] Nicomachean Ethics, bk. iv. ch. 3. From Peter's translation.
[2] See Theætetus.
[3] Plutarch's Life of Marcus Cato. Lives translated by Stewart and Long.

for a true characterisation of a great human, who with all his absorption in high philosophic themes believed in the maxim—*desipere in loco.*

That young "blood" of Athens, the beautiful and brilliant, but loose-principled and ill-starred, Alcibiades, whose connexion with Socrates is one of the unforgettable episodes in the everlasting romance of personal influence, is made by Plato to exclaim during a burst of vinous frankness, "You might very well compare Brasidas or Pericles to Achilles or Nestor, or other heroes of antiquity; but here is one who is comparable to no one at all except it be to a Silenus or a Satyr."[1] And by the author of "Xenophon's Banquet," already alluded to, Socrates is presented as arguing for his superior handsomeness on the ground that Sileni are the progeny of "naiads and nymphs divine." In the "Theætetus" we get a confirmatory glimpse of the good-humoured and playful way in which Socrates would allude to his outward man. It lights up his whole character, showing him free and easy in his manners, full of good nature, when you knew him, however apparently lofty in his general bearing before the outside world.

There was a story[2] told by Phædo of Elis, and repeated by the great Roman orator Cicero, to the effect that a certain Zopyrus, who had a foible for reading people's heads and divining their character, expatiated on the vices written on Socrates' face, whereat the rest of the company present, for the most part, strongly dissented, but Socrates said, "No, he is right; the vices are there, only reason has dethroned them." The story indicates the sensual strength and energy of the face, something in it that told of suffering and struggle, the ruggedness about

---

[1] Plato, Symposium, § 215.
[2] Gomperz, Greek Thinkers, ii. p. 48.

it of violent elemental forces, but also, far withdrawn, to those who could discern, a spiritual quality, a calm of power attained through victory.

(b) His Character

Aristoxenos, a pupil of Aristotle, tells of having heard his father, Spintharus, who came into personal contact with Socrates, say that his temper sometimes betrayed him into great improprieties of speech and demeanour.[1] In all probability his natural temperament was of the violent and explosive kind, and doubtless he found its control no pleasant pastime. But that he was guilty of improprieties of speech and demeanour may only mean what is otherwise clear enough that, with all his faculty for gentle persuasion and irresistible coaxing, when drawing on some modest youth or conceited charlatan into the vortex of argument, he was still a fragment of rude nature, rugged and simple, robust and healthy, not choosing his language always with a view to titillate the delicate tympanum of over-refined, effeminate ears. To people for whom the storm in a tea-cup is enough to induce a mild sea-sickness, the roll and swell and breakers of the real ocean must be a fearful terror. There were those who thought Jesus anything but controlled and restrained in parts of his speech and demeanour, but usually a knowledge of particular circumstances brings a more favourable and sympathetic verdict. So with Socrates. We read that, in the course of his discussions, he was often subjected to rough handling, being stoned, having his hair plucked, and being subjected to ridicule, but that he

---

[1] Fragments of Aristoxenos, 27, 28, *ap*. Frag. Hist. Græc, p. 280, ed. by Didot. Grote, Hist. of Greece, viii. p. 208 n., does not accept distrust of Aristoxenos by Ritter and Preller.

bore all with patience. Once, when he meekly submitted to a kick, his forbearance caused surprise. But he only said, " If an ass had kicked me, would I have taken the law of it ? "

Such stories may perhaps be exaggerated in details, and their source may be the undoubted antipathies he roused toward himself;[1] but the above answer has the genuine Socratic salt in it, and it no doubt faithfully preserves a characteristic superiority to personal revenge for insults. The Athenians were a most litigious species, with a very sensitive regard for their rights, but Socrates overcame the tribal weakness, for he remained a stranger to the inside of law courts all his days.[2]

Self-mastery was written deep over his character and life. He fought like a Hercules with the Nemean lions of doubt and appetite, and all the hydra-headed problems of intellectual and moral life, and he stands out before the world more than conqueror, winning his soul, and, if not knowledge, at least faith and trust and hope, where these alone are possible to win.

He was of the race of Jesus and the Buddha, one to whom we can admiringly and affectionately apply Meredith's lines :

> " We see through mould the rose unfold,
> The soul through blood and tears."

His life was a single-eyed pursuit of knowledge and virtue and a disinterested desire to spread them among others. Selfishness or worldliness had no place in his heart. He was brought up poor, but he had succeeded in gaining such knowledge, and was possessed of such native endowment, as might have put comparative wealth and affluence within his

---

[1] Apol., 23 A.
[2] Diogenes, ii. 5, 21, on the authority of Demetrius.

reach. He could have taken a high place among the travelling professors of the time, who charged large sums for their instructions and apparently lived like gentlemen, but he waved such a career aside as no temptation at all. Regarding himself always as an inquirer among inquirers, never as a teacher among pupils, he refused to accept money[1] from those to whom nevertheless his society was a liberal education. As Xenophon tells us, he lavished all he had, through his whole life, on others, giving the greatest benefits to all who cared to share them. Indeed we might apply to him, as the formula of life he adopted in relation to others, the words of the Apostle Peter: "Silver and gold have I none, but such as I have give I unto thee." "He stigmatised those who condescended to take wages for their society as vendors of their own persons, because they were compelled to discuss for the benefit of their paymasters. What surprised him was that anyone possessing virtue should deign to ask money as its price instead of simply finding his reward in the acquisition of an honest friend."[2]

His thought about life might be put into the grave and impressive words spoken by our own great sage, Carlyle, on that occasion when, as their Lord Rector, he addressed the students of his old University of Edinburgh: "Man is born to expend every particle of strength that God Almighty has given him, in doing the work he finds he is fit for; to stand up to it to the last breath of life, and do his best. We are called upon to do that; and the reward we all get—which we are perfectly sure of, if we have merited it—is that we have got the work done, or at least that we have tried

---

[1] Plato, Apol., 19 E. Xen., Mem., i. 6, 11. Diogenes Laertius, ii. 5, 27.

[2] Mem., i. 2, §§ 6 and 7.

to do the work. For that is a great blessing in itself; and I should say there is not very much more reward than that going in this world. If the man gets meat and clothes, what matters it whether he buy those necessaries with seven thousand a year or with seven million, could that be, or with seventy pounds a year? He can get meat and clothes for that; and he will find intrinsically, if he is a wise man, wonderfully little real difference." So Socrates. Life was a mission not a trade, for him. He construed it in terms of the highest. Not what we get, but what we give, to the world is our riches.

Thoreau, the American, wrote truly that "to be a philosopher is not merely to have subtle thoughts, nor even to found a school, but so to love wisdom as to live according to its dictates, a life of simplicity, independence, magnanimity, and trust." Like Rousseau he saw men born free but everywhere in chains, the life of civilisation a slavery for the meat that perisheth, and for a while he repudiated it and retired to the banks of Walden Pond, near Concord, there to live the philosophic life in a house built by himself and costing between £5 and £6.

But Thoreau was a bachelor, and he was only conducting an experiment. Socrates had to encounter four arguments against his world-renouncing interpretation of his call in a wife and three children, and with him it was no novel and short-lived adventure, but a mode of life faithfully followed for more than a generation. All the more worthy then is he of the name of a lover of wisdom.

He must have been quite a "character" in Athens, and that sound common-sense of his, that gumption which went right to the roots of things, sometimes took rather droll ways of expressing itself. His humour too, which was in the very bone of him, led him to actions which must have helped to increase the impression of eccentricity his quaint natural ways created. Once coming on a crowd of people staring at a fine horse, he stepped forward and asked the groom if the animal had much wealth. The fellow looked at him in surprise, thinking him hardly sound in mind to ask such a question, and, rather puzzled, replied, "How can a horse have wealth?" "Thereat" says Socrates, who narrated the incident, "I dared to lift my eyes from the earth, on learning that after all it is permitted a poor penniless horse to be a noble animal, if nature only have endowed him with a good spirit."

Right at the end of his career he could stand before his judges and say, "I am at the extremity of poverty on account of my service to God."[1] "He did not think wealth and birth a matter for reverence," says Diogenes Laertius, and if we go back to that magnificent Dialogue of Plato, the "Theætetus," a glorious anticipation of modern idealism, we shall learn to understand why he could despise them. It was because, like the Apostle Paul, he could say, "poor, yet possessing all things." We take this excerpt from one of the great passages of the world's literature:

"Hearing of enormous landed proprietors of ten thousand acres and more, our philosopher deems this to be a trifle, because he has been accustomed to think of the whole earth" (as the "Republic" puts it, he is a "spectator of all time and existence"); "and when they sing the praises of family and say that some one is a gentleman because he has had seven generations of wealthy ancestors, he thinks that their sentiments only betray a dull and narrow vision in those who utter them, and who are not educated enough to look at the whole nor to consider that every man has had

[1] Apol., 23 b.

thousands and thousands of progenitors, and among them have been rich and poor, kings and slaves, Hellenes and barbarians, many times over. And when people pride themselves on having a pedigree of twenty-five ancestors, which goes back to Hercules, the son of Amphitryon, he cannot understand their poverty of ideas." [1]

Pale, passing, poor, all other wealth and nobility to Socrates beside this of the mind and soul. Not what a man has but what he is constitutes his only title to rank and admiration. It is the thought that wanders through eternity, the emotion that is touched by all being, which is the great man's heritage. And he is rich indeed before whom the universe stoops to offer the gold and frankincense and myrrh of its own secrets, purposes, and works.

Socrates did his high thinking on pretty plain living and dressing. He had all the unconcern of a St. Francis about his own personal wants. There is a fragment from one of the plays of Eupolis, a comic poet of the time who had a considerable vogue, but of whose work no more than fragments have survived, in which a character delivers himself on this wise: "I hate this Socrates, this babbling beggar, who has meditated more than anybody else, but has never asked where he was going to get his dinner." [2] Aristophanes, greatest of the Comics, has various allusions to him and his disciples, which will demand considerable notice later. In the "Birds" he speaks of the faddists who were "dirty like Socrates," [3] "who lived in fasting and dirt, and played Socrates," [4] and in the "Clouds" he represents the wretched little coterie of Socratics as so stingy that they never

---

[1] Theætetus, 174, 175. [2] Fragment, 352.
[3] l. 1280. [4] l. 1282.

go to the baths or use unguents. They are a pale ghastly[1] lot, which does not, however, prevent them being also as black as coal.[2] These would have been unkind cuts at Socrates, if they were not comedy. There is nothing in Plato or Xenophon to suggest that the sage's appearance might have gained considerable advantage from a less economical use of soap and water. The indications are rather to the contrary, and would suggest that he knew the value of water, and had great delicacy of feeling in regard to the body. It might be a ponderous judgment which laid much stress on the very slender hints of an artistic treatment of character like Plato's, but at least he does state that before Socrates went to the famous "Symposium" he had bathed, and after an all-night flow of reason and feast of soul, instead of going to bed, he took a cold bath and proceeded to the duties of the day. Plato apparently could imagine him doing such a thing, and if Socrates was as black as Aristophanes painted him, then Plato was unconsciously playing into the hands of a cynical humour. Nor is it obvious why a philosopher who had no superstitions about water in life should suddenly succumb just before death.[3] Socrates, as we shall see directly, was averse to unhealthy negligence of the body.

In the matter of dress he dispensed with sandals altogether, following what was the indoor fashion[4] even outside. The latter practice would not have been such matter for remark unless it had been very rare. There is a fragment of Ameipsias where it is said of Socrates in regard to this economy that "he was born to be the curse of shoemakers."[5]

It was sometimes an advantage in the summer as

[1] ll. 835–7.   [2] l. 1112.   [3] Phædo, 115 A.
[4] Becker's Charicles, p. 445.
[5] Frag. 9. In a play The Tribon. See Diogenes Laertius, ii. 5, 28.

on the occasion where Plato pictures him walking along in the stream of the Ilissus with Phædrus, to cool and refresh himself under the scorching sun. But Socrates could do without the comfort of shoes in all climates and weathers. When campaigning at Potidæa, where the Athenians fought a battle with the Spartans in September 432 B.C., the other soldiers looked daggers at him because, while they kept indoors in the bitter cold or wrapped fleeces about their feet when they went out, Socrates trudged about on the icy roads quite unconcernedly in his bare feet and with a provoking curl of contempt on his lip.[1]

As for clothing, previous to this campaign of 431 B.C., Alcibiades relates that he had had Socrates to supper, and then he was wearing a " threadbare cloak " ;[2] he was struck alike by the man's wisdom and powers of endurance.

In all respects he was a model of the simple life. He only ate and drank as a rule when hunger and thirst intimated the legitimate and necessary claims of Nature, and at such times a good appetite provided all the sauce or spice that was necessary. His abstinence in these matters was a notorious characteristic, in allusion to which Aristophanes makes the Clouds promise old Strepsiades that if he also will join their cult he will be able to endure hardship, stand or walk without fatigue, never suffer from cold, nor be concerned about breakfast, and he will keep aloof from wine and gymnastics and other follies.[3] "Others live to eat," Socrates once said. "I eat to live."[4]

The same moderation and self-control characterised all his actions and passions ; if his face gave evidence of sensuality subdued, his face was a true witness, for

---

[1] Plato, Symposium, § 220.   [2] *Op. cit.*, § 219.
[3] Clouds, 413–16.   [4] Diogenes Laertius, ii. 5, 34.

Socrates held the reins tight on the lusts of the flesh and its bewitching pleasures. No historical figure gives a stronger impression of possessing an absolute power of peace over the rage and tumult of the heart's unquiet seas. Odysseus stopped the sailors' ears with wax, and had himself tied to the mast, as his bark sailed past the treacherous rocks where the fateful Sirens sang with baleful charm; but Socrates moved free and unfettered, with all his senses open, amid the siren music of pleasure, moved with a sense of absolute self-possession. He had made the " great renunciation," the decision for the higher as against the lower, for spiritual attainment as against self-indulgence. He had counted the cost, and he knew Hesiod's lines: " Wickedness may a man take wholesale with ease, smooth is the way and her dwelling-place is very nigh; but in front of virtue the immortal gods have placed toil and sweat, long is the path and steep that leads to her, and rugged at the first, but when the summit of the path is reached, then for all its roughness the path grows easy."[1] And with the substance of the teaching of Prodicus' famous allegory,[2] " The Choice of Hercules," he had the greatest sympathy, bringing out, as it does, that decided and final choice between virtue and vice, labour and ease, self-discipline and self-indulgence, which every youth must make whose life is to rise above mediocrity of achievement and be an enrichment to the world. The goals of all worthy living are both difficult and remote, and the means of their attainment sacrificial.

(c) Let us consider Socrates' severe self-restraint further and we shall be persuaded that, so far as Xenophon's recollections are concerned, it was not due to the motive which drove the monks in the

---

[1] Mem., ii. ch. 1, § 20. (Dakyns' translation.)
[2] See Mem., ii. ch. 1, §§ 21 ff.

middle ages to castigate and mortify the flesh. It was not due to a theory of dualism between body and soul, as a result of which the more a man crushed out all the natural impulses and desires of the physical side of his nature the purer and stronger would he become spiritually.

In this important matter of Socrates' theory and practice, the testimony of Plato and Xenophon is not wholly identical, because when we come to Plato's writings we find emerging in them a clearly marked dualistic doctrine. In the "Phædo," that superb dialogue on the Immortality of the Soul, in which rationalism touched with the emotion of mystic longing takes its highest flight and falls, we have Socrates delineated as one who desires to throw off this mortal coil—to depart and be with pure Ideas which is far better—and who, indeed, in life has been practising to die.

Philosophy in the "Phædo" is the dying to the body, and living to the Soul or Reason; it is the protracted struggle by means of Reason to rise entirely out of the sphere of sense and appetites and passions into the sphere of knowledge—where the mind sees clearly and not through a glass darkly. Here the body with its affections of pain and pleasure is a distorting and perverting medium, and only when we are wholly disengaged from it, can we look face to face with the eye of Reason on the Eternal Reality. Hence the practice of the presence of Death to which Socrates declares he has devoted his life.

Of the Socrates of the "Phædo," however, we think it may fairly be said, as of the Christ of the Apostle Paul, that it knows no more the master after the flesh, but after the spirit. Just as in the one case we have Jesus Paulinised, so in the other we have Socrates Platonised. We shall probably be convinced of this when we reflect that this view of Socrates' life and doctrine is closely and organically related in the "Phædo" argument to the doctrine of Ideas, which till recently nearly all scholars have regarded as, in this developed ontological sense, a vision of Plato not vouchsafed to the eyes of Socrates.

Besides, the "Phædo" presents, I think, some degree of positive assurance about the destiny of souls in the next world, which is not on quite the same key as Socrates' frank agnosticism, combined with the disposition to trust the "larger hope" which we have in the early dialogue "Crito." These two dialogues are contrary one to the other, and the "Phædo" as a historical document in this regard must take the lower place.

Again, then, we affirm our belief that Socrates did not live as an ascetic from the ascetic motive of a dualism of soul and body.

Turning to Xenophon we find that, like St. Francis of Assisi, he had a reverence and just regard for "brother ass" his body, for the very reason that if in your philosophical agonising you want to be free of the body and all the handicaps which it may lay upon the mind and reason, the best way is to keep it in good health.

It is not when the body is in good form, but when it is in bad form, that it hampers and restricts and deflects us in the higher race of the mental life. Rousseau wrote in "Emile": "All sensual passions find their home in effeminate bodies." "A feeble body makes a feeble mind." "The longer I live," said Sydney Smith, who was clergyman, philosopher, and physician all in one—" the longer I live, the more I am convinced that the apothecary is of more importance than Seneca, and that half the unhappiness in the world proceeds from little stoppages, from a duct choked up, from food pressing in the wrong place, from a vext *duodenum*, or an agitated *pylorus*. Old friendships are destroyed by toasted cheese, and hard salt meat has led to suicide. Young people in early life should be taught the moral, intellectual, and physical evils of indigestion." One of the shrewdest jokes ever launched was " Punch's " question, " Is life worth living ? " with the reply, " That depends on the liver."

Xenophon tells us that he neither neglected his own body, nor approved of others who neglected theirs.[1] Rather he inculcated the greatest attention to health, and food and drink, so that one might spend life as healthily as possible.[2]

He remonstrates with Epigenes on his poor-looking puny condition, telling him that healthiness is profitable not only from the point of view of all physical demands, but also from those of the mind. Poor health affects the understanding, it distorts observation and knowledge, it causes forgetfulness, lack of enthusiasm, distemper, madness often.

The body is the handmaid of the soul, and it should be made as beautiful as it can be.[3] He neither neglected his body nor approved of those who did, but advocated the natural claims of appetite combined with moderate exercise, as tending to a healthy body without trammelling the cultivation of the soul.[4]

" Let us not always say
  ' Spite of this flesh to-day,
I strove, made head, gained ground upon the whole !'
  As the bird wings and sings,
  Let us cry, 'All good things
Are ours, nor soul helps flesh more than flesh helps soul !' " [5]

---

[1] Mem., i. 2, 4.   [2] iv. 7, 9.   [3] Mem., iii. 12.
[4] Mem., i. 2, 4.   [5] Rabbi Ben Ezra.

Nor was Socrates' life a life that felt no attraction of pleasure, no urge of passion, no joy of fulfilled desire. Antiphon, looking at his frugal habits, thought he should be dubbed professor of misery, but Socrates points out that his food, though plain, is nutritious, and he brings to it the excellent spice of hunger. If he drinks only when he is thirsty, he enjoys it all the more. If he does not wear sandals, he is never troubled with sore heels.

His few wants leave him independent, superior to inconveniences that bother other people, and freer to face life's emergencies and duties, less tempted to shrink from dangers and hardships. Self-mastery, and moderation of the appetites, is the very foundation of all virtue, and it must be made the central thing of the soul.

It is the man who is thus master of himself and victor over greed and covetousness that men prefer for the executors of their property, and wards of their children ; it is he who can be trusted to rule well in the state and stand to his post in war ; he too whom people like for friend and guest, because he does not think of himself first. He is the man who is " dear to God, beloved by friends, and honoured by his fellow-countrymen."[1]

For all these reasons Socrates' life is, so far from being miserable, the happiest life of all—free from the decay and degeneration of soul which over-indulgence inevitably brings, and nearest to the life of God who has no wants or needs at all.[2] It is the most divine life on earth.

We thus see that Socrates practised self-control as a means of realising the highest and happiest

---

[1] The tones are of Xenophon, but one can detect the true Socratic note beneath.

[2] Mem., i. 6, 10. Cp. Diogenes, ii, 5, 27.

possible life of mind and spirit and body. The body was not to be thrown away as a useless or harmful thing, but to be cared for and used as an instrument of the soul.

Zeller seems to be right in the main when he says: "The self-control of Socrates, alike in Xenophon as in Plato, has not that ascetic character which has recently been attributed to it. . . . Here self-control is not the radical denial of pleasure to oneself, but the freedom of the consciousness of self, and the possession of self."[1]

"It was his professed purpose," writes Grote, "to limit as much as possible the number of his wants, as a distant approach to the perfection of the gods, who wanted nothing; to control such as were natural and prevent the multiplication of any that were artificial."[2]

"Up till now," he declared at his trial, "I will yield to none in the pleasure which life has brought to me. I think those live best who seek to be as good as they can be, and they with most pleasure who feel themselves growing 'from good to better daily self surpast,'" and that joy has been his.[3] His view was that of Aristotle at a later day that happiness is not amusement; it is not living the life of a vegetable, it is the exercise of the highest faculties of reason; the true happiness is that of the perfect man.[4]

Crito speaks of him as always of an amazingly happy, light disposition.[5] "His life at all times," says Xenophon, "was a marvel of cheerfulness and calm content."[6] He was a Mark Tapley in the flesh.

[1] Phil. der Griechen, i. Die Persönlichkeit des Sok., pp. 17, 18 (edit. 1844).
[2] History of Greece, vol. viii. p. 207.   [3] Xen., Mem., iv. 8, 6.
[4] Arist., Nicomachean Ethics, x. 6, §§ 2 and 6; 8, § 7.
[5] Crito, 43 b.   [6] Mem., iv. 8, 2.

Prof. Taylor has published a book[1] to show among other things that Socrates was a religious ascetic, and that he belonged to the ascetic sect of the Pythagoreans, maintaining an Orphic cult, one of the chief dogmas of which was that the body was a tomb of the soul, and that this life was really death, and that what men call death was really the opening into life, the escape from the prison-house—this "body of death," as St. Paul called it—into the pure, free activity of the soul. Prof. Taylor has argued for his views subtly and ingeniously, but he cannot argue away much evidence against them.

Neither the "Phædo" of Plato, nor along with it the "Clouds" of Aristophanes, appear to us to be the works on which such a view of Socrates can be securely based.

The personal reminiscences of Xenophon refer to a period of Socrates' life when he associated with him, that is perhaps from about 415 B.C. till 401 B.C.[2] when Xenophon went to Asia, so that the period of about two years which elapsed between the cessation of his intercourse with Socrates and the date of the events recorded in the "Phædo" hardly permit of a reconciliation of their accounts of Socrates' views on the body in relation to the soul.

There is the testimony both of the "Symposium" of Plato and that of "Xenophon," that Socrates, if an ascetic in his views, was sometimes a very jolly one, and of a non-teetotal variety. He could do his duty to the cup on rare occasions with no visible effect on himself, which argues either some little familiarity with it at other times, or almost incredible power of mind over body. "Though unwilling generally to drink,

[1] Varia Socratica, First Series, ch. i. pp. 29, 30.
[2] The exact dates are uncertain. See Dakyns' works of Xenophon, vol. i. introd. pp. 75, 76.

when he was compelled, he could beat everybody, and most amazing of all, nobody ever saw Socrates drunk."[1]

Aristodemus describes the close of the banquet in these words: "Eryximachus and Phædrus, and some others took their departure. I went to sleep and as it was late I slept soundly till cockcrow. The rest of the party were all asleep or gone, only Agathon and Aristophanes and Socrates were awake, and there they were sitting drinking out of a large cup, passing it round from left to right."

Socrates the while talked paradoxes about comedy and tragedy till the other two dropped into the arms of Morpheus, overcome with wit, wisdom, wine and weariness. He himself rose, went and had a bath, then turned to the usual avocations of the day.[2]

The Xenophontic "Banquet" has striking resemblances to Plato's, but of course there must have been considerable similarity about such functions, and the differences are just as striking. The change from the one to the other is like that which, however, Burns did not find it impossible to make from a distinguished and refined Edinburgh salon to the Jolly Beggar bonhomie of the Crochallan Club. The difference of atmosphere could be no greater than that to which Jesus accommodated himself, when one day he fared with a sympathetic Pharisee and on another ate and drank with publicans and sinners.

Socrates apparently had a large nature which was sometimes as conspicuous for geniality as at others for refinement. He could play the polished gentleman with a Protagoras or a Prodicus, and also the hail-fellow-well-met with roystering cronies. The Aristophanic portrait of the hungry, cadaverous, round-shouldered, hollow-chested indoor student must have

[1] Plato, Symposium, 220 a.   [2] Plato, Symposium, 223.

been irresistibly comical to the Athenians, because so palpably absurd.

In the Xenophontic "Banquet" he gets quite hilarious, and jokes, in a mood inebriated only partly with mere good-humour, on the unfortunate features of his outer man. At one point [1] he gets the length of declaring he would like to take a few turns at dancing, for the movements lend added grace and animation to the human form divine. Of course the idea of this stout old philosopher tripping it on the light fantastic toe sends the company into fits of laughter. But he assures them that he indulges the terpsichorean art at times in private, for the benefit of his constitution. No wonder the graceful Charmides stood aghast on accidentally coming upon the elephant at its evolutions! For a historical parallel we should have to go to Dr. Johnson, who was accused in the papers of taking lessons in dancing. "And why," he asked, "should not Dr. Johnson add to his other powers a little corporeal agility?"

Of course we won't swear to the exact truth of everything in our authority, but the spirit of the thing may be taken as true, and it all goes to indicate the boyishness, the lightheartedness, the jollity on occasion, of this man whose inner mind and soul were at heavy wrestle with the mysteries of life and problems of thought. Restless doubt and inquiry had not added a drop of bitterness, sourness, or dolefulness to the essential sweetness and gaiety of the disposition he showed. He seemed to spend his life in irony and jest on mankind, says Plato.[2]

He puts the brightest face on things because, in spite of all his hardships, endurance, and deprivations, he has the joy of having saved his soul, won the glorious privilege of being independent, and so lived

[1] Ch. ii.   [2] Plato, Symposium, 216 E.

as to feel the highest of all pleasures, that "of becoming better oneself, and of acquiring better and better friends."[1] He merely took poverty in his stride, as an incident, not as something to point to, and give himself airs on. It was no pose with him. Once referring to Antisthenes, who had turned the rent in his cloak out so that it could be seen, Socrates quietly said, "I can see his vanity through the hole in his coat."

Simplicity and sincerity marked his ways with himself and others. All his desire was to be, not to seem. He had a mission to fulfil and he was straitened till it should be accomplished. He was happy through all; but the mission was the only thing worth consideration.

[1] Mem., i. ch. 6, § 9.

CHAPTER IV

DOMESTIC LIFE

"This is my prayer to thee, my lord: Strike, strike, at the root of penury in my heart.
"Give me the strength lightly to bear my joys and sorrows.
"Give me the strength to raise my mind high above trifles."
—RABINDRANATH TAGORE.

VULGAR report has it that the saints are very difficult beings to live with, and we can well imagine it to be so. We have even heard of a doubtful species who were saints abroad and devils at home, a hybridism which points to lack of care in the breeding of the virtues and disqualifies them in popular estimation. Any man, however, who has given himself as a hostage to God in some great absorbing cause will be apt to forget those trifling but charming adaptations which constitute the amenities and graces of social life. Even a person's abnormal sensibility may make him " gey ill to deal wi,'" as in Carlyle's case. When a poor mortal can't digest anything but chickens and refuses to have *them*, because he can't stand their preliminary dying cries, we can forgive the impatience of his sturdier brethren who rejoice in the *dura ilia messorum*, and we mark how virtuous may be the qualities that render us hardly tolerable to our fellows. Even the authentic saint is apt to be a thorn in the flesh of those made of poorer stuff, for his unworldliness is like to be a source of constant irritation. Often he is able to live for other people because somebody else lives for him, and naturally he rather despises their office. Mary has a sister Martha who cooks and washes at home. The saint eats his dinner as though he ate not, which is far from pleasing to those who had the cooking of it. His spiritual zeal creates material problems he cannot stoop to solve.

Socrates was one of the easiest saints in the world to get on with, whether at home or abroad, and yet he must have made things difficult for his wife, and she reciprocated in her own way. Xanthippe, doubtless affectionate enough, but a coarse-grained, ordinary woman, could have done without her husband's philosophy, if he had brought home more cash, and occasionally fewer friends. Socrates would not teach for money, his services were either above or beneath reward, and she had to adopt the same estimate of hers. He would not do his work for anything but love, and she had to keep the house going on the same commodity. She deserves more sympathy than she has usually got. We can sympathise with her under the unhappy necessity of performing

> "that hardest task of man alive
> To make three guineas do the work of five."

We don't exactly know what her philosophy of life was, normally, but there must have been moments when it came perilously near Bernard Shaw's doctrine adapted for domestic use, "The crying need of the nation is not for better morals, cheaper bread, temperance, liberty, culture, redemption of fallen sisters and erring brothers, nor for the grace, love, and fellowship of the Trinity, but simply for enough money."

It has to be confessed that Socrates' household economy is wrapped in mystery. Demetrius of Phalerum, who wrote a book on him, declared in it

DOMESTIC LIFE

"that Socrates not only possessed a house, but also seventy minæ (*i.e.* £284, 7s. 6d.) which were borrowed by Crito."[1] Plutarch does not accept this statement, holding that it sprung from a desire to relieve Socrates of the stigma of poverty. Demetrius' mind must have been a piece of queer psychology if he thought he could overthrow the united testimony of Plato and Xenophon, and even in Athens in those days, though money had three or four times the purchasing power it has among us, £284, 7s. 6d. could hardly represent wealth. Anyhow, the "Œconomicus" of Xenophon suggests a much more modest capital. "If I could find a good purchaser, I suppose that the whole of my effects, including the house in which I live, might very fairly realise five minæ" (*i.e.* £20, 6s.). So he is represented as saying to Critobulos, and not only so but he further declares that it is ample and sufficient for his wants.[2] The verdict of Boeckh is that, put out at current rates of interest, the portion of this available for investment would not bring sufficient return to provide Socrates and his wife with barley, not to mention other necessaries, or the maintenance of his three children. The point is discussed in "The Public Economy of Athens" by Boeckh, who is inclined to doubt the statement in the "Œconomicus" on the ground that the history of the ancient philosophers is so corrupted by myth and legend. If it is not to be credited for that reason, then it is difficult to know where the line that divides truth from something else is to be drawn in Xenophon's writings, especially as all the evidence goes to show that Socrates lived in extreme poverty. After all the claim to credence of a document like the "Œconomicus" is on a very different footing from that of biographical

---

[1] Plutarch, Life of Aristides, ch. i.
[2] Ch. 2, § 3.   [3] *Loc. cit.*

writers in the Christian era. But Boeckh goes on, "Assuming Xenophon's account to be entirely correct,"—and what motive, we ask, could Xenophon have to give an aggravated account of Socrates' poverty?—"it must be thought that the mother of the young sons maintained herself and two children either by her labour or out of her dowry, while Lamprocles supported himself; and that the domestic economy for which Socrates was so celebrated consisted in keeping his family at work."[1] We have not information to decide on these circumstances. What Xanthippe's dowry might be is a matter of mere speculation, but in all probability it would not amount to much. While for her labour, that must have been at the best but a broken source of income, if we assume with the records that the three children of Socrates were all by her. The youngest was with his mother in the prison on the morning of Socrates' death, which may perhaps be ground for inferring that the child was then of tender age, and not to be left out of the mother's care. If so there must have been a lapse of many years between the eldest and youngest, because Lamprocles was quite a youth before his father died, and able to form an independent judgment on his mother's character. In any case there must have been times, at the birth of the children, when expenses were heavier than usual and Xanthippe's labours not available.

There is the possibility that while he refused payment for the privilege of association with him, yet some of his friends, who were well supplied with this world's goods, might be in the habit of relieving the financial strain for his wife. On the other hand, there is evidence against such bounties, unless of course they were given to Xanthippe without Socrates'

[1] Public Economy of Athens, bk. i. ch. 20 (Eng. trans., 2nd edit., revised 1842). Quoted also in Holden's Œconomicus, p. 110.

personal knowledge. For to Critobulus he says his exiguous property is quite sufficient to meet his wants, and if he ever did need any assistance he was quite sure he had friends who would be only too willing to render help. They would make some contribution, to themselves a mere trifle, which would be a deluge of plenty to him.[1] We have already noticed his delicacy in money matters, and his extremely sensitive regard for his independence. It was a matter of report that he had declined the offer of Alcibiades to give him land on which to build a house,[2] and on another occasion the invitation of Charmides to accept some slaves for the purpose of making money by them.[3]

We gather then that Socrates' household subsisted on a sum that would be incredible did we not know that living in Athens was altogether cheaper and simpler than in modern societies. If we could have visited his home we should have found it intolerably bare and mean, judged by modern ideas, for even the well-to-do Athenian house[4] was far removed from being a mansion, up to and at the period of the Peloponnesian War. They might be one story, but generally consisted of two stories, the lower comprising the public rooms, and the inner or women's apartments, where the females lived in an unhealthy confinement which reminds us of the Zenanas of India to-day. The upper story, which in some cases was reached by an outside stair abutting on the street, and which itself might overhang the lower story,

---

[1] Œconomicus, ch. ii.
[2] Diogenes Laertius, ii. 5, 24, on the authority of the Recollections of Pamphile.   [3] *Ibid.*, § 31.
[4] Cp. Couat, Aristophane, p. 194. Zimmern, Greek Commonwealth, *ad loc.*; Becker's Charicles, *ad loc.* Tucker, Life in Ancient Athens, pp. 54, 55.

could be used for the accommodation of the domestic menials, where such were possessed. The material used in building was commonly brick or wood,[1] and sometimes stone. The roofs were flat, and the lighting got partly from above, partly through doors, though windows in the walls were also a method employed to some extent. The heating was done by fires, but it is supposed there were no properly constructed chimneys, and that the smoke escaped in the way in vogue in the old Scotch country cottages, *i.e.* through a hole in the roof. The upper story, where it existed, must have been rather in the way from this point of view, and in that case the smoke had to get away as best it could through apertures and doors. The floors in early times were of dried earth, but in the fifth century we also find them made of paving stones or pebbles set in cement.[2] Becker in "Charicles" says they were, as a rule, only plaster. In the more elegant houses diverse patterns might be wrought on the floor.

As for the walls they were merely whitewashed until Alcibiades introduced the innovation of painting them. Socrates appears to have been averse to this application of art, for he complains that "pictures and decorations deprive of more pleasure than they give."[3] So at least it is stated among some other very trite and commonplace remarks ascribed to him, and if it is to be understood at all, the sentiment must have been called forth by rather crude attempts at mural decoration.

As for furniture, it was very scanty in all probability, consisting of rude beds, couches, chairs, stools, portable tables, cupboards, with necessary utensils and vessels

---

[1] Xen., Mem., iii. 1, 7. Whibley, Companion to Greek Studies, § 623 ; Tucker, *op. cit.*, p. 58.
[2] Whibley, *op. cit.*, § 623.
[3] Mem., iii. 8, 10.

for cooking and for the table,[1] which when out of use adorned the floor or walls.

Altogether then, taking Socrates' establishment as a poor one, below the ordinary Athenian standards of comfort, the impression we form of it is that it must have been what to us would be an intolerably bare and plain habitation, without touch of art, possessing only such beauty as utility rigorously interpreted gives, a habitation, however, which would demand the very minimum of outlay to keep it up to its humble best. A coat of whitewash now and again for the walls would be the extent of normal outlay to keep it in decent order.

The cost of living in other respects was likewise very low at Athens, the habits being simple. At table knives and forks were not in use, solid food being eaten with the fingers, while for liquid dishes a metal spoon or a chunk of bread sufficed.[2]

The average Athenian took three meals a day; breakfast, partaken of immediately on rising;[3] lunch about noon after the marketing was done; and dinner in the evening, when the duties of the day were over and one could enjoy oneself, and, on occasion, some genial society, as well as one's viands. How many meals Socrates usually took is, of course, quite another matter. That would depend on circumstances and the state of appetite. He regarded food as a matter of minimum importance, to be regulated by need rather than by rule. He might very occasionally indulge in luxuries like fish and poultry and hare at a grand banquet given by some friend on a great occasion, but at home, as all accounts relate, he dined abstemiously on the plainest fare. Vegetarian dishes were the order

---

[1] Whibley, *op. cit.*, § 624. Cp. also Xen., Œconomicus, ch. 9, § 6.
[2] See Becker's Charicles, p. 320 (Eng. trans.).
[3] Arist., Aves, 1285.

of the day, being cheapest, and consisting mainly of barley bread and porridge, also vegetables like onions, leeks, beans, lettuce, and cabbage. Butcher meat was also at times, but sparingly, eaten by the people. Olives and figs, nuts and fruit cakes, were run on for dessert, the last enjoying great favour at Athens, with a reputation like Bath buns in the south, or Eccles cakes in the north of England. The poorer people, of course, did not enjoy all this variety and, inexpensive as such diet was, it does not by any means represent the possible minimum of subsistence. A man like Socrates especially could easily cut out a number of these items as superfluous. Plato imagined people in more primitive times to live " on barley and wheat, baking cakes of the meal and kneading loaves of the flour." [1] And what the Scotch could nourish a strong, healthy, and brainy peasantry on, would not be too plain for Socrates, and would mean extremely little outlay.

We can get an idea, from information scattered through the Comedies of Aristophanes, as to the prices of such commodities. Enough to make a repast might be got for a half-obol,[2] or three-farthings in our money, according to the statement in the "Frogs"; in the "Wasps,"[3] the judge Philocleon can feed a family of three persons on $4\frac{1}{2}d$.

From the "Plutus" we learn that a cloak might cost about thirteen[4] or seventeen shillings,[5] and a pair of shoes about six shillings and sixpence,[6] but these can by no means represent minimum prices. "A man could keep himself on twopence halfpenny a day; at that outlay he could have some bread, olives, and some fish or meat. Fourpence halfpenny

---

[1] Repub. 372 b.   [2] Arist., Frogs, 554.
[3] ll. 300, 301.   [4] Assembly of Women, 412.
[5] Plutus, 982.   [6] Plutus, 983.

DOMESTIC LIFE

sufficed to buy bread, provisions, and drink for a family of three persons. Food and fire did not cost a family more than one hundred and eighty-two drachmas, or about eight pounds. In addition there was rent and clothing. A house could be had at an annual rental of from five to ten pounds. Clothes and shoes did not cost more than from fifty to sixty drachmas, *i.e.* from about forty-four to fifty-three shillings. Thus, says Couat, a family could live on three hundred and twenty-five francs a year, *i.e.* about sixteen pounds."[1] "The most moderate person required for living $1\frac{1}{4}$ obols a day (*i.e.* about 2*d*.), which in a year of 360 days gives a sum of about £3." For four persons that means £12, and at the rate of 12 per cent. this demands a capital of £144 for food alone.

The earnings of workmen were correspondingly small, pay varying from five obols to two drachmas, in our money sevenpence halfpenny to one and sevenpence halfpenny. The salary paid by the state to soldiers for time spent in military manœuvres was at the rate of fourpence halfpenny a day.

From facts like these it is possible to understand to some extent the smallness of Socrates' estimate of his own property, and to get an idea of what an insignificant sum it would be possible for him and his family to subsist upon by denying themselves all but the very necessaries of life, and with the help of Xanthippe's vigorous management, assuming it to have taken an economical bent.

The question arises in regard to Socrates' married life, whether Xanthippe was the only wife he ever had. We quote the following passage from Diogenes Laertius: " Aristotle says that he (Socrates) had two women in

[1] Couat, Aristophane, p. 192. Cp. Boeckh, Public Economy of Athens, bk. i. ch. 20 (Eng. trans.), pp. 109 ff. (1842).

marriage; in the first instance, Xanthippe, of whom Lamprocles was born; then Myrto, the daughter of Aristides the Just, whom he took without dowry; she became the mother of Sophroniscus and Menexenus. Some say he married Myrto first; some, that he had both at the same time, *e.g.* Satyrus and Hieronymus the Rhodian. For, they say, the Athenians, wishing to increase the population, on account of the lack of men, decreed to marry one woman as wife and to beget children by another. Hence Socrates' action." [1] Of these statements it is certainly not true that Xanthippe was the first wife of Socrates, and was succeeded by Myrto, for Socrates was the husband of Xanthippe at his death, and the mother of his youngest child. She was also admittedly the mother of his eldest—Lamprocles. So that, if he ever had been married to another woman before Xanthippe, he either had no children by her, or for some inexplicable reason no writer has made any allusion to them. The same comment will hold of any hypothetical relationship with a woman after his marriage with Xanthippe. The idea has to confront three improbabilities: (*a*) the purpose of the relationship, if it was to replenish a population reduced by war, was not in Socrates' case attained; or (*b*) if it was, no mention is made of the progeny, which is hard to account for, since the three by Xanthippe are mentioned, a number which hardly represents any zeal for the state in its need, when we remember that many years must have intervened between the birth of the eldest and youngest; (*c*) the improbability arising from Xanthippe's feelings in the matter, which, if they were like her sentiments generally, must have been strong and decisive against rivals.

The story in a milder form is contradicted by Plutarch in his Life of Aristides,[2] where he refers to it in

---

[1] Diogenes Laertius, ii. 5, 26. [2] Ch. 27.

the following terms: "Demetrius of Phalerum, Hieronymus of Rhodes, Aristoxenus the musician, and Aristotle (if we are to believe the treatise on Nobility a genuine work of his) say that Myrto, the *granddaughter* of Aristides (Diogenes says the *daughter*) lived in the house of Socrates the philosopher, who was indeed married to another woman, but who took her into his house because she was a widow destitute of the necessaries of life. These authors are sufficiently refuted by Panætius in his writings on Socrates."

It would have been extremely interesting to know what Panætius had to say on this matter, but as it is, we must either be content to dismiss the episode as pure legend, or be satisfied that any base and carnal motive for his conduct is out of the question as inconsistent with all that is most sure and certain about his character.[1]

This, however, has to be granted, that his relations with Xanthippe were not of the most fortunate, partly for reasons concerned with the status of women generally in Athens at that time, and partly on account of Xanthippe's own peculiar temperament, which had the one advantage of being a foil to set off the patience and goodness of heart of her philosophic husband.

(*b*) The sentiments and conceptions of woman and her sphere in Athens were such as to make it almost impossible for a wife to be the intellectual companion of her husband, unless when she was possessed of marked native talent. That intellectual culture and acquirement which boys got from schools and tutors and the free intercourse of social life was denied the Athenian girl, and she grew up (ordinarily) with merely domestic interests and accomplishments. There were women who had fitted themselves for intellectual

[1] See the remarks of Professor A. E. Taylor in Varia Socratica, pp. 61, 62.

companionship with men and who enjoyed free and unfettered intercourse with them, but they belonged to a small class apart, which was not the one from which an Athenian would choose his wife; they were the free-lances of society, outside the pale of civil rights and beneath the recognition of the respectable of their own sex. The life and interests of the respectable female were cribbed, cabined, and confined; the home was her sphere, almost her prison, and her duties were those of the faithful wife, mother, and mistress of the home. She was seldom to be seen on the street; it would even have shocked propriety for her to do her own marketing; and as Pericles declared, in his famous Funeral Oration, the less she was on the tongues of men for good or evil the better. Using Xenophon's metaphor of the ideal wife, she was the queen-bee living always in the hive, and directing her workers in the doing of their various duties. She was a delicate combination of the German Hausfrau and the English mid-Victorian, the quintescence of domesticity and propriety. Cranford itself had nothing to show more fair in the way of delicacy, modesty, and ladylikeness, what is called in these last days the "womanliness of woman." Only we fear that to cover the effects of her indoor life she took to the rouge-pot, a pardonable weakness surely, since it sprang from the self-effacing desire to be pleasing to her husband. Intellectually she was always a minor, and was thought better so.

It will be interesting, and not, we hope, altogether unilluminating with regard to Socrates, to get as fair an idea as we can of the facts about the Athenian wife. It will show that we ought not to judge of Socrates' married lot by standards not then demanded or expected.

That woman was inferior and regarded as such is,

on the whole, true.¹ In answer to a question put by Socrates, in the "Œconomicus" of Xenophon, which gives a very charming, if also to us at times an unconsciously amusing picture of the ideal domestic life, Isomachus, the interlocutor, speaks in this wise regarding his docile and exemplary mate: "Well-skilled? What proficiency was she likely to bring with her when she was not quite fifteen at the time she wedded me, and during the whole period of her life had been most carefully brought up to see and hear as little as possible, and to ask the fewest questions, or do you not think that one should be satisfied if at marriage her whole experience consisted in knowing how to take the wool and make a dress, and seeing how her mother's hand-maidens had their daily tasks assigned to them? For as regards control of appetite and self-indulgence she had received the soundest education, and that I take to be the most important matter in the bringing up of man or woman." [2]

(c) The objects of marriage are stated in the oration of Demosthenes against Neæra as being "in order to beget legitimate children and to have a trustworthy guardian of the home and all in it." [3] Isomachus, in the "Œconomicus," says: "Did it ever strike you to consider, dear wife, what made me choose you as my

[1] Plato, in Repub., v. p. 455, says: "In almost every employment the male sex is vastly superior to the other. There are many women no doubt who are better in many things than many men; but speaking generally the case is as stated"—a perfectly English sentiment, rather more strongly put by Aristotle: "Even a woman may be good and also a slave; though the woman may be said to be an inferior being and the slave is absolutely bad" (Aristotle, Poetics, 15, 1). Plato in the Laws desiderated education for girls to enable them to take their place by men.

[2] Œconomicus, 7, 5, 6.

[3] p. 1386. Cp. Gomperz, Greek Thinkers, ii. p. 382; Grote, Plato, ii. p. 2 n.

wife among all women, and your parents to entrust you to me of all men ? It was with the deliberate intent to discover, I for myself and your parents on behalf of you, the best partner of house and children we could find, that I sought you out, your parents acting to the best of their ability made choice of me. If at some future time God grant us to have children born to us, we will take counsel together how best to bring them up, for that too will be a common interest and a common blessing if haply they shall live to fight our battles, and we find in them hereafter support and succour when ourselves are old."[1] The chief ends of marriage are " first and foremost to perpetuate the races of living creatures, and next to make provision for sons and daughters to render support in old age."[2]

There is nothing in this that might not be assigned by any contemporary writer on the subject to-day. And one really sees no reason for the assertion that in Greece the married relation was a sensuous one in a degree in which it is not so among the mass of people now. The Apostle Paul himself, while setting up celibacy as the ideal for the Corinthian Christians, still advised them to marry if their passions were too strong ; it is better to marry than to burn.[3] And Bernard Shaw has attacked the marriage institution of England as being to a large extent describable in terms of St. Paul's lower alternative. And who can deny that it is by ordinary conventional sentiment taken as a charter by which any and every indulgence of sexual passion is legitimised and consecrated.

It may be said that the better education and wider interests of women to-day permits of and makes possible a truly spiritual union between man and

[1] Œconomicus, ch. 7, §§ 11 and 12. (Dakyns' trans.)
[2] *Op. cit.*, ch. 7, § 19.   [3] 1 Corinthians, ch. 7, v. 9.

woman—a companionship in life's ideal interests which purifies and transfigures the merely sensuous bond. That is of course true, but we should be wrong in supposing that the same transfiguration was not possible to the Greeks.

It is nothing to the contrary by any means that the relationship did not usually originate in romantic sentiment and love's young dream, that marriage was the result of an arrangement between the bridegroom and his parents, on the one hand, and the parents of the bride on the other, and that the two were often unacquainted with each other previous to the event which was of such import to both. If the mode of selection was artificial and rather prosaic, we must recollect that it is the only one we consider good enough for our royal families, and the one which plays a larger and larger part as we ascend in the scale of society. Moreover if, as Xenophon hints, it was based on a reference to the end of marriage as the production of offspring for the state, and carried out with a view to the best accomplishment of that end, it was only the kind of thing which the " advanced " people in our own society, styled Eugenists, would very much like to see more prevalent among us.

(d) Woman was regarded as an inferior creature, so she is still; but that does not prevent her from enjoying special privilege and deference. Anyone who knows our society knows that the gentlemanly attitude to the fair sex, chivalry and gallantry in their higher refinements, are quite compatible with a good deal of latent cynicism in the views of women, and a very pronounced belief in their essential mental inferiority to the male.

In Greece there was much that went to neutralise female inferiority, and make the male attitude to it in many cases something other than one of " contemptuous toleration," as it has been described.[1] In certain respects, with all its narrowness of mind and restriction of liberty, womanhood was the object of special deference and respect, and a high ideal in the way of modesty and purity was demanded.

Marcus Cato said that "a man who beat his wife and children laid hands on the holiest things," and we can find in Aristophanes indications that as regards woman that was also the Athenian view. It is bad enough that Pheidippides beats his father—it is disgraceful; but that he should even threaten to beat his mother is an intolerable enormity. Strepsiades can make no terms with the causes of such unnaturalness.[2] The plays of Æschylus and Sophocles breathe the sense of a certain rare dignity, propriety, and delicacy, as the characteristics of womanhood. Weak, foolish, and baneful the sex may be, but it is more, it stands out as a thing to be reckoned with for good or ill. In the "Electra" of Euripides one finds expressed, in the conduct and on the lips of an old peasant, those feelings of chivalry towards the weaker sex which denote the respect it commanded.

Isomachus finds in his ideal wife one who will share his joys in days of gladness, enter into his sorrows in days of trouble.[3] She is the real partner in his inner life, even though excluded from public interests. The Athenian, like the average educated German, wanted to find in his home a haven where the ripples and waves of business cares and political strifes did not come;

> "Thou hast enough with fields and kine to keep;
> 'Tis mine to make all bright within the door.
> 'Tis joy to him that toils, when toil is o'er,
> To find home waiting, full of happy things."[4]

---

[1] Godley, Socrates and Athenian Society, p. 124.
[2] See Clouds, ll. 1442 ff.
[3] Xen., Œconomicus, ch. 9, § 12.   [4] Euripides, Electra.

DOMESTIC LIFE

Certainly we smile at the eagerness of Isomachus to relate to Socrates "instances of the large-mindedness" of his wife, shown in the readiness with which, as he says, "she listened to my words and carried out my wishes"—it is so exquisitely English. Nor was this the only side to the picture. With all her conventional subordination she was not always without the immemorial power to subdue superior strength. "You see that little boy," said Themistocles once to his friends, "the fate of Greece is in his hands, for he rules his mother, and *his mother rules me*, I rule the Athenians, and the Athenians rule Greece."

If we may be permitted to quote from the "Œconomicus" again, in spite of Gomperz's statement,[1] that Xenophon's works are no true picture of Athenian life and sentiment: (Husband to wife)—"The greatest joy of all will be to prove yourself my better; to make me your follower; knowing no dread lest, as the years advance, you should decline in honour in your household, but rather trusting that, though your hair turn grey, yet in proportion as you become a better helpmate to myself and to the children, a better guardian of your home, so will your honour increase throughout the household as mistress, wife, and mother, daily more dearly prized, since it is not through excellence of outward form but by reason of the lustre of virtues shed forth upon the life of man, that increase is given to things beautiful and good."[2] In the "Banquet" it is mentioned as if it were something not at all very remarkable that Niceratus adores his wife and is adored by her.[3]

At its best married life was thus a happy union in which the feeling of inferiority or superiority was

---

[1] Greek Thinkers, vol. ii. p. 382.
[2] Œconomicus, vii. (Dakyns' trans.)
[3] Xen., Banquet, ch. viii. (Dakyns' trans.)

effaced, and at its worst a relation from which the law permitted release to the woman under certain circumstances, so that she was not entirely at the mercy of a callous husband. Woman, then, was no mere chattel without rights; technically she was the inferior, the man was the head of the wife, as in the Pauline Ethic, but in practice it depended a good deal on the persons concerned.

The case of Socrates himself is instructive, though we do not class him as an ordinary Athenian. After allowing for the natural tendency to work out the typical example of the other-worldly philosopher and henpecked husband in one, we must allow some truth to common gossip, and recognise that under Socrates' humble roof Xanthippe was master of the situation. Whether by reason of constitution or of circumstances, or of both combined, she had developed into a quick-tempered, sharp-tongued, petulant woman. She had not any of the power of Mrs. Wiggs of the Cabbage Patch to lock up her troubles and lose the key. She was apt to be querulous in speech and volcanic in action. And we can sympathise with the alacrity of Socrates, which comes out as a little natural touch in the "Œconomicus," whether consciously or unconsciously. Isomachus expresses a fond desire to treat the philosopher to some instances of that large-mindedness of his wife which showed itself in her willingness to do what he wanted; and Socrates replies, "What sort of thing? Do, pray, tell me, since I would far more gladly hear about a living woman's virtues than that Zeuxis should show me the portrait of the loveliest woman he has painted." The sentiment is thoroughly Socratic, but is there not also a drop of pathos in the question? Still the reminiscences and anecdotes go to show that Socrates, ample-minded, big-hearted, easy-going, with all his restless rapier-like intellect, treated the honest but fiery Xanthippe with the best of good-humour and consideration, for he knew the virtues in her motherly heart.

Alcibiades once said that her rating was intolerable. " Oh," said Socrates, " I'm used to it as one gets used to the noise of wheels. Besides *you* don't find the noise of geese intolerable ! " A. ' But they give me eggs and young ones.' S. ' And Xanthippe gives me children.' "[1] On another occasion, as the gossip goes, he compared himself, as husband of a fiery wife, to a trainer who has to deal with spirited horses. When he can manage them, he has the satisfaction of knowing he need fear no others.[2] One day she was giving him a rating in the presence of some friends, and concluded her tirade by flinging some water about him, whereat the philosopher good-naturedly contented himself with remarking, " Did I not tell you Xanthippe was thundering, and it would soon rain ? "[3] It reminds one of the story told of St. Basil. The Saint was haled before an angry magistrate, who threatened that he would tear out his liver. To this Basil politely replied, " Thanks for your intention ; where it is at present it has been no slight annoyance." Asked his advice whether a man ought to marry, Socrates wittily replied, " In either case you will repent it." Such was ancient gossip.

His excellent and forbearing conduct in the home seems to have been a proverb in the ancient world, and not without an influence for good. Marcus Cato expressed himself to the effect that he would " rather be a good husband than a great statesman, and that what he especially admired in Socrates was his patience and kindness in bearing with his ill-tempered wife and stupid children."[4]

[1] Diogenes Laertius, ii. 5, 36.   [2] *Op. cit.*, ii. 5, 37.
[3] *Op. cit.*, ii. 5, 36.   [4] Plutarch, Life of Marcus Cato, ch. 20.

In every direction he was, as we have seen, a man of extraordinary self-restraint, and the root of it lay, we think, in his capacity to see things steadily and see them whole. Outbursts of anger and retaliation against individuals are generally due to a temporary lapse of memory under present excitement, a defect of rational vision, during which the object is not seen entire, but is caught at a rapid, partial, or unfavourable angle; in such an instantaneous, fragmentary view there is nothing to counteract the impulse of resentment. But Socrates at such testing moments could keep the whole object in full view of the whole eye, and the reaction was determined accordingly. He saw not merely Xanthippe the termagant, but Xanthippe the sharer of his burdens, the companion of his poverty, the mother and nurse of his children, the wife who no doubt at bottom loved him from her heart.

Lamprocles, one of their sons, on a certain occasion lost his temper with his mother, and when his father remonstrated, he alleged in excuse that nobody could stand her cantankerousness. Socrates took him in hand and showed how unjust and ungrateful he was, in view of all he owed to his mother. "The mother conceiving bears her precious burthen with travail and pain, and at the risk of life itself—sharing with that within her womb the food on which she herself is fed. And when with much labour she has borne to the end and brought forth her infant, she feeds it and watches over it with tender care, not in return for any good thing previously received, for indeed the babe itself is little conscious of its benefactor and cannot even signify its wants, . . . and for many months she feeds it night and day, enduring the toil, nor recking what return she shall receive for all her trouble. . . . And this mother who is kind to you and takes such tender care of you when you are ill to make you well again, and to see that you want for nothing which may help you; and more than all who is perpetually pleading for blessings in your behalf and offering her vows to heaven—can you say of her that she is cross-grained and harsh?"[1]

Behind her faults then Socrates saw the essentially good mother. Nor should we fail to note the piety of the home, so precious a possession of the ancients, which is here indicated. We shall have to deal later with the religion of Socrates, but no treatment of domestic life would be right which omitted all reference to the domestic pieties and the religious feeling which pervaded the common life of the people, and out of which arose the sacred rites of the family hearth. In passing one may also draw attention to the fact that the attitude here depicted does not bear out the Aristophanic representation of him as, in intention and spirit at all events, an underminer of filial piety. Socrates taught doctrines whose tendency was to work as solvents of merely sentimental conventions, where sentiment is out of place, but there was nothing in that which at all weakened the duty of a just deference and gratitude to parents, any more than it would be legitimate exegesis to take the teaching of Jesus that unless a man hated brother and sister and father and mother he could not be worthy to be his disciple, and interpret it as teaching actual hatred of one's own flesh and blood as condition of loving humanity, which would be an extraordinary inversion of their real spirit and tendency.

We have seen then the calm, reasoned attitude of Socrates in the home, his recognition of the essential work and worth of the woman whose irritability must have often been a thorn in the flesh. The elements

[1] Xen., Mem., ii. ch. 2. (Dakyns' trans.)

of violent domestic unhappiness and strife were there, but the steady and completely disciplined character, and the all-round vision of Socrates, saved the situation, so far as salvation was possible, and kept him cheerful and genial through all.

(e) He brought the same reconciling spirit to bear on all family relationships, holding that members of a family are meant to be a help and blessing to one another. The family is an organism whose members, like eyes and hands and feet in the body, make up for each other's deficiencies and contribute to the common unitary life. Domestic squabbles were for him the sign of a species of stupidity, of a lack of the common-sense to give and take, to overlook and forgive. For the want of this spirit the divine meaning and purpose of the family is frustrated. It is intended to be a little commonwealth of those who co-operate each with each to the advantage and good of all alike.[1] The parents out of natural affection must sacrifice and labour for their children's weal, and the children must honour and respect their parents. The home thus becomes a school of character and a centre of happiness. The chapter on Socrates' education has already brought out the fact that in Greece generally the hearth was a centre of religious and moral guidance and instruction, a place for the first stages of character-building, and an altar whose priest was the father.[2] There is nothing in Xenophon's "Reminiscences," or anywhere outside the Platonic Dialogues, that we know of, to suggest that Socrates felt, as Plato did so deeply, that the institutions of the family and of property had failed to produce a high enough type of citizen, and that that result would only be achieved by breaking down family walls, and introducing a

---

[1] Mem., ii. 3, 19.
[2] Cp. Fustel de Coulanges, La Cité antique.

state communism in which all narrower, more domestic loyalties would be submerged, and loyalty to the one father and mother, Society, alone remain. That we believe was left for the rationalism of a thinker in whom sentiment was much less deeply rooted than in the rationalism of Socrates. The latter was, in the words in which Lord Houghton was characterised by G. W. E. Russell, "that most precious combination —a genius *and a heart*. He warmed not only both hands but indeed all his nature before the fire of life." Family relationships as well as social relationships were in his view capable of being made an indispensable enrichment of life.

CHAPTER V

PUBLIC LIFE

> " Ah, forge of God, where blows
> The blast of an incredible flame, what might
> Shapes to what uses there
> Each obdurate iron or molten fiery part
> Of the one infinite wrought human heart;
> In tears, love, anger, beauty, and despair,
> Throbbing for ever, under the red night?"
> LAURENCE BINYON.

(a) SOCRATES AS FRIEND

IN Athens men were citizens first and anything else after that. " An Athenian citizen," says Pericles, in the oration put into his mouth by Thucydides—" an Athenian citizen does not neglect the state because he takes care of his own household. We alone regard a man who takes no interest in public affairs, not as a harmless but as a useless character." [1]

Loyalty to the state's welfare must condition and circumscribe all other loyalties. Home life with us is richer than with them. We recognise that the home is the best school for society, that it is there we first learn the love and brotherhood, the mutual forbearance and self-sacrifice, which we must later apply in the wider relationships of the community. It is in the warmer, more genial atmosphere of the family we train those seedlings which we must plant out in the world to clothe it with beauty and fruitfulness.

[1] Thucydides, bk. ii. ch. 40.

At the same time it must be confessed that there is in human nature, as we are acquainted with it at present, a strong tendency to give up to the family what was meant for mankind. It is an enlarged form of selfishness, which checks and frustrates various reforms which would be for the good of the nation as a whole. What we want is more public spirit which will bring men and women outside their excellent homes to think and work disinterestedly for the common weal. We in this land have never appreciated as the Greeks did how much we owe to society and its organisation in the way of secure life, economic resources, accumulated culture, and developed morality; indeed, we are its debtors for everything which enriches personality and makes life worth living. If we are above the condition of Hottentots and Sandwich Islanders, it is because of the social heritage into which we have entered.

Socrates, at any rate, cannot be accused of subordinating public to home duties. In a town of citizens he was distinguished for his public ardour, though it was exposed to misrepresentation or lack of recognition because it did not run in the conventional channels. No figure was more familiar in the market place and other haunts of public resort,[1] like the Gymnasia. Anywhere where two or three people were gathered together you might find Socrates in the midst. He could hardly have been of the tribe referred to contemptuously by Robert Louis Stevenson, "who have plied their book diligently and know all about some one branch or another of accepted lore, come out of the study with an ancient and owl-like demeanour and prove dry, stockish, and dyspeptic in all the better and brighter parts of life," though that is the picture of him which Aristophanes sketches, making him live

[1] Mem., bk. i, ch. 1, § 10.

a rusty-musty existence in an underground cellar where he and his followers get pale grubbing after pale "notions," their faces "bruckit wi' dirt," as Scotch folk say.

"Socrates," says Laches, "is always passing his time in places where the youth have any noble study and pursuit." He might be found sitting in one of the various tradesmen's shops surrounding the market, where Athenians would often turn in of an afternoon and pass the hot time of day resting and conversing, or under the porticoes of buildings, or perhaps walking beneath the shade of the plane trees which Cimon had had planted in the market.

The market, or Agora, was the very centre of Athenian life, the "hub of the universe," where the hum of talk and discussion for ever floated among the cries of hucksters, who stood at their booths or stalls and shouted out their wares in bustling rivalry, and where each class of goods had its own position and area. The market was a large, rambling, irregular space, stretching from the Pnyx to the Inner Cerameicos. More especially from nine in the forenoon till about twelve it presented a scene of animated bustle, moving knots of men, gentlemen or slaves, busy making their purchases; of women comparatively few and these of low or ambiguous social standing.

It will help us to réalise the bright scene, the varied background, in which Socrates moved, if we quote the description of the market place [1] given by Becker in his "Charicles": [2]

"The market place was filling fast when Charicles entered it. Traders had set up their wattled stalls all over it, with their goods exposed on tables and benches. Here the female bakers had piled up their

---

[1] See also Whibley, Companion to Greek Studies, p. 536.
[2] P. 61 of Eng. trans.

round-shaped loaves and cakes, and were pursuing with a torrent of scolding and abuse the unlucky wight who happened, in passing by, to upset one of their pyramids. There, simmered the kettles of the women who sold boiled peas and other vegetables; in the crockery market, hard by, the potmen were descanting on the goodness of their wares. A little way off, in the myrtle market, chaplets and fillets were to be sold, and many a comely flower-weaver received orders for garlands, to be delivered by her in the evening. All the wants of the day, from barley-groats up to the choicest fish, from garlick to the incense of the gods; clear pure oil, and the most exquisite ointments; fresh made cheese, and the sweet honey of the bees of Hymettus; cooks ready to be hired, slaves, male and female, to be sold,—each and all were to be found at their customary stalls. There were others, who went about crying their wares, while every now and then a public crier crossed the ground, announcing with stentorian voice the arrival of some goods to be sold, or the sale of a house, or perhaps a reward for the apprehension of a robber, or a runaway slave. Slaves of both sexes, as well as freemen, kept walking up and down, bargaining and inspecting the stalls, in search of their daily requirements.

"The fish market bell was just ringing as a signal that the hour of business had arrived, and forthwith all streamed in that direction, to lose no time in completing this all-important purchase. The way to the money changers led Charicles directly across this part of the market. And it was truly amusing to behold how the eager buyers tried all their arts of persuasion to move the hard-hearted dealers, who stuck doggedly to their prices. 'What's the price of these two pike, if I take the pair?' asks a greedy gourmand in his hearing. 'Ten obols,' answered the fishmonger, scarce deigning to look up. 'That's too much,' said the other, 'you'll let me have them for eight, I'm sure?' 'Yes, one of them,' was the reply. 'Nonsense,' said the would-be purchaser; 'come, here are eight obols.' 'I told you the price, sir; and if you don't like it you can go elsewhere,' said the inexorable dealer, with the most perfect nonchalance. Such scenes as this were of frequent occurrence, and Charicles would have liked to witness more of them, but that Manas was with him bearing the important casket."

It was in this bustle then Socrates lived his life and pursued his mission. He was as true a city bird as any Cockney. He never went away from Athens but for military service except on the very rarest occasions. Only one such occasion is referred to by him in the "Crito,"[1] and it is asserted to be the only one. Three are mentioned by Diogenes Laertius,[2] with the authority from which he quotes, one of them being a stay at Samos with Archelaus when Socrates was still young. The record shows his heart was within the dear old walls. Athens to him was something like London to Johnson: "Why, Sir, you find no man at all intellectual, who is willing to leave London. No, Sir, when a man is tired of London he is tired of life; for there is in London all that life can afford."

Not that he was insensible to the charms of natural beauty, and could not feel the spell of the country. He once told Aristippus,[3] that the ideal place for a church was away in some lonely spot, high up, whence the eye could look across the landscape. There about the worshipper would be peace and tranquillity and the emotion of the long look into the distance. In the "Phædrus," if we may take the little dramatic

---

[1] Crito, 52 b.   [2] ii. 5, §§ 22, 23.   [3] Mem., iii. 8.

touches as true to the spirit of Socrates, and there is much justification for doing so on artistic grounds, we find the master by no means untouched by natural beauties. He agrees that it is more refreshing to walk on the country roads than in city promenades.[1] When Phædrus has led him to a quiet spot beneath a plane tree, he exclaims enthusiastically, " By Hera, what a retreat ! This plane-tree is large and high. And the height and woven shade of the Chestnut altogether lovely ! And what glory of blossom, as if to fill the place with finest scent ! And the spring beneath the plane is most delicious about our feet with its fresh cold water. It seems to be sacred to Nymphs and Achelöus, from these figures and offerings. How exquisitely sweet and delightful the air that breathes in the place, ahum too with a chorus of crickets, summer's harmony. Best of all the gentle grassy slope, just made for the head to recline on luxuriously ! You could not have been a better guide, my dear Phædrus."[2] He has entered into the very feeling of nature's scenes and scents and sounds. But if he had been asked whether he cared much for Nature, we imagine he would have made Browning's reply, " Yes, a great deal, but for human beings a great deal more."

He was the " poor lover of discourse," the seeker after knowledge and wisdom, and it was in men and books he found his best instructors. Men and books were his passion. As he says in " Phædrus "[3] " he was afflicted with a weakness for listening to speeches."

" Hold up a book before me and you may lead me all over Attica and the wide world." It reminds us of Lord Macaulay, in a letter to his sister Margaret : " If I had at this moment my choice of life, I would bury myself in one of those immense libraries, and

[1] Phædrus, § 227.   [2] Phædrus, § 230.   [3] § 228.

never pass a waking hour without a book before me." One infers from the Platonic dialogues that Socrates possessed a wide, profound, and studied knowledge of the literature of his country.

Ruskin believed that great authors used words with painstaking accuracy and premeditated significance, so that only by minute verbal study do we extract the full flavour and richness of their writing; every word carries involved overtones which only the tutored ear can distinguish and appreciate. Now, many people read by the line or sentence, a few by the page; Socrates was a word-reader. He read critically and with the understanding. Like our own John Locke he did not believe in merely skimming along without a comprehension of each part as one proceeds. It was thorough reading; he hated lazy, superficial acquaintance with literature, and it was a trait of his character which rather irritated and annoyed people who treated language in an offhand, cavalier sort of way. His searching, analytic method of dealing with literature struck others as the unhappy pedantry of a bore, rather than, as it was, the delicate individualising power of the lover.

Another reason for his love of the city was his love of society. He had a genius for friendship.

> " The grace of friendship—mind and heart
> Linked with their fellow heart and mind;
> The gains of science, gifts of art,
> The sense of oneness with our kind;
> The thirst to know and understand,
> A large and liberal discontent;
> These are the goods in life's rich hand,
> The things that are more excellent."

These lines perfectly express Socrates' views. Plato and Xenophon confirm each other on this matter. Even his thinking was social and co-operative and, like

Emerson, he might have said, "We want but two or three friends, but these we cannot do without; they serve us in every thought we think."[1]

"I am one of those," Plato makes him say in the "Lysis,"[2] "who from my childhood up have set my heart upon a certain thing. All people have their fancies. Some are fond of gold, others of honour. Now I have no violent desire for any of these things. But I have a passion for friends. And I would rather have a good friend than the best cock or quail in the world or even than a horse or a dog (note the quiet irony). Yes, I should prefer a real friend to all the gold of Darius or even to Darius himself. I am such a lover of friends as that." Or, as Xenophon recalls him expressing it: "I too, Antiphon, having my tastes, even as another finds pleasure in his horse and his hounds, and another in his fighting and cocks, so I take my pleasure in good friends; and if I have any good thing myself I teach it to them or I commend them to others by whom I think they will be helped forward on the path of virtue."[3]

The Athenians, as a whole, were a sociable people, and they dined on occasion at one another's houses, holding symposia, from which however the women were excluded, this latter circumstance not tending to improve the tone of such gatherings. Besides this they also formed themselves into little social clubs,[4] at which they had meals together, each member paying his contribution to the common expense. The Socratic circle seems also to have followed this custom. It was what we might call a small philosophical club, in which the delights of friendship became a stimulus and help to intellectual pursuits. As Socrates ex-

---

[1] In a letter to Carlyle.   [2] Lysis, 211 E.   [3] Mem., i. ch. 6.
[4] Cp. Laches, 179 b. Whibley, Companion to Greek Studies, § 612.

presses it in the "Protagoras," "All men who have a companion are readier in deed and word and thought, for they can co-operate in their discoveries." It is this high aim that gives Socratic friendship its true note.

The "Memorabilia" and the "Lysis" express the same doctrine that it is only between the good that friendship strictly speaking can exist. Men only want the friendship of the good, for only from such can any benefit be derived; "to win the love of good men we must be good ourselves in speech and action."[1] Friendship lives in an interchange of sympathy, help, and gratitude,[2] and is, in the highest sense, unselfish, a beautiful rivalry in mutual service.[3] "Friends have all things in common," was a Greek aphorism about friendship approved and adopted by Socrates.[4]

Accordingly, in his view, it is only possible between those who have overcome selfishness; its foundation is self-control, mastery of all the lower passions and desires. It is for those who have control over the pleasures of the body, who are kindly disposed and upright in all their dealings.[5]

Friendship ought to be a bond uniting all the good everywhere, and yet experience shows the good often opposed to each other. The very desire for possession of the things that are lovely and of good report creates strife and discord, not to mention that which is stirred up by anger and avarice and envy in individuals and nations.[6]

"Nevertheless," says Socrates, full of faith's and love's glowing optimism, "through all opposing barriers friendship steals her way and binds together the beautiful and good among mankind. Such is their virtue that they would rather possess scant means

---

[1] Mem., ii. ch. 6.
[2] Mem., ii. ch. 6.
[3] ii. ch. 6.
[4] Repub., 424 A. Lysis, 206 E.
[5] Xen., Mem., ii. ch. 6.
[6] Mem., ii. ch. 6.

painlessly than wield an empire won by war. In spite of hunger and thirst they will share their meat and drink without a pang. Nor bloom of lusty youth, nor love's delights, can warp their self-control; nor will they be tempted to cause pain where pain should be unknown. It is theirs to eschew not merely all greed of riches, not merely to make a just and lawful distribution of wealth, but to supply what is lacking to the needs of one another. Theirs is to compose strife and discord, not in painless oblivion simply, but to the general advantage. Theirs also to hinder such extravagance of anger as shall entail remorse hereafter. And as to envy they shall make a clean sweep and clearance of it; the good things which a man possesses shall be also the property of his friends, and the goods which they possess are to be looked upon as his." [1]

The teaching of the Platonic dialogue "Lysis" is to the same effect. Because of the impulse Friendship gives to excel in benevolence and kindly deed, it is a thing of incomparable worth. It grows with the years like a beautiful tree bearing its fruit, because it is rooted in good soil. Friendship is the daughter of the Heavenly Love, it is itself heavenly, all its inspirations are noble and generous. It enters not only into the joys and gains, but into the sorrows and losses of others, so enlarging the personality and purifying the morality of men. Such being its divine descent and nature, it is not possible in any genuine sense between the selfish or the evil. It is above these because it means Harmony, and the evil have no harmony of nature even with themselves; in them the lower is at victorious war with the higher, and the soul is in a state of insurrection and anarchy. Evil is selfishness, friendship is unselfishness. The good alone can truly and deeply unite.

[1] Mem., ii. ch. 6, § 23.

Socratic Friendship thus conceived is, like the Christian Love, a principle which is to bind the good, the elect, together, in a community which brings within its sweep those of all classes and nations. One feels that Socrates is expressing the consciousness of principles and affinities that are in their nature supra-national, simply human without qualification or restriction. We shall have to allude to the point again in discussing his ethics in relation to the treatment of enemies.

We must pursue Socrates' teaching about Friendship along another line no less important. It was to be a relationship growing out of the soul and its affinities, not out of the body and its appetites. In this matter Socrates came to his time as an apostle and reformer. Here he stands out as a man sent by God to his day and generation. His doctrine of Friendship was revolutionary and redemptive to the Athens of that day, in respect of one of its social customs.

All injustice and partiality avenges itself sooner or later on a society. We cannot fail of the true human law with impunity. On this Æschylus and Shakespeare shake hands across the centuries:

> " While Time shall be, while Zeus in heaven is lord,
> His law is fixed and stern;
> The wage of wrong is woe."[1]

The Athenians denied womanhood a free equal life; it was unnatural, and from it as a root grew unnatural vices as an evil fruitage on the tree of life. The romance which should have gathered round woman twined like a noxious growth about boyhood. "It was the masculine beauty of youth that fired the Hellenic imagination with glowing and impassioned sentiment," says Grote,[2] and Gomperz points out that

---

[1] Æschylus, Agamemnon. Trans. House of Atreus, p. 72.
[2] Plato, vol. ii. p. 3.

these attachments not infrequently led to " devotion, enthusiastic, intense, ideal, the sensual origin of which was entirely forgotten." [1] The form and comeliness of these boys often, however, became an infatuation to mature men, in whom the love of beauty was a very passion. The springs of a sexual attraction were stirred, incomprehensible as the fact may be to us, and it led to practices which were and could only be demoralising and disastrous. It disturbed the sanity of age and corrupted the innocence of youth. Socrates' doctrine and example were directed against these friendships in whose flower curled the worm of sensuality.

Alcibiades, in the "Symposium," relates how he had used every wile and device to tempt Socrates into the illicit pleasures of love, playing upon the philosopher's well-known susceptibility to physical beauty. He had subjected him to the very keenest temptations in order to stir up his amorous passions, but all in vain; Socrates could not be corrupted. He came out of the trial of his virtue as by fire unscathed, and poured contempt on Alcibiades' arts.[2] Whether or no we can accept every detail of this confession of Alcibiades in his cups, whether or no we can take the confession as a whole as at all truly biographical, at any rate it does give dramatic expression to what must have been a recognised characteristic of Socrates, that he would have nothing to do with the sensual practices connected with boy-love.

Xenophon gives similar testimony, telling us that Socrates warned others against the perils of these amours. He remonstrated with Critias on his relations with Euthydemus, "knowing that his love was carnal,

[1] Greek Thinkers, ii. p. 380.
[2] See Symposium, §§ 217–219, and cp. Plutarch's Life of Alcibiades, chs. 4 and 6.

of the body," appealing to his sense of self-respect and honour, pointing out that such conduct was a degradation of pure love; and when this proved unavailing, mightily offended the proud Critias by resorting to irony in which he likened the latter's ways to hoggery.[1] In another case he adopted a more bantering tone, where we might think it impossible to be too serious and grave, but he was an inveterate jester, without being one iota the less serious and earnest. There is no more intense and concentrated man alive than George Bernard Shaw, yet John Bull, with his unconscionable ponderosities, thinks him capable only of flippancy and jest. Behind all that, however, is an earnestness deep almost as life. Grapeshot may in some circumstances be more effective than powder and ball. And we don't measure feelings by weight. So with Socrates.

Critobulus, a man of sense, has, the master hears, given a kiss to a fair son of Alcibiades, wherefore he ought to be called a libertine, who is ready to leap into fatal flames. "Poor soul, what do you expect your fate to be after that kiss? Let me tell you. On the instant you will lose your freedom, the indenture of your bondage will be signed; you will be driven to spend large sums on hurtful pleasures; you will scarcely have a moment's leisure for any noble study; you will be driven to concern yourself zealously for things which no man, not even a madman, would choose to make an object of concern."[2] Socrates advises such an one caught in these infatuations to run helter-skelter from the zone of danger; let him go abroad till he gets cured, for it is the poisoning of manhood.

[1] Mem., i. ch. 2, §§ 29 and 30.
[2] Cp. Xenophon, Banquet, ch. 4, §§ 24 ff., on Socrates' warnings against the passions.

Socrates then clearly saw this moral cancer in contemporary manners, and he sought to recall his fellow-men to the truth that it is not such love but the love of the mind and the soul which leads to the surest and highest exaltation. The charm of wisdom never weakens nor betrays nor disappoints—" She is better than rubies and all the things that can be desired are not to be compared unto her." He saw friendship as a pure ideal of mutual co-operation in pursuit of the soul's highest goals, and of such a character were the friendships of his life. There is a spiritual gravitation which makes the mutual attraction of souls the greater the nearer they are in spirit and purpose to each other.

" Do you ask to be the companion of nobles ? Make yourself noble and you shall be." The men who gathered about Socrates, some older, some younger, were men who, like him, yearned for the heights, whose heart panted after the waterbrooks of Truth and Reality. Nor was there any limit, in the master's view, to the value of a companionship like that. It was there, in the leap of a kindred emotion, in the light caught from one another's eyes, in the thought that kindles from soul to soul, that one reached the best in one's own or in another's mind.

It would seem that the little Socratic group formed a club, a common enough thing in Athens as we have remarked, and those who took part in the meetings brought their own contribution to the common meal, Socrates' method being that, while some brought more than others, all should share freely and alike.[1] It may have been these meetings and not any Orphic-Pythagorean religious community, such as Professor Taylor suggests, which lay at the bottom of Aristophanes' idea of the Phrontisterion or " Notion-den "

[1] Xen., Mem., iii. ch. 14.

in the "Clouds." These club meetings became a common feast of wit and wisdom. If Socrates or Simmias or Cebes or Hermogenes or any of the others came across any good thing among the written treasures of the wise of old, they seized upon it and brought it to the club,[1] and together those present discussed it.

It was a little Literary and Philosophical Society. We can imagine what times they had together. What discoveries! what enthusiasm!—a group of searchers gathered round Socrates the Searcher. He sat among them like a kind of god, feeding on nectar and ambrosia, or like a Dr. Johnson, only without the "I am Sir Oracle" tone. We can imagine their meetings, breaking up late at night or early in the morning, as described in Plato's "Symposium," the enthusiasts going out beneath the dark blue vault and the cold bright stars, their mind aglow with intellectual ecstasies, their heart a tumult of ardours! Pale, passing, poor to Socrates all carnal passions and enjoyments beside these stirring raptures of the soul's high loves. There is a splendid passage in Xenophon's "Banquet" where Socrates, amid the night's fun and rollicking laughter, stands forth as the prophet of this marvellous, this more spiritual and loftier love in man.

He speaks of the transitoriness, the imperfection, the selfishness, and dissatisfaction of mere carnal loves, in contrast with the abiding growth, the unselfishness, the sharing of each other's joys and sorrows in true love, where the passion for holy friendship leads to sweet offices and a bliss which company life from youth to eld.

With Socrates, then, it is always the soul that is the real thing. Man is not his body but his mind; so, to love the body is not to love the man's self, but only

[1] Mem., i. ch. 6, § 14.

his property, for the soul is the man and it is superior to and rules the body.[1]

In the "Symposium" of Plato also the mystery of Spiritual Love is unfolded in glowing language by Socrates, but he repeats the revelation as being not his own but given him by Diotima. This may be interpreted as a mere device of the Socratic irony. Socrates always took the rôle of the agnostic. Or it may be taken to suggest that in this oratorio of Love there are some notes which Plato felt to be not quite the voice of Socrates. Here Love is more metaphysical than in Xenophon; it is concerned with transcendental beauty, Beauty Absolute. "And the true order of going and being led by another to the things of love is to use the beauties of the earth as steps along which one mounts upward for the sake of that other beauty, going from one or two, and from two to all fair forms, and from fair forms to fair practices, and from fair practices to fair notions, until from fair notions he arrives at the notion of Absolute Beauty, and at last knows what the essence of beauty is."[2]

There is nothing in that which goes beyond the historical Socrates, but this Beauty is further defined as "absolute, separate, simple, everlasting, which without increase or diminution, or any change is imparted to the ever-growing and perishing beauties of all other things."[3] In this conception of the Absolute Idea as a separate self-subsistent reality we have the Platonic element, though Socrates has recently been credited with holding also that theory.[4]

We can't discuss that question now. Socrates at least led up to the very door if he did not enter it before Plato, and we shall quote a passage from the "Symposium" that thrills with Socratic tones, and which

---

[1] See 1st Alcibiades. 130, 131. [2] Plato, Sympos., 211. [3] *Ibid.*
[4] By Professor A. E. Taylor in Varia Socratica.

has an intrinsic charm, making it too fine to be omitted :

"These (preceding) are the lesser mysteries of love into which even you, Socrates, may enter; to the greater and more hidden ones which are the crown of these, and to which, if you pursue them in a right spirit they will lead, *I know not whether you will be able to attain.* But I will do my utmost to inform you and do you follow if you can. For he who would proceed aright in this matter should begin in youth to visit beautiful forms ; and first, if he be guided by his instructor aright, to love one such form only—out of that he should create fair thoughts ; and soon he will of himself perceive that the beauty of one form in general is his pursuit, how foolish would he be not to recognise that the beauty in every form is one and the same ! And when he perceives this he will abate his violent love of the one, which he will despise and deem a small thing, and will become a lover of all beautiful forms ; in the next stage he will consider that the beauty of the mind is more honourable than the beauty of the outward form. So that if a virtuous soul have but a little comeliness, he will be content to love and tend him, and will search out and bring to the birth thoughts which may improve the young, until he is compelled to contemplate and see the beauty of institutions and laws, and to understand that the beauty of them all is of one family, and that personal beauty is a trifle; and after laws and institutions he will go on to the sciences, that he may see their beauty, being not like a servant in love with the beauty of one youth or man or institution, himself a slave mean and narrow-minded, but drawing towards and contemplating the vast sea of beauty, he will create many fair and noble thoughts and notions in boundless love of wisdom ; until on that shore he

PUBLIC LIFE

grows and waxes strong, and at last the vision is revealed to him of a single science, which is the science of beauty everywhere." [1]

The evidence in its entirety goes to show that the love Socrates advocated was pure. Zeller says he does not abolish the *eros* or love toward boys, but retains it as the innocent basis of a higher and spiritual attraction.[2] Why the innocent basis of such a love for the intellectual and spiritual progress of youth should be abolished, one cannot imagine. Sorel[3] takes a graver view and holds that, though Socrates neither practised nor taught immorality, his preaching of the higher love or friendship was yet an idealisation of vice, which cut at the roots of the family life, and while it did not by any means initiate, at any rate accelerated, the evil tendencies of the time.

All we can say here is that to our mind the statement that Socrates' doctrine of love and friendship aggravated the evil of his time is tantamount to saying that the apostolate or the discipleship of Christ cut at the roots of family life, that the Reformation aggravated the vices of Catholicism, and Lord Shaftesbury's legislation only led to deterioration in factory life.

Socrates rather stands out as a great moral and spiritual prophet and reformer, the censor of contemporary vices, the revealer of a better way. He is the apostle of a Love and Friendship than which there is nothing more beautiful and winning in all the creations of the mystic souls of men. It lifted men into a community above class, nation, tribe, a community in the pursuit of things spiritual and universal, things honest, true, lovely, and of good report.

[1] Plato, Symposium, 210. (Jowett's trans.)
[2] Zeller, Philosophie der Griechen, 1842, i. p. 18.
[3] Le Procès de Socrate, pp. 95, 96, 234.

It differs from the Christian "philanthropia" in that it comes to men on the heights, while the latter seeks them in the depths. Men must rise to the love of Socrates, the Pauline love descends to them.

But such antitheses fail to seize the redemptive and renewing potency of Socrates' ideal to an age and people such as he had to do with. It was an Athenian evangelism rapt and glowing, at once an individual and a social gospel. And it must be claimed for it that it was not merely a doctrine, an ideal, for Socrates, but the very life of the prophet himself. It is when doctrine and life, thought and deed, are thus fused into a whole that glows and burns through the living personality of a man that we get gospels not theories, and that men are drawn into communities, under the moving inspiration and moulding influence of a master. And Socrates had this power, he drew a band of enthusiastic and devoted disciples around him, composed of those in whom he had found or in whom he created the self-same spirit as was in himself. These were Crito, Simmias, Cebes, Plato, Chærecrates, Chærephon, Hermogenes, Phædo, Xenophon, Alcibiades, Antisthenes, and others, who came for longer or shorter periods within the magnetic spell of his great enthusiasm—his Amor intellectualis. Diogenes Laertius gives an account of the call of Xenophon to follow Socrates, which is curiously like the account of Jesus calling his disciples, in its suddenness and the ready submission it evoked. Xenophon must have been quite a youth, and was very beautiful to look upon. That would attract Socrates. One day then, in a narrow lane, he met this fine-looking, modest youth, and in his quaint, unconventional way, put out his staff and blocked the passage. Then he proceeded to question Xenophon as to where various commodities might be got, the youth being ready in his replies. "And where are the fair and noble to be found?" Xenophon was surprised at this and could not answer. "Then follow me and be taught," said Socrates. And he followed and became a hearer. Xenophon was permanently influenced by his association with the master, and we know the gratitude, admiration, and esteem in which he held him.

Euripides, the poet, was also strongly influenced by Socrates. Aristophanes, in the "Frogs"[1] satirises him for his spirit and views, which are much the same as those attributed to Socrates in the "Clouds." He makes Euripides say:

> "This was the kind of love I brought
> To school my town in ways of thought;
> I mingled reasoning with my art
> And shrewdness, till I fired their heart
> To brood, to think things through and through;
> And rule their houses better too."[2]

Euripides also has introduced gods of his own, in harmony with the materialism of the schools—Ether, Vocal Chords, Reason, which will compare with the Clouds, Air, and Tongue he, in his comical spirit, accuses Socrates of worshipping. It is evident the poet sails in the same galley with the philosopher a few years younger than himself. Verrall, in his "Euripides the Rationalist," gives a serious exposition of Euripides' attitude to the orthodox gods and mythology, showing it to be one of criticism and repudiation. He had the spirit which, as Aristophanes puts it, "questions all things," the very spirit of Socrates.

It was not through writing, but through the direct and living influence of spirit on spirit, through the power to attract and deeply impress the young and eager intellect and aspiration of Athens that Socrates made such a profound mark on his day and generation.

[1] 405 B.C.   [2] Gilbert Murray's trans.

(b) Socrates as Citizen

The Athenian citizen had to play many parts. Under the democratic regime he was soldier, politician, judge, as well as family man and perhaps also trader. And we now turn to see how Socrates conducted himself in these various capacities.

As a soldier he took part in various campaigns in the Peloponnesian War, which broke out in 432 B.C. In September of that year he was present at the Battle of Potidæa, in which Potidæans and Corinthians, whose colonists the former were, though under tribute to Athens, fought against the Athenians, who, according to the inscription, "gave their lives in barter for glory and ennobled their country."[1] Alcibiades says that in this campaign Socrates and he messed together, so that he had an opportunity of witnessing his extraordinary feats of endurance, "in which he was superior to everybody."[2] It was here he once stood absorbed in meditation from dawn till evening and right on through the night till next morning, and that in what Alcibiades describes as a "tremendous winter"; but Alcibiades had delicate tastes. He also bears his testimony to Socrates' courage in battle, by telling how the philosopher saved his life, by refusing to leave him when he had been wounded, and rescuing him and his arms.[3]

The same unruffled courage was displayed at the Battle of Delium in 424 B.C., when the Athenians were utterly routed by Bœotians and Thebans after a stubborn fight.[4] Socrates was one of the seven thousand heavy-armed, and after the day had turned

---

[1] Bury's History of Greece, p. 393.
[2] Plato, Symposium, 220 A.
[3] *Ibid.*, 220.
[4] Thucydides, bk. iv., chs. 93–96.

PUBLIC LIFE

against them and the Athenians were in full flight, Alcibiades, who was on horseback and could see what was going on, relates that he came up with Socrates, who was just as Aristophanes had described him in the streets of Athens, " stalking like a pelican and rolling his eyes, calmly contemplating enemies as well as friends, and making very evident to all and sundry that whoever attacked him would be likely to meet with a stout resistance ; " and in this way he and his companion, Laches, escaped, for persons of this class are never touched in war, those only being pursued who are running away headlong."[1] It was of this episode that Laches declared that if only all the others had behaved like Socrates the honour of Athens would have been saved.[2]

He was also on the field at Amphipolis in 422 B.C. when the dashing and brilliant Spartan general Brasidas fought the Athenians under Cleon, that versatile and influential demagogue[3] whom Aristophanes had pilloried and flogged so ruthlessly in the " Knights."[4]

On all these occasions Socrates could later look back and feel he had done his duty as well as it could be done.[5] As he told his judges he had always stuck to his post without a thought of flinching, believing that the post of duty was the post at which God had placed him.[6] Duty for Socrates was a religious conception, and law a sacred thing which must not be violated by the arbitrary act of any man. No one was further removed than he from the spirit of anarchy and lawlessness. Obedience to duly con-

---

[1] Symposium, 221.   [2] Laches, 181 b.
[3] Thucydides, bk. iv., ch. 21.
[4] On Aristophanes' portraiture of him, see Couat, Aristophane, pp. 142-153.
[5] See Plato, Apology, 28 E.   [6] Ibid., 28 E.

stituted authority was confirmed by the sanctions of religion, and the man who broke them and failed of fidelity would find that he had only thrown himself into their power, when they rose against him before the Judges of the other world.

The same deep and sacred loyalty to Athens and her constitution was conspicuously shown at the very end in his conscientious objection to escaping from prison and the city at the pleading of Crito and his friends, who were anxious that he should avail himself of comparatively easy means of avoiding the death penalty and find asylum elsewhere. He refused, in terms in which, as Grote has remarked, " he is made to express the feelings and repeat the language of a devoted democratical patriot." [1]

His career was marked by another striking exemplification of this loyalty, as well as of his absolute fearlessness and integrity.

In 406 B.C. the war with Sparta—the Peloponnesian War—was still dragging its weary length along and in that year the Spartan and Athenian fleets met at the islands of Arginusæ off the coast of Asia Minor, the latter achieving a complete victory.[2] The Athenian generals detailed off two captains with ships to attend to the disabled vessels and pick up the wrecked crews, while the rest of the fleet pursued the enemy. A violent storm arose which prevented the carrying out of this which in the eyes of the Greeks was a sacred duty, and the sailors were left to perish. The report of this caused the greatest furore at Athens; indignation boiled among the people. So intense was the feeling against them in spite of their report

---

[1] Plato, vol. i. p. 430.

[2] For details of the whole episode, see Xenophon, Hellenica, bk. i. ch. 6, § 30 ff. and ch. 7. Cp. Holm, History of Greece, vol. ii. ch. 28.

PUBLIC LIFE

of having done all that could be expected to save the sailors, it was decided by the Popular Assembly, contrary to the wise and equitable provisions of the Statute Book, to try the nine generals *en bloc*, and give an immediate single vote upon their guilt and fate.

Socrates stood out against this procedure as illegal and unjust,[1] and amid menace and hooting persisted in his attitude. He would do nothing contrary to the law. "He was king of himself with something sublime in him." In spite of him, however, and his unflinching stand, others, who agreed as to the illegality of the proceedings, were browbeaten and threatened in an excited and uproarious assembly till they submitted. The vote was summarily taken and eight generals condemned, the ninth, Theramenes, having saved his skin by turning traitor on the others. The six of them who were present in Athens were put to death.

The moral victory, however, lay with Socrates, the man of rock-like integrity, for the fickle and turbulent mob afterwards repented of its crime, and Callixenus, who had introduced the motion for this inequitable mode of voting, starved himself to death on account of the revulsion of popular feeling against him.[2]

"He is strongest who stands most alone," says Ibsen, and in this instance Socrates and the right proved stronger than the Athenian populace and the wrong. The fact is that, in his cool self-respect, the quiet but haughty way in which he would stick to his own judgment in total indifference to consequences and the opinion of others, whoever they might be, mark him as of the order of true greatness. One

---

[1] Hellenica, ch. 7, § 15.
[2] Xenophon, Hellenica, i. ch. 7 (end). Cp. Holm, History of Greece, vol. ii. p. 503.

cannot but smile at his sober, imperturbable, and unostentatious reverence for himself and his own convictions of things. You could as soon have moved Mount Parnassus from its firm base as him from right. He rested on it with all his elephantine weight and smiled and winked at the assaults of mosquitoes.

The following instance must be told in the few and sufficient words in which Plato makes Socrates tell it at his Defence, when standing his trial:

"When the Oligarchy was in power, the Thirty sent for me and four others to come to their room. They commanded us to go and fetch Leon the Salaminian from Salamis, that he might be made away with. It was their way to implicate as many people as possible in their crimes. But I showed them that, to use a vulgar expression, I did not care a rap about death, that all I cared for was not to do anything against the right of man or the law of God. Strong as it was, the government could not terrify me into wrong, for when we left the Council-room the four others went to Salamis, but I walked away home. That would probably have meant death for me, only the government was shortly after broken up." [1]

If these facts show anything they show that the imperturbable strength and integrity of the character of Socrates rested on a lofty patriotism supported by a profound personal religion, and a deep devotion to the principles of Justice.

We shall have to speak of Socrates' religion later, but here it may be said that the Divine and the Invisible beset him behind and before; its eyes, he felt, were ever upon him. "How could he do this evil and sin against God?"

The laws of the state were man's attempts to lay down as well as he could the restrictions and condi-

[1] Plato's Apology, 32 C, D.

tions necessary if he was not to injure his own welfare, but realise his Good, the real ideal of his life, the end laid down by the divine appointment. Wilfully and maliciously to transgress these laws for one's own selfish purposes was thus to offend against Heaven. The only excuse for breaking one law is that you are keeping a better. Prove that these human enactments are not the law of God and their authority and sacredness are gone. The only absolutely inviolable thing in the world is the Good, the Ideal. But so long as laws are recognised as finger-posts on the long journey to human perfection, so long we must keep them standing and follow their directions—aye, even though it mean the sacrifice of life and self. No man must prove traitor to the Ideal or anything that leads to it. It is a small matter whether *he* live, a great matter whether the Good be kept alive.

He would brook no tampering with the behests of Conscience. To him that inner voice spoke in tones more awful and subduing than the thunders of popular convention or passion or caprice. Two days before he drank the hemlock, Crito was with him in prison, urging him to avail himself of easy means of escape, and trying to get round his obstinacy in refusing to entertain the idea, by reminding him that his passive acquiescence in this *coup de grâce* on the part of his enemies would bring a stigma of cowardice and spiritlessness on his own name and that of his friends in the eyes of the public, and turn them into a laughing-stock. To which Socrates replies that the one consideration for him is whether the suggestion is morally right. " For now as always I am not the man to be moved by anything but that reason which approves itself to me as the best. What a man must fear in this world or in the next is not the opprobrium of the mob of shallow and ignorant people, but the disapprobation of the man—though there be only one—who is wise and knows."

" Prove me wrong by right reason," he seems to say with Luther before the Diet at Worms, " and I shall alter. Otherwise recant I neither can nor will. For it is perilous to go against Conscience. Here I stand, I can do no other. So help me, God."

No trimmer of sails this, no catcher at the popular breeze, but a true captain of life steering by the immovable stars, in the teeth of wind or wave.

The state which has such citizens is truly blessed; they are the salt which preserves it from going to decay, whether or no they feel called to join in active politics. They save by what they are, more than by what they do. For " character " as Emerson says, " teaches above the will."

Socrates then fulfilled the military and judicial functions which devolved upon him, but he kept aloof from the game of politics which so fascinated his fellow-citizens. He preferred being a philosopher and prophet to being a politician. Looking at the life of the city he came to the conclusion that there were plenty of people anxious to direct and conduct its affairs, but few capable of conducting them well. There was a glut of rulers but a scarcity of thinkers. Politics had not enough science in it, nor economics enough ethics, and on that fact he believed the state would founder. The Athenian democracy was by no means an idyllic or angelic phenomenon. If Pericles held up before it its more ideal self, in his Funeral Oration, we do not lack pictures of its weaknesses and vices, perhaps exaggerated by prejudice, in the works of Aristophanes and Plato. The former satirises it in its judicial capacity as being swayed by personal whims and petty spites and the arts of clever flattery. Such was its morale that the informer and the rhetorician held it in the hollow of their hand. Politically, he represents it as a silly egotistical old dotard, the victim of sharpers and blusterers and demagogues, with none of the qualities or qualifications of true rulers. It was in such a state of nerves as to feel safe only when ruled by the bottom dogs. This aspect of democracy, with its comical touch of caricature, is brought out in the "Knights," where it is suggested to the Sausage-seller that he should become a political leader and rival the power of Cleon.

"S.S.: But I know nothing, friend, beyond my letters,
And even of them but little, and that badly.
DEMOSTHENES:
The mischief is that you know anything.
To be a demus-leader is not now
For lettered men nor yet for honest men,
But for the base and ignorant. Don't let slip
The bright occasion which the gods provide thee."

. . . .

"A brutal voice, low birth, an agora-training;
Why, you've got all one wants for public life.
The Pythian shrine and oracles concur." [1]

But there is no Aristophanic humour in Plato's vehement denunciation of the state of things in his "Republic" and "Theætetus." [2] He thrashes the mob unmercifully as a hysterical, loud-mouthed bully, insisting upon its own arbitrary and confused ideas and visiting those who dare resist it with "disfranchisement, fines, and death." [3] It is a many-headed, unphilosophical monster which rears about it a brood of sophists, sycophants, and flatterers, who minister to its whim and pleasure. That is its law of survival of the fittest in Plato's view.

This state of matters will account for Socrates'

---

[1] ll. 218 ff. (Rogers' trans.)
[2] See Republic, 496; Theætetus, 173-175.
[3] Rep., vi. 494.

abstention from politics. It was not that he was above the city and its concerns, or that they were beneath him, but that as an active partisan he would be in for a job whose tools were too dirty for him to handle, because he did not know the way to compromise and cajole, and would be sure to rouse a brood of jealousies and antipathies which would hurry him off the face of the earth before his work was half-done, and also because he had bigger aims and ends and satisfactions to strive for than fell within the scheme of a merely political programme. It was not at the superstructures but at the bases of life he must work. He could not give up to party what was meant for mankind. It was a deepening and clarifying of the whole consciousness of the people which was wanted. And that would involve an attitude of censorship and criticism which in political life would mark a man out as a victim on party altars.

In his "Apology" Plato makes him state quite definitely the reason for that aloofness from citizen activities which in Pericles' phrase makes a man not merely harmless but useless.

The divine sign, he said, opposed his going in for politics, and that quite rightly, " for you know well enough, Athenians, that if I had long ago taken up politics, long ago I should have met my fate, and been of use neither to you nor to myself. Oh, you needn't get indignant at hearing the truth. There isn't a man who will escape, if he offers genuine opposition to you or any other crowd and prevents injustices and illegalities from taking place in the city. The man who is out for no sham fight in the cause of justice, if he wants to live even a short time, must be a private not a public citizen."[1]

(c) What then was this mission laid on him by God?

[1] Apology, 31 D, E, 32 A.

It had a twofold aspect. (1) It was a crusade against Ignorance. (2) It was a crusade for Virtue. And the two lay very near each other in Socrates' thought. It was an intellectual, ethical, and social mission in one. If we had to sum it up in one phrase, we should say it was a gospel of Efficiency—all-round Efficiency.

(1) The Crusade against Ignorance. We have already seen Socrates as a youth entering into the shadows of the everlasting No; all the scientific and philosophic knowledge of his time utterly failed to satisfy him, or throw any light on the riddle of existence. He had learned his own ignorance, and he never forgot the lesson.

In this condition a strange thing happened. His friend Chærephon, a headstrong, impulsive youth, actually asked the Oracle at Delphi whether there were a wiser man than Socrates, and the response was "None."[1] This rather staggered Socrates, who was deeply conscious of being wise in no matter, small or great. It puzzled and troubled him, for he could not venture to doubt the truth of what the Oracle declared. That would be sacrilege. Accordingly he must justify the paradox to himself. So off he set to those who enjoyed the reputation of wisdom— politicians, poets, and artisans—thinking that the Oracle would surely be proved mistaken. On the contrary, however, Socrates found that, wise and knowing as they were in their own conceits, they were really quite ignorant, the only difference between them and himself being that he knew he was ignorant and they did not. Incidentally he took occasion to enlighten them on the point, however, and for his pains roused more hatred and antipathy to himself than gratitude. Superficial convention, complacent sham, bottomless cant, were the order of the day—and he

[1] Plato, Apology, § 21.

turned the sharp piercing ray of his dialectic upon them. He had a revealing touch! Of the politicians, he says that, like himself, none of them knew anything "beautiful and good," only they had an idea they did, while he entertained no such illusion.[1] His experience too was that it was those who enjoyed the highest reputation who were really most deficient, and those who were reckoned inferior who had most sense and gumption in their composition.[2]

As for the poets, they taught by a kind of instinct and inspiration better than they knew or understood. Question the best and most painstaking of them on their works, and they were like children. The poetic faculty created in them what was only an illusion of wisdom.

The artisans did know some things and could do them, but as in the case of the poets, their capacity in one direction led to a claim to wisdom in others which was without foundation.

This process of showing up the limits and the superficiality of men's knowledge created a mistaken notion that Socrates himself must have knowledge on those matters in regard to which he was able to prove the ignorance of others. But he disclaims any such pretension. He has learned that God alone is truly wise, and that what the Oracle was trying to teach him was that the wisdom of man was little and naught; and that he who, like Socrates, realises this, is the wisest of men. "And so even now" (over seventy years of age) "I am still going about seeking out and questioning any whether among citizens or foreigners, whom I think to be wise, in accordance with the will of God. And when to my mind he turns out not to be wise, then, with God's help, I show him that he is not. And on account of my absorption in this mission, I have

[1] Apology, 21 D.   [2] *Op. cit.*, 22 A.

had no time either for public or domestic affairs, but I am in extreme poverty because of this service of God."[1]

It was the sense of this call to a higher service, far exceeding in importance and value any merely political functions and duties, the service of bringing men to see how shallow their conceptions and judgments were, how poor their whole stock-in-trade of genuine knowledge, how slight their touch with realities—it was that which compelled Socrates to treat everything else in the world as negligible. This one thing he must do, drag people out of their snug little caves of illusion, and set them in their nakedness face to face with Reality. That was the first step toward wisdom and salvation.

Get to know thyself, what thou really art, what thou really hast. Strip off all that clothing of the mind which thou hast borrowed, all these categories and formulæ and ready-made judgments which thou hast adopted; these only prevent thee from getting into touch with the reality of thyself and of the universe. They are no real possession and they prevent thee from attaining that humility, that sense of utter present insufficiency, which is the beginning of any true hope for thee! Thy knowledge is ignorance, God alone is wise.[2] Thy wisdom is just to know that!

We shall in dealing with Socrates' religion discover traits that relate him to the mystics of the world, and here we would point out that Socrates' attitude seems to be that of an *intellectual mysticism*. He has experienced the mystery of the universe, the vanity of human knowledge; he has renounced the wisdom of man, and the world of that wisdom; he has felt that in God alone is knowledge and truth, and he has entered into the grace of that self knowledge which is Humility.

---

[1] Plato, Apol., 23 b.   [2] Apology, 23 A.

Except that the experience is gone through in terms and stages *preponderatingly* intellectual—for no such experience is entirely of the intellect, but involves the whole character in every part of it—how does this differ from the experience of religious or moral mysticism in general?

Let us take the following description from Miss Evelyn Underhill's fine book on "Mysticism,"[1] and the similarities will be obvious:

" Primarily then the self must be purged of all that stands between it and goodness; putting on the character of reality instead of the character of illusion or ' sin.' It longs ardently to do this from the first moment in which it sees itself in the all-revealing radiance of the Uncreated Light. ' When once love openeth the inner eye of the soul for to see this truth,' says Hilton, ' with other circumstances that attend it, then beginneth the soul to be really humble; for then through the sight of God it feeleth and seeth itself as it is, and then doth the soul forsake the beholding and leaning upon itself.'

" So, with Dante, the first terrace of the Mount of Purgatory is devoted to the cleansing of pride and the production of humility. Such a process is the inevitable—one might almost say mechanical—result of a vision, however fleeting, of Reality; an undistorted sight of the earth-bound self. All its life it has been measuring its candlelight by other candles. Now for the first time it is out in the open air and sees the sun. ' This is the way,' said the voice of God to St. Catherine of Siena in ecstasy. ' If thou wilt arrive at a perfect knowledge and enjoyment of Me, the Eternal Truth, thou shouldst never go outside the knowledge of thyself; and by humbling thyself in the valley of humility thou wilt know Me and thyself, from which knowledge

[1] Evelyn Underhill, Mysticism, pp. 241, 242.

thou wilt draw all that is necessary. . . . In self-knowledge, then, thou wilt humble thyself; seeing that, in thyself, thou dost not even exist.'"

Not of course that the recognition of the vanity of ordinary human knowledge and of one's own knowledge, combined with the sense of God as alone wise, in itself affords sufficient ground to call Socrates a mystic of the intellect. We believe he must be classed with the Mystics because of that, along with other characteristics which he displayed and which will be referred to in their place. Meanwhile in the total view of him which one wishes to attain this mystical strain should stand out prominently. It suggests the fact that while his criticism was intensely negative, it had a positive motive behind it, one might say a religious motive, for illusion and error fill the soul with husks so that the hunger for the true bread is suppressed, and man remains so far separated from God and reality. And to that extent genuine morality becomes impossible. All his criticism was a mere preliminary to search for true knowledge upon which alone morality could be securely founded, and morality with Socrates was the great thing. It was, however, in this aspect of it a knowledge to be gained not from the study of nature but from the analysis of human experience, and a discrimination and clarification of its confused ideas and principles. It had a social as well as an individual aspect, and must be the basis of the conduct of states as well as of personal conduct. The democracy whose deficiencies we have referred to must also enlist in its concerns the knowledge which saves.

It was thus part of the mission he diligently pursued to unmask that profound ignorance of upstarts and haranguers which Aristophanes burlesqued and to make Athens aware that its government demanded something more than ability to gull the mob and get elected.

In season and out of season he seems to have prosecuted this task of deepening and clearing the politics of Athens. He scorched vain and flippant pretension by thrusting it into the fire of his ridicule. The government of a state is too complicated and serious an affair to be trusted to any but men of trained talents and expert knowledge. It should be an affair neither of blood nor of ballot, but of brains.

He showed up the futility of appearing to be wealthy, brave, and strong without the reality, or of getting a position which one has not the ability to fill. It simply means that when the testing-time comes, comes disaster and disgrace with it. " I call that man a cheat and no small bit of a cheat, who would get other people's money by false pretences; but he is by far the worst impostor who deludes people into thinking he is fit to rule a state when he is nothing of the kind." [1]

In this crusade his double in modern times is Thomas Carlyle, that other blaster of bubble-heads and enemy of all sorts of sham, insincerity, and superficiality. Carlyle despised contemporary politics as a huge palaver and the House of Commons as a little gibbering-gallery. He screeched with every bit of bile in him for the man of talent, the king or true-knowing man, so that the ills of human things might at last be righted or put in the way of being righted. The aristocrat of knowledge and talent must rule, it is the virtue and salvation of all others to obey: " If thou do know better than I what is good and right, I conjure thee, in the name of God, force me to do it."

That was Socrates' view of the matter. Liberty and Equality were to him as to Carlyle the cult and cant of mediocrity. To worship them was to consecrate and crown not the human maximum but the human minimum; it was to suppress nature and silence

---

[1] Mem., i. ch. 7. Cp. bk. iii. ch. 6; bk. iv. ch. 2.

PUBLIC LIFE

facts with a battle-cry. To see no mountains and valleys in the world, see nothing but a level plain, is to see wrongly, and to see wrongly is to act disastrously. When the post of pilot for a ship is vacant, we do not all claim to be equally fitted for it, neither do we offer it to the man who proves himself to have the glibbest and most dexterous tongue; we give it to the trained man, the expert, the pilot, the man who has studied navigation, ships, and seas.[1]

Similarly with the ship of state. Only he is qualified to steer it who knows what port it is destined for, and how to get there. The statesman must have learned human nature and its goal, he must have learned also the ins and outs of what concerns the social life and its maintenance, he must be philosopher and economist. How else can he be anything but a falsity, and what else can falsity be but failure?

The same view is taken by Plato in the "Republic," and his sentiment so far is quite Socratic. It is not the order of nature or of common-sense that the uninstructed sailors should, either by cajolery or force, take the place of the captain, who has been trained to the business.[2] Accordingly in the state "one or more of the true philosophers shall be invested with full authority and contemn the honours of the present day, in the belief that they are mean and worthless; and that, deeply impressed with the supreme importance of right and of the honours to be derived from it, and regarding justice as the highest and most binding of all obligations, he shall, as the special servant and admirer of justice, carry out a thorough reform of his own state." [3]

But such reform in Socrates' view should only be undertaken by one who is conversant with facts.

[1] Mem., i. ch. 2, § 9; iii. ch. 9, § 11.
[2] Plato, Republic, § 488.   [3] *Op. cit.*, § 540.

No reformer, no idealist, no man whatever, has any right to lay his hand to the duty of re-making or ruling society till he has made himself familiar with its structure, its laws, its details, any more than he would have a right to tamper and fumble with a delicate and complex piece of machinery if he were ignorant of the details of machine construction. Socrates saw that in his day the condition of the people was such as to demand for its betterment what Professor Jones, in his book on " The Working Faith of a Social Reformer," has declared to be most requisite in our own time : " No one who is interested in the social well-being of the people will deny that amongst the deepest needs of our times is the need of clear light upon the broad principles of social well-being, *the need, in short, of a science of social life.*" It is out of the marriage of the true ideal with the knowledge of facts and conditions, in the brain of the thinker, a marriage both partners in which must respect and reverence each other, that all sound, healthy, and saving reform and rule is born. The Ideal must be instructed by facts, the facts must subserve the Ideal.

The fact that the first six chapters of the Third Book of Xenophon's " Recollections " are devoted to illustrating Socrates' activity in trying to make his fellows realise the supreme need of full and accurate knowledge to the successful conduct of any public post of responsibility, indicates the importance Socrates attached to science in political and social affairs.

The sixth chapter gives a most amusing instance of Socrates' humour and irony brought into subtle play for the purpose of drawing out a conceited youth, who aimed at the highest offices of state and gave his friends concern because of his entire lack of gumption, to see that he was really ignorant. Socrates took him in hand and cross-examined him with the aid of a little judicious flattery, and succeeded in showing him that he was altogether without that knowledge of affairs which would be absolutely necessary to success in the office.

For the sake of the blend of common-sense and ironic humour of it, as well as to further exemplify Socrates' work in this line, we quote the reminiscence of another occasion in which he had to deal with the conceit of youth and its danger to the state, when there is no solid attainment behind it. He pictures such an one beginning his public speech in this exalted strain: "'Men of Athens, I have never at any time learnt anything from anybody: nor if I have ever heard of anyone as being an able statesman versed in speech and capable of action, have I sought to come across him individually. I have not so much as been at pains to provide myself with a teacher from amongst those who have knowledge. . . . However, anything that occurs to me by the light of nature I shall be glad to place at your disposal.' How appropriate would such a preface sound on the lips of anyone seeking, say, the office of state physician, would it not? How advantageously he might begin an address on this wise: 'Men of Athens, I have never learnt the art of healing by help of anybody, nor have I sought to provide myself with any teacher among medical men. Indeed, to put it briefly, I have been ever on my guard not only against learning anything from the profession, but against the very notion of having ever studied medicine at all. If, however, you will be so good as to confer on me the post, I promise I will do my best to acquire skill by experimenting on your persons.'"[1]

The true democracy then for Socrates is and can only be an equality of opportunity, a liberty to all

---
[1] Mem., bk. iv. ch. 2, §§ 4 and 5. (Dakyns' trans.)

to develop the gift that is in them by having access to the sources of education and training, but it can only embody its right idea when pains are taken to put the wisest and ablest at the head of its concerns, and when its members are not of the opinion that in the affairs of free government every man has an equal claim to office and power. Democracy must be ordered and disciplined.

Socrates' claim to be called a social reformer in the strict sense has been denied by Professor Joël as against the view of Döring. Joël holds that neither in history nor in Xenophon does Socrates stand out as a social reformer, and such an idea could only have arisen in an age like the present, when social reform has risen to such prominence in men's thoughts. "Wherein," he asks, "does the social reform of Socrates consist? There is not a word of Socialism. A strengthening of the principle of democracy it cannot be, just as little a reversal or alteration in the balance of power in the state (Döring, pp. 373, 375), no change at all, indeed, of the external organisation of society (Döring, p. 369), but only a dealing with spiritual factors. Not the State, the Constitution, the economic system, the relations between citizens, are to be reformed, but the citizens themselves. In a word, Socrates wants no *social-reform* but its opposite, *individual-reform*. It is no economic amelioration from above, it is not a socialising, or a levelling, or a unifying, but an accentuation of differences, an "aristocratising" (Döring, p. 384), an inner elevation, and even in the 'Memorabilia' an increase of specialisation. Allow the 'Memorabilia' to be quite historical for the moment, where does Socrates speak of his social-reform?"[1]

Now we believe it true that Socrates was far more

[1] Joël, Der Echte und der Xenophontische Sokrates, vol. II. pt. ii. p. 955.

concerned with individuals and character than with programmes and systems, but in this connexion Joël distinguishes too sharply between what is individual and what is social. In Socrates' mind these terms do not exclude one another, nor are they "opposites." The reform of the individual would soon manifest itself in social reforms and improvements. And there was one matter in which he would certainly have altered the method of election to state offices, viz. that in which resort was had to election by lot. His whole conception of government by knowledge and skill was opposed to any method of deciding the occupancy of leading positions by arbitrary methods.

How exactly he proposed to secure the choice of the best to rule we do not know, and perhaps he had not considered, beyond the primary need of diffusing the idea that for public posts it was the trained and efficient men and not the talkers who alone should be considered as eligible. Only when the democracy had been educated up to that conception, fundamental, indisputable, and indispensable, would the necessity arise to think out some specific means for giving effect to it. But at least choice by lot would have to go. *That* the "Memorabilia" do teach.

Moreover, in the early chapters of the Third Book already alluded to, it is *social* reform, improvements in the condition of society, the increase of its prosperity and happiness, that are contemplated as a result of the heightened efficiency of its rulers and servants. Hence one cannot see why we should not be justified in speaking of Socrates as a social reformer. Surely the connotation of that term will extend to anyone whose aim is the amelioration and improvement of society and social service as such, and Socrates certainly desired such improvement and stated certain conditions of its attainment.

Alike for the purposes of social and individual life it was requisite not only that one should know the facts which have a bearing on the right discharge of duty, but also that one should know oneself intimately, have a true and just estimate of one's powers, so that one won't attempt what is beyond one's capacity, and won't be afraid to venture on what lies within it, and thus deprive society of useful services, which it ought to have. It is possible for a man to attempt too much because of conceit and egotism, but it is also possible for him to attempt too little through self-depreciation. Xenophon relates how Socrates would deal with any case of the latter kind he came across. The instance given is Charmides, the son of Glaucon, who was a brother of Plato. Here was a man of insight and ability, who shone in private gatherings, evincing a fine gift for administration, yet the state was deprived of his valuable gifts because he recoiled from the battles of the Assembly which were with noise and garments rolled in blood, metaphorically speaking. He thought he would be nowhere in such bustle. Socrates reasoned with him on this timidity before " dullards and weaklings " when among experts he could give an excellent account of himself. " Is it the fullers among them of whom you stand in awe, or the cobblers, or the carpenters, or the coppersmiths, or the merchants, or the farmers, or the hucksters of the market-place exchanging their wares, and bethinking them how they are to buy this cheap and sell the other dear ? "[1] As well might a man face trained athletes and then cower before amateurs. " My good fellow, do not be ignorant of yourself! Do not fall into that commonest of errors—theirs who rush off to investigate the concerns of the rest of the world, and have no time to turn and examine them-

[1] Mem., bk. iii. ch. 7.

selves. Yet that is a duty which you must not in cowardly sort draw back from: rather must you brace yourself to give good heed to your own self; and as to public affairs, if by any manner of means they may be improved through you, do not neglect them. Success in the sphere of politics means that not only the mass of your fellow-citizens, but your personal friends and you yourself last but not least, will profit by your action."[1]

Joël would doubtless see evidence of Cynic influence upon Xenophon's account in the last sentiment, but there is nothing in it as it stands which, even if cynic, might not also be Socratic. And the whole passage shows that Socrates had not lost either interest or faith in, or loyalty to, the Athenian state. He considered it a man's duty to render what service he could to society. But the passage also brings out the emphasis he laid on this affair of self-knowledge, and that is our present point. He sometimes quoted the inscription on the temple at Delphi, " Know thyself,"[2] because the knowledge of self includes the awakening of the mind to what it does really know and what it really does not know. To know oneself is, in Carlyle's phrase, "to know what one can work at," but to be thorough it also involves a searching examination of one's ideas and general mental and moral stock-in-trade. A cross-examination of Euthydemus reveals that, with all his conceit of his own knowledge and ability, he has never really thought out the ideas and criteria which he applies to experience and conduct, he calls certain things right and others wrong on the basis of mere tradition and convention and common-sense, and it is only when pressed by Socrates that he finds his easy-going moral judgments break down,[3] and learns that if they are to be securer

[1] Mem., bk. iii. ch. 7.   [2] Mem., bk. iv. ch. 2.   [3] *Ibid.*

and more valid than mere opinion, he will have to sift and define them a great deal more by the processes of reason and thought. Yet until we have come to a sure and certain knowledge of right and wrong, good and bad, how can we be in a position to come to proper decisions in regard to our conduct, either as individuals or as citizens?

Conduct is three-fourths of life, and the three most important fourths to Socrates. It cannot be escaped. Life is action, and yet, when the truth is told, hardly any have really considered the moral principles which lie at the very heart of it and give it its character. Our conduct is not action, it is muddle, a thing of accidents. Socrates felt it was high time this sort of thing should cease and conduct be cleared up, and based upon consistent and irrefragable principles. Only so do we attain self-determination and self-possession. These are appropriated from the world of human experience only through criticism and reason. Freedom is a function of intellect, and intellect is the highest and most intimate expression of personality. We *are* our ideas and principles even more than our volitions and acts; the former are our inner selves, the latter but their expression in the world, according to varying circumstances.

The self then, in a moral point of view, became the one great central object of Socrates' mission. He turned from the study of natural science, which he found unsatisfying to the demands of his intellect, and comparatively remote from the unescapable exigencies of life, to the urgent task of a moral reconstruction based upon the purified certainties of thought and reason, summed up in the term " self-knowledge."

We cannot in deference to the indications of Aristophanes which Prof. A. E. Taylor has sought to justify by subtle means and through reference to Plato, depart from what has been the traditional view that Socrates did turn from natural science as his main interest to an absorption in ethical matters. That does not by any means signify that he absolutely closed his ears to the scientific speculations of others, or cut off from memory what he had previously learned of them in youth. What it does signify is that he found no rest or satisfaction in science, was persuaded that, as prosecuted in the schools of Greece, it would never solve the riddle of the universe, that indeed that riddle could only be solved by penetration into man's moral experience, that both intellectually and practically it is man who is the fundamental object of interest to man. He is the microcosm in and through whom alone we shall understand the macrocosm.

Plato, Xenophon, Aristotle, all bear witness to this transference of the centre of gravity of Socrates' interest from the physical to the ethical, and the complete subordination of the former to the latter, nay, even its elimination from his discussions. Plato is as emphatic and uncompromising on this point as Xenophon. In the "Apology" he represents Socrates as referring to Aristophanes' caricature in the "Clouds," where he is set forth as an inquirer into " the things in heaven and beneath the earth," presumably what we should call the phenomena of astronomy and geology, and teaching others these things. He is seen turning in the air and declaring that he is walking on it, and a lot of other nonsense, " things of which," says Socrates, " I understand nothing at all. I do not speak as one who holds such science in dishonour, if there should be anyone who has knowledge of such things. . . . But for myself, O Athenians, I have neither part nor lot in these studies. I challenge any of you to speak and declare it, if you have ever heard me make the slightest reference to such topics in my discussions, and there are many of you who have heard my conversations." [1] There can be no ambiguity about these words, and they are from Plato. Moreover, the dominant interest of what are recognised generally as the earliest Platonic dialogues is an interest not in nature—that is absent wholly—but in moral ideas, Friendship, Courage, Temperance, and so on, which goes to substantiate the attitude expressed in the " Apology," and the inference one readily draws from the autobiographic part in the " Phædo " already given.

It is the same with Xenophon. There Socrates is set before us, busy with the search after the essential nature, the definition, of Piety, and Courage, and Temperance, and Prudence, &c.[2]

" He set his face against all discussion of such high matters as the nature of the Universe, how the cosmos, as the savants phrase it, came into being; or by what forces the celestial phenomena arise. To trouble one's brain about such matters was, he argued, to play the fool. He would ask first, Did these investigators feel their knowledge of things human so complete that they betook themselves to lofty speculations? Or did they maintain that they were playing their proper parts in thus neglecting the affairs of man to speculate on the concerns of God? He was astonished they did not see how far these problems lay beyond mortal ken." [3] Then he goes on to justify the last sentiment by reference to the interminable conflicts of the different schools of physical philosophers. " One sect has discovered that Being is one and indivisible. Another that it is infinite in number. If one proclaims that all things are in a continual flux, another replies that nothing can possibly be moved at any time. The theory of the universe as a process of birth and death

[1] Plato, Apology, 19 b, c, d.   [2] Mem., i. ch. 1.
[3] Mem., i. ch. 1. (Dakyns' trans.)

PUBLIC LIFE

is met by the counter theory, that nothing ever could be born or ever will die."[1]

Xenophon gives another reason why Socrates scorned these physical and metaphysical speculations, viz. his scepticism as to their utility. "Do such explorers into divine operations hope that when they have discovered by what forces the various phenomena occur, they will create winds and waters at will and fruitful seasons? Will they manipulate these and the like to suit their needs?"[2]

Whether or not Socrates actually regarded men whose interest was the physical universe in general as fools, whether or not he used the argument of the comparative uselessness of such inquiries—and we see no reason why one, disillusioned with such studies and feeling intensely the immediate and urgent necessity to rationalise and so secure and fortify morals as at once concerned with Athenian as well as human well-being, should not in his zeal press the argument about utility—at any rate the main point is made sufficiently plain, that Socrates took no direct personal interest in scientific studies.

Aristotle's testimony is to the same effect. "Socrates," he says, "though confining his examination to questions of moral conduct and giving no study to the nature of the universe as a whole, sought *within the moral sphere* for the Universal, and was the first to concentrate his attention on definitions."[3] Statements to the same effect are repeated by him at various places, *e.g.*, "Socrates concerned himself with the ethical virtues and was the first to seek to give definitions in regard to them by the universal."[4] "He gave up inquiry into nature."[5]

---

[1] Mem., i. ch. 1, § 14.   [2] Mem., i. ch. 1.
[3] Metaphysics, A 987, b, 1. Taylor, Aristotle on his Predecessors, p. 100.   [4] Metaphysics, M 1078, b, 17.
[5] De Part. Anim., i. 642 a, 28. Cp. Ethics Eud., i. 1216, b, 2.

In the face of all this it appears rather perverse to tumble into line with a comic poet like Aristophanes, and hold that Socrates actively maintained his early interest in nature. But this is what Sorel does, arguing for the view that Socrates was a follower of Anaxagoras, and that the denial in Plato's "Apology" refers only to astronomy, whose objects, the sun and stars, Socrates regarded as divine, and therefore not amenable to human calculation and knowledge, while in other respects he remained an Anaxagorean, and the Athenians were not wrong in charging him with that heresy.[1] All we can answer to this is that the words of the "Apology" naturally construed, explicitly refer to more than the science of astronomy, and as regards Anaxagoras, the implication Socrates meant to convey in his reference to that philosopher at the Defence was that he was not an Anaxagorean. The "Phædo" is to the same effect. Sorel has simply missed the obvious, or refused to see it under some Aristophanic mesmerism.

Taylor, who also advocates the view that Socrates continued his active interest in scientific speculation and inquiry to the last, disposes of the Aristotelian dicta by the following interpretation, which does not at all strike us as the natural meaning of the language: "It is in this sense, in the sense that Socrates was occupied in the discernment of the 'ideas' of the things which are unseen, that I should understand the well-known statement of Aristotle that his 'business' was concerned with 'ethical matters,' the affairs of a man's soul, and not with 'nature' in the Aristotelian sense, the world of that which is born and dies" (p. 245).

But Aristotle himself, from the quotations just given, will be seen to explain what he meant by "ethical matters," and it is "the moral sphere," and "the

---

[1] See Le Procès de Socrate, pp. 139–144.

moral virtues"; it is not the distinction between the eternal world of ideas in Plato's sense, and the world of sense, for how could Socrates in concerning himself with these "ideas," be said to have no concern with the world of sense, if, as Professor Taylor says elsewhere (p. 88), he did not separate the "ideas" from the "phenomena of the world of sense" but insisted all through on their positive relation? In that case his concern was with both worlds. No, the Aristotelean distinction, interpreted in the obvious natural sense, is that between the realms of ethics and of natural history.

It is to fail to grasp the significance of Socrates' experience, even while seeking to confer an honour on his intellectual interests, if we try to rescue him in spite of himself from an attitude, if not of contempt perhaps semi-humorously expressed, at least of comparative indifference to, and personal detachment from, scientific speculation and inquiry in regard to the universe. For the attitude of agnosticism into which he was driven by the use of merely scientific categories threw him back with fuller abandon upon human categories, and drove him to look upon the world as a moral and religious phenomenon, only to be understood in the light of the revelation of the religious spirit and by the help of the categories of moral experience. His very rationalism, pressed to the furthest limits carried him over the boundaries of materialism into a higher philosophy whose primary demand was that man should penetrate to the mystery of his own nature, and in its secrets read the meaning of the world.

In comparison with this service which the depth and thoroughness of his method and his experience have rendered to the human spirit, the fact of his dropping the pursuit of the sciences is unimportant in determining our estimate of his greatness. *Non omnia possumus omnes.*

It is seldom that a perfect balance can be maintained of all the helpful and legitimate interests of human life, and such balance is almost impossible and would be, perhaps, an obstacle in the case of those who are called to be apostles of one special aspect of the Ideal.

The fundamental and the crowning knowledge, then, is the knowledge of self, for with that all the commonplace illusions amid which men ordinarily live begin to vanish away like mist rent in pieces by the sun's rays.

And so he went about persuading and compelling people to get at the truth regarding themselves, to get a face to face view of realities. The salvation of man lies in getting away from mere appearances, the confusion of inert minds. He thought it his God-appointed business to help people to do that who failed to do it for themselves.

He went out and in amongst all classes of the people —poets, teachers, leaders, artisans—on this quest after sure knowledge. Cobblers, vendors, ne'er-do-wells, it mattered not, he took to do with all. One time you would see him sitting in a shoemaker's shop, soon after he might be found in an artist's studio. He was no respecter of persons or trades. Distinctions of birth, class, wealth, were simply nothing to Socrates. High and low, rich and poor, being men, were alike to him, so long as he had anything to learn or teach, bearing on his life-work.

One of the most salient features of the personality was his combination of sincere humility with unusual mental alacrity and cleverness. Socrates' mind was incisive; it could perform the dissection of a man's intellectual tissue with the fineness and delicacy of a perfect surgical instrument. Other men's minds cast shadows in the neighbourhood of Socrates' intellectual brilliance. And too often a faculty like this goes with personal conceit to make a combination by no means pleasing. Indeed, in spite of its sharpness, such a character affects us as repugnant. Conceit kills any reverence we may have for cleverness.

Socrates' character, however, was too large, too solid for the flippancies of egotism. Its fundamental note was seriousness, though with many an overtone of jest and joy.

And so we find in him a continual recognition of his own ignorance while criticising the pretended knowledge of others. He did not himself pretend to the knowledge which he too often discovered did not exist in others who did pretend to it. If, in anger at being shown up, they rounded on him and told him he knew no better, he only smiled in their face and said it was true.[1] That was not all. No one could have an argumentative battle with him without being compelled in their heart to acknowledge his insight and penetration, and hence the idea that his profession of ignorance was purely ironical and assumed. This is what is known as Socratic Irony. But it was only mere irony to the superficial knower. Socrates had a deeper standard or estimate of what constitutes true knowledge, and he knew that he himself could not attain to it. This ideal of his was always a problem with which he was wrestling, a problem that continually baffled even his brain. His life was a wrestle with ideas, for ideas. He must know exactly what he is talking about instead of using conventional words and phrases in the conventional way to express conventional meanings.

That is the sort of thing which prevents progress. Men are misled by words, and will not be at the trouble of examining into privileges which certain words have obtained by heredity, and which ought perhaps to be taken from them.

[1] On all this, Theætetus, 150.

This is especially so in the most important of all the phases of practical life—viz. the moral.

We glibly call things or actions good, just, right, courageous, pious, etc., without even asking ourselves, Am I right in so calling them? Do they really merit the title? What *is* goodness, justice, right, courage, piety, and so on? I am trading in doubtful, perhaps in counterfeit, coin, till I have asked and answered the question, What is the real and true meaning of these ideas?

Only then shall the voyage of life be guided by the fixed stars in the heaven of thought, and not by wandering and inconstant lights. We must get behind slightly superficialities of speech to the deep underlying, changeless, and absolute realities of the moral consciousness.[1] Then we shall be able to make progress, drawn on by the profounder gravitations of truth, instead of being tossed hither and thither at the caprice of language. The greatest foe of a strong and right morality is ignorance. What the world needs is knowledge. So we see Socrates as the apostle of the eternal in morality. His attitude is a messenger to all that is young in the world. It proclaims that the great hindrance to advance in the world's conduct is custom, tradition, hearsay, make-believe, and lack of penetrating thought. We are too apt to oppose anything which does not come with the certificate of recognised values. We forget that there may be a discovery of new values and a " transvaluation " of old.

Dogma is the old man of the sea that hangs about the neck not only of an emerging religion, but of a rising morality. Men and women assume that it is a sufficient reason for the existence of a particular code of judgment and action that it has got itself to exist. The actual custom becomes the tyrannical

[1] The seeker of concepts and not instances, Theætetus, 147.

law. The external banishes the internal to endless exile. Convention corrupts the world. Socrates is against all that. The actual must always be criticised and corrected by the ideal—the old fact by the new thought. The mind of man is the sole authority, the sole source of revelation. Its pronouncements are alone sacred. Whatever cannot justify itself before the bar of conscience, or stand the light of reason, though it were hoary with eld and entwined like the ivy with ancient sentiment and gnarled prejudice, must be torn from the soil, if the primroses and crocuses of the fresh spring are to have room to take root and grow, as heralds of another summer of the soul of man.

Socrates was Athens' prophet of the soul, of the inward life—the life of reason, judgment, thought.

(b) The rationalism of Socrates, however, was not a bare abstract rationalism. It was his method, his instrument, but the man himself was far more than a logic-chopping machine. He had soul as well, and it was the life of the soul in its richness and fullness he sought. He took it all as his province. There are writers, like Joël in an extreme degree, and also Gomperz, who fall foul of Xenophon, on account of what they are pleased to regard as his commonplaceness and philistinism.[1] To such, Socrates is the pure rationalist and dialectician, bones with the flesh off, only the skeleton of a man. We think Xenophon on the whole, so far as it went, gave a reliable enough picture of his subject, though naturally he may have brought some features which attracted him into more prominence and passed lightly over others in which he was not so much interested. No doubt Socrates said, as every man must say, many things

[1] Cp. Prof. Bury on Xenophon in " Ancient Greek Historians," p. 151.

which are not brilliantly metaphysical, and it was surely permissible to him to have interests and sympathies that were not purely philosophical. He was a full-blooded philosopher and lover of wisdom, and that means he was a lover of life and of experience on other sides than the intellectual; it means that he must have felt, as assuredly he seems to have done, that the intellect is made for life, and not life for the intellect. He was indeed a Professor of Life, and took the greatest interest in all that concerned it, all its problems and ideals.

Virtue and the soul were his care, as not only Xenophon but also Plato sufficiently attests,[1] and it was for their sake that he indefatigably advocated the necessity of accurate knowledge.

We are unstable, inconsistent, unprogressive and futile, because we lack knowledge, which, in the Socratic sense, means contact with Truth and Reality, instead of relatively to the fickle changing shows of things. It is only expressing the same thing to say that we must get deeper than the senses. These do not carry us down into the soul and essence of things; in them the accidental and essential come united together and confused, and it is only by the process of thought and reflexion that we can strip off the modes and fashions with which Reality is clothed, in which it is "half revealed and half concealed," so that we can apprehend it in its pure, perfect, unchanging being.

It is easy to see that such communion with Truth has and always must have a revolutionary aspect, that it is the principle of continuous reform and endless advance. It is this which keeps man and the world young, and we do not wonder that Socrates gathered the youth about him and stirred their

[1] Apol., 31 a, b.

enthusiasm, and that it was the youth above all to whom he was drawn.

Of course it was inevitable in a society with any elements of conservatism in it that an inspiration of that kind, carried into effect upon current modes of belief and conduct, should set up ferment and antagonisms, and Socrates became a man marked out for suspicion and hate.

But it was never his way to throw up a line because of its consequences to himself. It seemed to amuse him more than anything else to notice the nervous excitement of people to protect themselves against him. It was the amusement of conscious power of the man who has given himself and all he has in hostage to Truth, who is prepared to be snuffed out with the false if he be false, and asks no victory for himself but that of the Truth, whose slave he is. George Fox himself was no more devoted and disinterested in showing up the hollowness of vain profession and groundless convention, and the Athenians found the one about as great a nuisance and terror as the English did the other, and it is not unlikely that as possible victims would get out of the way when they saw Fox bearing down on them, so at Athens Socrates would be avoided by some who did not relish the prospect of being shelled as clean as oysters by a few dexterous strokes of the Socratic dialectic. Here is Macaulay's verdict, in which he suffers a good deal more than he need have done, from sympathy with the Athenians, perhaps because he fails to remember the *bonhomie* and good humour of Socrates the iconoclast : " I do not much wonder at the violence of the hatred which Socrates had provoked. He had, evidently, a thorough love for making men look small. There was a meek maliciousness about him which gave wounds which must have smarted long, and his command of temper was more provoking than noisy triumph and insolence would have been." [1]

We don't doubt about the wounds and smarts, but surely there is little to drop tears over when conceit and swagger and philistinism mourn. And it was in a good cause.

Socrates went about as a sort of sage let loose or minister at large, to whom people sometimes had recourse in difficulties and who was always ready to enter into their interests, and learn from them what could be learned. He gives us the impression of one largely skilled in literature and the human heart, a man withal of "self-reverence, self-knowledge, self-control," well fitted in all respects to be a good guide, counsellor, and friend.

We have no desire to submerge this aspect of his activity expatiated on by Xenophon and vouched for by Plato, in which the moral and spiritual interest ranging over all life stands out predominant—the great peak about which the lesser heights cluster.

It is all included in the meaning of the term "philosopher" as Socrates understood it. To him philosophy meant wisdom in the largest sense, not only the intellectual penetration to the essence of things, but also a way of life, an attitude of the whole soul, the achievement of a just perspective in life, a right balance of its various interests, according to the disposition, and under the control, of God; to be a philosopher means to see life steadily and see it whole at every moment so that one's conduct in all its forms is the result of a right appreciation of values on the part of the agent. To live such a life, realise such a character, and to stimulate and lead others to the pursuit of it was a great part of Socrates' mission, a

[1] Life and Letters, ch. xiii.

part which he could not on any terms give up. His determination on this point was as fixed and unalterable in the presence of his judges, as that of Luther before the Roman Catholic dignitaries and plenipotentiaries at Worms. " I can do no other. So help me, God."

" To do wrong," he said, " and to distrust the better, represented by God or man, *that* I know to be wickedness and disgrace." [1]

" I honour and love you, Athenians, but I will rather obey God than you, and as long as I have breath and power in me, I shall never cease to be philosopher nor to admonish and censure any of you I meet, saying, as has been my wont—' My friend, as an Athenian, of that city greatest and most renowned for wisdom and strength, are you not ashamed to make your care the amassing of as much wealth as you can, and glory and honour, while you neither care for nor give your thought to prudence and truth or to making your soul as good as you can ? And if any of you disputes the point and says he *does* care, I shall not let him off and leave him, but I shall question him and examine him, and, if I find that he has not acquired virtue but claims to have, I shall reproach him with treating the things of highest value as of least value, and esteeming the less important as the more important. This I shall do with old and young, stranger or citizen, especially the citizens as closer linked to me by blood. For I tell you God calls me to this work, and I believe that no greater blessing has ever befallen you in this city than my service to God. For I go about doing nothing else than persuading you, old and young, to transfer your interest from the body and from wealth and to concern yourselves with so much fervour only for the highest perfection

[1] Apol., 29 b.

of soul possible to you. I say to you that virtue does not come from wealth, but from virtue comes wealth and all other blessings to men both individually and socially. . . . Such is my teaching, and I shall not give up, no, not if I had to face many deaths."[1] "I am a man who has never had the wit to be idle during his whole life, but has been careless of what the many care about, wealth, and family interests, and military offices, and speaking in the assembly, and magistrates, and plots, and parties. Reflecting that I was really too honest a man to follow in this way and live, I did not go where I could do no good to you or to myself; but where I could do the greatest good privately to every one of you thither I went, and sought to persuade every man among you that he must look to himself, and seek virtue and wisdom before he looks to his private interests, and look to the state before he looks to the interests of the state; and that this should be the order which he observes in all his actions."[2]

It was in the capacity of a minister in spiritual things, stirring up the conscience of the people, reproaching them when they confused life's true values, and subordinated the supreme ends of human existence to what were only means and instruments, that Socrates likened himself to a gadfly,[3] which keeps stirring up a great and noble steed when it gets slow and tardy in its movements. It is *his* function to keep the Athenian State from falling into a drowsiness and sleep of its better part and highest faculties, by continually exhorting its citizens, like a father or elder brother, to strive after virtue and make it their paramount business.[4]

The dialogue "Clitophon" also bears testimony to the importance which Socrates attached, and the

---

[1] Plato, Apol., 29 d-30 c.   [2] Apol., 36 b, c; cp. 38 a.
[3] Apol., 30 e.   [4] Apol., 31 b.

place which he gave, to this mission of virtue. There also in terms and phrases which recall the "Apology," he is spoken of as one who has given himself to a crusade against the conception of life's happiness as consisting in the amassing of the goods that perish ; there also he is represented as going about trying to awake the Athenians out of their indolence and sleep as regards the true aims and values and blessedness of human activity, and as exhorting them to the study and acquirement of virtue, as more necessary than any other part of education,[1] whether that of the intellect or of the body ; there also we are told that he held up the soul and its interests as supreme over every other human concern.[2] Clitophon indeed acknowledges, what Xenophon insists on in the " Recollections," that Socrates had no rival in the power to stimulate youth in the pursuit of the things pertaining to the soul's welfare,[3] in wakening them out of the dogmatic slumbers of the ordinary conventional fashion of life to a sense of their spiritual needs, though he adds that Socrates could give no help, indeed was rather an obstacle, when it became a matter of achieving the end of virtue and attaining happiness—a criticism which rather confirms the belief that there was vacillation and uncertainty in Socrates' ethical teaching, and that, in accordance with his own disclaimers, he never reached philosophical rest in the possession of fixed positive truth. The iron of doubt that had entered deep into his soul in youth was never wholly extracted. To him it was only given to walk by faith, not by knowledge, though he never ceased to pursue the quest of the latter, because he was convinced that until we attain clear and sure knowledge in the realm of ethics, we can never develop true and settled virtue, to help to produce which, individually

[1] Clitophon, 407 c, d. [2] *Ibid.*, 410 d. [3] *Ibid.*, 410 e.

and socially, was the one cardinal enthusiasm and interest of his earthly career. For this mission he continued poor; for this he sacrificed all other ambitions and pleasures; with a single eye he did this work of God, trying to instil a higher consciousness into his fellows, to promote among them nobler manners, purer laws, juster relations, better life, seeking no reward and taking none; except the peace of his own conscience, the approval of God, and the gratitude and affection of those who could appreciate the good he did.

It becomes us whensoever in our hearts we recount the names of those who have laboured humbly and faithfully in this world as disciples and slaves of the soul and of virtue, those who in their day and generation have been saints and apostles of the life of the spirit and belonged to the great order of the good, who have loved good for its own sake with a passionate love, whose lives have been the light of men, —it becomes us to remember among them that unwearied devotee who, borne on by his inner faith and convictions, pursued his ministry for virtue's sake, scorned, unheeded, hated, by most of his fellow-citizens, in the public haunts and highways of Athens, in its shops and its houses, among high and low, rich and poor, artist and artisan, at the call of God and the need of man; an exile from convention by the privilege of reason, a pilgrim from dogma and error by the same privilege; one who "marched breast forward, never doubted clouds would break," and who believed in the True and the Good shining beyond the veils of human ignorance and delusion.

He was just the man to be counsellor and friend to others in need because he could see all matters in the clarifying light of reason and from the highest and broadest point of view, and we now turn to get acquainted with his principles and teachings on some of the greater matters of life, as they emerge from his handling of the personages and facts he came across in daily life, as he pursued this ministry at large.

We shall close this section with the fine characterisation of him by Joël:[1] "He warned and was misunderstood, did citizen duty and was misrepresented, went about the streets and came not to knowledge—he brooded in his soul and remained an enigma to himself. He was the " selbstlosen Socrates "—the selfless Socrates. He gained his life in losing it."

[1] See Der Echte und der Xenophontische Sokrates, vol. II, pt. ii, p. 961.

CHAPTER VI

HIS TEACHING ON WORK

WE shall see that the great determining principle which Socrates brought to bear in deciding the problems of thought and life was that of reason, the reason which sits throned within, and whose oracles if listened to would dissipate those difficulties which confront us because we are hidebound by convention and public opinion. Inner Reason dictated not only the sage's advice to, but also his relations with, others, as we shall immediately illustrate, and it lay at the root of his greatness. "I am a man who at all times can only be persuaded by reason approved on reflection."[1]

Mr. Arnold Bennett has said with considerable truth that "brain alone is the enemy of prejudice and precedent, which alone are the enemies of progress. And this habit of originally examining phenomena is perhaps the greatest factor that goes to the making of personal dignity, for it fosters reliance on oneself and courage to accept the consequences of the act of reasoning. Reason is the basis of personal dignity."[2]

This was eminently so with Socrates. His advance upon the main body of mankind was due to the fact that in him Thought and Reason sat upon Olympus and judged the world. Other people accepted things, Socrates judged them. He took the law and order of the day into avizandum; he asked whether it had

[1] Plato, Crito, 46 b.   [2] The Human Machine.

anything to say for itself worth listening to before the bar of an enlightened Reason.

It is related that Margaret Fuller, one of a brilliant coterie of literary spirits in America, once said "I accept the universe." The statement of Miss Fuller was repeated to Carlyle in his grim shades at Chelsea. "Gad, she'd better!" was his laconic comment.

There is a sense in which we must all accept the universe and be thankful, and the Calvinism in Carlyle's bones laughed at any poor female biped who made a fuss about so simple and inevitable a fact. But if we must accept the universe, we ought first to be sure what the universe is. If the Actual says, "I am the universe," and soul says, "I am the universe, and I am better than the Actual," then Socrates, like Carlyle himself, would say, "Let the soul have it." Man's soul is in the world not to submit to it, but to subdue it, for after all the human soul is the organ of the Soul of the world, through which the latter utters its deeper, truer reality. And the nature of the soul is, in its Socratic view and in the Greek view generally, above all else, Reason.

What Reason condemns is damned, what Reason approves is law, Reason being of course not mere formal logic; but the trained and educated insight of wisdom and knowledge.

There is an incident for which Xenophon vouches as having come within his own personal experience, when Aristarchus, one of Socrates' friends, met him with downcast spirit and disconsolate face. The philosopher bade him unbosom his miseries; and out came a tale of woe. Aristarchus's home had been made the asylum and refuge of all his penniless female relations, fourteen souls all told living under his roof, at a time of crisis in Athens, when food was scarce, money likewise, and no chance of either buying or borrowing, on his eaten-up securities.

It was indeed a pickle—these ladies all to be kept alive; and nothing to do it with!

Socrates at once saw daylight through the darkness, and a sun behind the clouds.

He horrified the already overwrought, anxious Aristarchus by suggesting the simple expedient of setting these free-born relations to work on baking and sewing and dressmaking.

It would bring in the much needed guineas, it would afford that occupation of one's time and faculties without which proper manhood and womanhood is impossible, and it would create an atmosphere of good temper and happiness instead of that of jealousy and dejection and sourness.

After some objection on the score of the indignity of work for well-born ladies, Socrates' plan was tried; and with great success. The prospect of Aristarchus' home brightened, and he was relieved of the worry and anxiety of a very delicate and difficult situation.

Sometimes Socrates would drop into an artist's studio or tradesman's shop, and converse with the man on the principles of his art or craft, the idea being probably not so much to enlighten them as to learn from them facts about their work and its methods, which he could use to illustrate and support his own logical and ethical theories. Socrates had genius enough to see that the common life about him was of as much use to philosophy and as closely and essentially related to its aims and objects and conclusions as any department of human activity. He brought philosophy out of the schools into touch with the ordinary life of ordinary men, and so made it a more living and practical and serious thing. It was like the sunlight which must illuminate not only stately buildings and public offices, but small back shops and private stores, and be of all the more worth for it.

It was, indeed, made a matter of criticism that in his philosophical discussions he would keep his arguments haunting about shoemakers and tanners, and blacksmiths' shops, thus making the august muse smell of leather and old iron, and other nasty common things.

But here again Socrates took the point of view not of the senses, but of thought and reason. A bad smell or a dusty exterior might be part of the noble order of the universe. We might just as well be as democratic as Reality itself.

And here we come in view of another of those dim clustered isles which gather themselves out of the monotonous level of the grey sea of custom and convention, that lies about the world's rare up-towering souls.

In Athens, as is well known, there were two widely separated social classes—the free-born citizen and the slave. It was the business of the free-born to guide and govern their city, it was the business of the slave to work for the free-born.

Thus in Athens manual labour was generally looked down upon as disfiguring and "low." Even in a master-mind like Plato's, we often hear echoes of this uncomplimentary estimate of trade and labour. Plato believed that man was meant to be an artist, but the artisan is a slave in spirit, his occupation stains his soul, warps his mind, and so injures the delicate harmonious beauty of the full-petalled and symmetrical bloom of life.

Socrates saw deeper than Plato. Socrates', I believe, was a fuller and more balanced mind than Plato; he had more catholic sympathies, a larger heart, hewn out of common humanity.

And to him it was given to see that " all work is

noble and alone noble," as Carlyle put it ; that honest labour, which plants a stalk of grain or a flower where before was nothing, is the very mission of this life and of all who live. Socrates, it was, in Athens, who saw clearly the " perennial sacredness of work." He, too, would have proclaimed to all and sundry, " Produce, produce, were it the pitifullest infinitesimal fraction of a product ; in God's name, produce it."

Disgrace, so he taught, never lies in the kind of work a man does, if it is useful and needful. Idleness is the only disgrace. But there are people who are extremely busy idling, and others who seem to be idling who are really busy with life's most important work.

Of the former class, who would be as well if not better doing nothing, are dicers and gamblers and others engaged in occupations that are injurious to themselves and others. These Socrates classed as " idle drones." Work to be worthy of the name must have some social utility, and those who get their wealth by means that adds not a jot to the real wealth and welfare of society are simply parasites, who live on the sweat of their fellows, eating the honey others gather through the industrious day.

On the other hand, not every man who is not engaged in what is popularly or conventionally called " work " is an idler. There are some who called Socrates a meddlesome fellow who lounged about doing anything but useful work. Socrates repudiated that charge.

One can imagine Socrates Redivivus thumping Robert Louis Stevenson on the back in lusty appreciation, when he had written in his " Apology for Idlers " : " Perpetual devotion to what a man calls his business is only to be sustained by perpetual neglect of many other things. And it is not by any means certain that a man's business is the most important thing he has to do." That was the view out of which all Socrates' public activities grew; that was his *Apologia pro vita sua.*

Moreover, he believed that the true joy of life comes from the sense of work well done. As a modern teacher finely puts it: " No impulse is too splendid for the simplest task: no task is too simple for the most splendid impulse."

He was once asked what he regarded as the best business and pursuit of man, and he replied: " Doing well." He did not mean by that, good fortune. Success as such was to him little enough. " In my creed, that man is successful who by dint of learning and practice does a thing well," or " tries to do his duty."

" These are the best men, and nearest to the heart of God, who if farmers do their farming well, if doctors their doctoring, if politicians do their best in politics. But the man who does nothing well is useless to men and no friend of God." [1]

" Whatever you do," he is reported to have said to an old friend he met after he had missed him for a long time, and whom he advised, being out of employment, to use his gifts as an agent on somebody's estates, and never mind the cant about it being slavish to work for others, " *Whatever you do, do it heart and soul. and make it your finest effort.*"

" *Act with all your might*" was a favourite aphorism of Socrates taken from Hesiod, and even to-day its adoption would mark a revolution in vast areas of our industries and business. There are few things more wanted to send the world spinning merrily forward than the reintroduction into our modern industry of the whole heart and will and might. We miss the zest, the glorious zest, of labour that carries us along as on

[1] Mem., iii. ch. 9.

a spring-tide. " I eat my heart out when I am not up to the neck in work," said St.-Beuve.

No one can fail to be impressed with the thoroughness and enthusiasm with which through life Socrates himself pursued his high calling—a calling ever to learn, ever to examine, ever to move on from that which is found wanting to that which is securer and more perfect. He sat as " Grandpa," at the feet of Connus, but that was only one sign of the passion of devotion of his whole being to life's whole ideal—the ideal of Knowledge, Reason, Good. To the end he felt he was only battling at the closed gates, that he had never got entry within the mystery at whose altar it was his consuming desire sometime here or hereafter to bow, with the light of knowledge in his eyes—but he never resigned the quest, nor gave up the pursuit. He lived for it with all his might, and with a good heart he was able to die for it.

Professor Joël has argued, as he has on other features of Xenophon's delineation, that in ascribing to Socrates this advocacy of all honest labour, this sense of the dignity of work and the disgrace of idleness, we find another instance of effect of Cynic ideas and doctrine upon Xenophon's mind; that it was Antisthenes and his followers who regarded no work as too mean, and who thus broke down the time-honoured division between the two great classes of the free citizens who never soiled their hands with labour, and the artisans. He maintains that the intellectualism of Socrates would not tend to an appreciation of artisan work, and that indeed he gave up his own craft.[1]

We can see no good ground for this position, based on the gratuitous assumption that if a doctrine and

[1] See Der Echte und der Xenophontische Sokrates, vol. II. pt. ii, pp. 1025, 1026.

attitude can be shown to be Cynic, *ipso facto* it cannot have been Socratic. It is a queer principle of criticism, and there is plenty of evidence in Plato as well as in Xenophon that Socrates did not despise art or artisans, while it is obvious to all who understand the circumstance that his abandonment of his early trade had nothing to do with any feeling that it was mean and unworthy. He abandoned it for the same reason for which he eschewed the gentlemanly life of politics.

His attitude towards labour was exactly that of the great German mystic Tauler: "One can spin, another can make shoes; and all these are gifts of the Holy Ghost: I tell you, if I were not a priest, I should esteem it a great gift if I was able to make shoes, and would try to make them so well as to be a pattern to all."

CHAPTER VII

TREATMENT OF ENEMIES

REASON and Reflection are radical forces, much more so than is sentiment; and just because more radical in their standards, they are more Catholic and universal in their judgments. Their function and tendency is to strip off the accidental and transient and penetrate to the essential. We have just seen how Socrates, by appealing to the Reason within, was at once carried to a view which broke down the great conventional distinction between the class of the free who toiled not neither did they spin, and the class which had to toil and spin for them, a distinction which in any case was counting for less and less in the public life of Athens, as the Aristophanic drama shows.

The critical principle applied by Socrates not only cut at the root of the conventional opinion in regard to labour which set up a cleavage within the same society, but it was bound also to operate as a solvent for the unnatural divisions and relations between members of different societies.

If a man, *e.g.*, ought to love his neighbour as himself, the inference of Reason is that he ought also to love everybody else's neighbour as himself. The consideration as to whether a man lives in the same street and the same society or in another street and different society, makes no difference from the point of view of the Reason in the way in which you ought to treat him. Taking them simply as individuals, the colour of men's skin, or their position geographically on the surface of the globe, does not affect the fundamental rights and duties which the Moral Law imposes as between them and ourselves. This was one of the great principles of the Practical Reason in the thought of Kant, who expressed it in the imperative so to act as if the maxim on which you act were to become through your will a universal law of nature. That means that *ethically* every person must have equal value for us, and we must treat all in the same spirit, and it leads to what may be called a rational or ethical Humanitarianism in which all such divisions and antipathies and hatreds as have no justification in reason and morality are abolished.

The question is, did Socrates see all to which the principle committed him, and did the vision liberate him from the ordinary ethic of his time, which drew a sharp line between friends and enemies, and sanctioned opposite modes of conduct toward them? "It is commonly held to redound to a man's praise," he says in conversation with Chærecrates, "to have outstripped an enemy in mischief or a friend in kindness,"[1] a quotation of ordinary sentiment which it is worth observing occurs in a talk in which Socrates is pressing Chærecrates to take the initiative in healing the quarrel which has arisen between him and his brother. He advises him to go and frankly offer his hand to his brother in reconciliation. He will be sure to find his generosity reciprocated, but even if it should not be so, then "at the worst you will have shown yourself to be a good, honest, brotherly man, and he will appear as a sorry creature on whom kindness is wasted."[2]

But Socrates had a very high ideal of family re-

---

[1] Xen., Mem., bk. ii. ch. 3, § 14.   [2] *Ibid.*, § 17.

lationships, and brotherhood was a natural tie which he believed God intended should bind members of the family together closer than hands and feet, or ears and eyes, in a community of mutual good;[1] and the "Recollections" don't represent Socrates as inculcating the same attitude in the case of mutual enemies in general. Take the following words addressed to Critobulus by Socrates, who assumes the rôle of an agent for promoting friendships:

"If you will authorise me to say that you are devoted to your friends; that nothing gives you so much joy as a good friend; that you pride yourself no less on the fine deeds of those you love than on your own; that you never weary of plotting and planning to procure them a rich harvest of the same; and lastly, that you have discovered a man's virtue is to *excel his friends in kindness and his foes in hostility*. If I am authorised thus to report of you, I think you will find me a serviceable fellow-hunter in the quest of friends, which is the conquest of the good."[2]

It would seem as though Socrates had failed of his own principles in this matter, and that the pressure of environing ideas was too strong for the fidelity of his own spirit to itself. We confess we find it difficult, in virtue of the impression which the whole character of the man makes upon us, and which we have tried to convey, in preceding pages, to believe that Socrates could be satisfied with such an attitude of mind towards his enemies. It conflicts with all we know of him, in his bearing towards others. We are not convinced by Professor A. E. Taylor's "Varia Socratica" that Socrates was actually a member of a Pythagorean brotherhood, but he was intimate with Pythagoreans, and it is not

[1] Xen., Mem., bk. ii. ch. 3, §§ 18, 19.
[2] Xen., Mem., bk. ii. ch. 6, § 35.

credible to us that one whom they affectionately recognised to be greater than themselves should have fallen below the moral level of the teaching of their school, which was, according to Aristotle, that they were "never to injure anyone, but endure patiently wrongs, and injury, and, in a word, do all the good they could." This was the very doctrine that Socrates practised. It was he of whom his jailor at the last could say that he was unlike other prisoners, for he had never railed at him, but had spoken only kindly words, and showed nothing but courtesy and benevolence; of whom Demetrius, quoted by Diogenes Laertius, could relate that once when he was kicked by some cad in passing, he only laughed, and when his friends expressed astonishment at this meek and mild behaviour, asked whether when asses kicked him he was to have the law of them;[1] of whom Xenophon himself says that "he was never the cause of evil to the state, was free of offence in private as in public life, never hurt a single soul either by deprivation of good or infliction of evil, and never lay under the imputation of any such wrong-doing"; who, according to Plato's "Apology," found at heart no cause of anger against his accusers or those who condemned him to death,[2] and could say in the presence of his fellow-citizens that he had never intentionally wronged anyone;[3] who held that men do not commit wrong except because of ignorance, error, or illusion, not seeing the true character and consequence of their action. Could such an one believe in the doctrine of retaliation or of injuring enemies?

We confess we derive little consolation from Professor Joël's theory that Xenophon's account would be influenced by the Cynic doctrine that Justice consists in

---

[1] Diogenes Laertius, bk. ii. ch. 6, § 21.
[2] Apol., 41 d.   [3] Apol., 37 a.

strict reciprocity, paying back in the coin in which you are paid, an eye for an eye and a tooth for a tooth, and that what Xenophon gives us is not the historical Socrates but the Cynic sage.

The fact is, Xenophon himself has presented us with Socrates in another aspect, as taking a great view of humanity, very much akin to that he had of the family—a view in which the good among mankind are presented as forming one great community and brotherhood.

"Soc. Seeds of love are implanted in man by nature. Men have need of one another, feel pity, help each other by united efforts, and in recognition of the fact show mutual gratitude. But there are seeds of war implanted also. The same objects being regarded as beautiful or agreeable by all alike, they do battle for their possession; a spirit of disunion enters, and the parties range themselves in adverse camps. Discord and anger sound a note of war: the passion of having more, staunchless avarice, threatens hostility; and envy is a hateful fiend.

"But, nevertheless, through all opposing barriers friendship steals her way, and *binds together the beautiful and good among mankind.* Such is their virtue that *they would rather possess scant means painlessly than wield an empire won by war.* In spite of hunger and thirst, they will share their meat and drink without a pang. Nor bloom of lusty youth, nor love's delights can warp their self-control; nor will they be tempted to cause pain where pain should be unknown. It is theirs not merely to eschew all greed of riches, not merely to make a just and lawful distribution of wealth, but to supply what is lacking to the needs of one another. Theirs is it to compose strife and discord not in painless oblivion simply, but to the general advantage. Theirs also to hinder such extravagance of anger as shall entail remorse hereafter. And as to envy, they will make a clean sweep and clearance of it; the good things which a man possesses shall be also the property of his friends, and the goods which they possess are to be looked upon as his. Where, then, is the improbability that the beautiful and noble should be sharers in the honours of the state not only without injury, but even to their mutual advantage?"[1]

Socrates' doctrine is that friendship can only exist between the good: evil disintegrates and divides. But goodness takes no account of national divisions. Wherever the good are, they are friends of the good: they need each other, and they help each other. In their hearts are none of the things which create strife and enmity. Here, then, is the recognition of a kingdom of peace and goodwill, a kingdom of mutual affection and service, a kingdom of God, which takes no account of artificial national divisions. It is a kingdom of the Spirit, and all who have the Spirit belong to it.

This, then, was the plane on which Socrates' thought moved, the purer, wider air he breathed; and the soul which lived at these heights could not have been completely held by any inferior doctrines of morality. We can be quite sure that he would recognise only the highest standards in conduct that were known to him. Aristotle informs us that Socrates held that no one would choose, if he had the choice, injustice rather than justice in action, nor cowardice rather than courage, nor any vice in preference to the corresponding virtue?[2] The philosopher who cherished such views was likelier to pity the poor misled wrong-doer and seek to set him right, than to exact revenge or cause him further injury. The consistency of his practical con-

[1] Xen., Mem., bk. ii. ch. 6, § 21 ff. (Dakyns' trans.)
[2] Aristotle, Magna Moralia, i. 9, 1187 a.

duct with his doctrine of ill-doing as ignorance, drives us to accept the unanimous testimony of the Platonic dialogues, which is to the effect that to return evil for evil on a man would only be to aggravate the evil.

In the "Apology," Socrates states his inmost conviction that "to be unjust and to disobey any one better than oneself, whether God or man, is contrary to duty and honour." The point, then, is as to whether or no it is unjust to render evil for evil, or under any circumstance to injure a fellow-creature. And to that we reply in the first place, that if doing evil is the result of ignorance, then to retaliate in like manner *is* unjust and wrong, and can only be the result of ignorance also, and we suggest that Socrates was not so dull and obtuse as to fail to recognise the obvious inference from his own principles.

Nor can we fall back on the idea that his conception of justice was, in itself, too confused and imperfect to exclude the maxim of retaliation. Socrates had got beyond the current position on this matter. "In questions of just and unjust, fair and foul," he says to Crito, "which are the subjects of our present consultation, ought we to follow the opinion of the many and to fear them; or the opinion of the one man who has understanding? Ought we not to fear and reverence him more than all the rest of the world; and if we desert him, shall we not destroy and injure that principle in us which may be assumed to be improved by justice and deteriorated by injustice?"[1]

"In spite of the opinion of the many, and in spite of consequences whether better or worse, shall we insist as before, that *injustice is always an evil and dishonour to him who acts unjustly?*

"Cr. Yes.

"Soc. Then we must do no wrong?

[1] Plato, Crito, 47. (Jowett's trans.)

"CR. Certainly not.

"SOC. *Nor when injured, injure in return, as the many imagine;* for *we must injure no one at all?*

"CR. Clearly not.

"SOC. Again, Crito, may we do evil?

"CR. Surely not, Socrates.

"SOC. And what of doing evil in return for evil, which is the morality of the many—is that just or not?

"CR. Not just.

"SOC. *Then we ought not to retaliate or render evil for evil to any one whatever evil we may have suffered from him.*"[1]

The same conclusion is put into Socrates' mouth in the Republic":[2]

"SOC. If, then, someone says that it is just to render to each what is due to him, by that understanding that injury is due to enemies, and service to friends, such an one would not be wise in so expressing himself. He has not spoken the truth. For it has been seen that *in no circumstances is it just to injure anyone.*" Socrates' argument has turned on the point, to him self-evident, that nothing that is right and good can possibly do hurt or injury to anyone.

In the "Gorgias" Plato makes him declare that the worst evil that can ever befall a man is to do wrong,[3] and that if it were a choice between acting unjustly and suffering unjustly, between doing wrong and having wrong done to himself, he would choose the latter.[4]

In these dialogues, then, there is not a quaver of uncertainty about the conviction that the just and good man will never repay injury with injury but

---

[1] Plato's Crito, 49. (Jowett's trans.)
[2] Bk. i. 335 e.
[3] Plato, Gorgias, 469 b.   [4] *Ibid.*, 469 c.

always with good, and it fits in beautifully with Socrates' character.

Are we to suppose, then, that Plato gives us the truth, and that Xenophon was mistaken and inconsistent in his reminiscences of the master's teaching on this theme? We should have no hesitation in taking that position, only there is one other dialogue ascribed to Plato—the fragmentary dialogue "Clitophon"—in which Socrates is taken to task for the obscurity and ambiguity of his opinions on certain matters, and this very question of the treatment of enemies is mentioned. Clitophon speaks thus to him: "Finally, Socrates, I applied directly to yourself, and *you told me that it was the principle of justice to injure enemies and do good to friends.* But *afterwards it came out that the just man never injures anyone, for he acts with a view to the good of everybody in everything.* And this was my experience not once or twice but for a long time, so I gave up my persistency, having come to the conclusion either that while you were without a rival in stirring up people to the concern of virtue, but could do no more . . . either you do not know really what justice is or you do not choose to communicate your knowledge."

This is a most interesting and significant passage, and the vacillation which it attributes to Socrates is not without commentary and witness in the Platonic literature at large. It has the note of authenticity about it, and on the strength of it we would suggest that while Socrates had long risen in spirit and sympathy above the ethics of contemporary orthodoxy, yet in the realm of theory it cost him a prolonged struggle to shake himself quite free of the views in which his upbringing had been steeped, and which were strongly entrenched in the social and even religious authorities around him. He experienced a protracted duel between the loftier and the lower conception of moral obligations, and in the end the loftier vanquished, so that he found it impossible to conceive that a just man would do any injury to any fellow mortal, even if injured by him. In his speculations and discussions he would start off from the generally accepted hypotheses on the subject; but would by the force of his own reasoning always be driven to the higher point of view. Perhaps, indeed, it would be on the whole the most fitting inference from the evidence before us to hold that, in accordance with his usual method, he only laid down the accepted opinion as a point of departure from which he could set out and carry others with him to the recognition of its untenability and the acceptance of his own real view, a method which was obviously liable to create misunderstanding in those who did not clearly grasp it. The contradiction alluded to by Clitophon would thus receive explanation as being due to the fact that he mistook for an admission what was only a concession for the purposes of an argument, whose issue was its overthrow.

Reviewing all the evidence, we may take it as certain that Socrates practised, and practically certain that before his death he taught, the doctrine of returning good for evil, that "neither injury, nor retaliation, nor warding off evil by evil is ever right." [1]

Emerson achieved an insight into moral law which led him to pronounce in his own oracular way that "the good man has absolute good, which like fire turns everything to his own nature, so that you cannot do him any harm." [2]

But 400 years before Christ Plato put the same deep spiritual truth on the lips of Socrates, who after his sentence of death calmly declares that "*no evil can*

---

[1] Plato, Crito, p. 49 d.   [2] Essay on "Compensation."

happen to a good man in life or in death." [1] Virtue makes its possessor invulnerable; all things, even the rage of enemies, work together for good to those who love the good and are good. They are the protégés of Heaven; " *neither they nor theirs are neglected by the gods."* [2]

With such conviction as that it would indeed be a degradation of self, not to say a grave inconsistency, to entertain the idea of revenge. Let a man be true to the divine law and ideal within him, and he has already conquered his enemies and the world. He can afford to do only good to every man, whether friend or foe. It is the same idea as was later promulgated by the Cynics, that all things were theirs. Spiritually they appropriated the universe. " The Cynic hath begotten all mankind, he hath all men for his sons, all women for his daughters; so doth he visit all and care for all. Thinkest thou that he is a mere meddler and busybody in rebuking those whom he meets? As a father he doth it, as a brother, and as a servant of the Universal Father, which is God."

It is worthy of grateful recognition that the principle of overcoming evil with good, which is the very flower of Christian ethic, was thus the possession of the great thinkers of Greece some centuries before Jesus and Paul inculcated it. And yet we must recognise a certain difference. Its root was not the same in Greek philosophy and in Christian teaching. In the former it was rather the flower of reason, in the latter the blossom of love. Perhaps in the case of Socrates we may say it was the fruit of both, as in that of Jesus; it grew not only out of his beautiful love but also out of his sweet reasonableness. We should not be doing more than justice to the Athenian saint to say that it was the natural product alike of his mind and his heart as they lie open to us in these

[1] Apol., 41 d. [2] *Ibid.*

wonderful records. The keenness of his intellect, the geniality of his nature, and the largeness of his soul, all led him to it, and it is as high as morality can take us.

Let us remember that for him all evil and wrongdoing has its origin in ignorance, ignorance of the true Good. That good, if we could only see it clearly, would be recognised to be one and the same for all. In it or moving towards it we are all in harmony and at peace. We only become enemies as we lose sight of the Highest and turn our hearts to lower and relative goods, poor deluded fools, divided not only from others but divided within ourselves. With the Apostle, Socrates could devoutly say, "Avenge not yourselves, beloved. For it is written, Vengeance is mine; I will repay, saith the Lord."[1] Only that Socrates would have said that the man who does evil takes revenge on himself.

[1] Romans, ch. 12, v. 19.

CHAPTER VIII

THE STATE AND THE INDIVIDUAL

WE have already to some extent set forth Socrates' attitude to contemporary society, but we must now further elucidate his doctrine and especially try to clear away one or two partial and imperfect views of it.

The principle of good-will and of well-doing, otherwise the law of mutual service, underlay the whole social organisation of man in Socrates' view of it. Nowhere more than in Athenian thinkers has the idealistic conception of the state prevailed. Society did not originate in, nor does it exist for, nothing more than the protection of individuals in the enjoyment of their own life and the realisation of their own ends. Society comes into being because we human beings have need of one another, because we are so constituted and made that we can be a great help to one another. That was alike the Platonic and the Socratic doctrine. Socrates has been called the great individualist, and he was the superman whom Greece had to produce ere it could produce the Saviour (Joël). He rose above the existing state, and out of the world within him created an ideal state. He was the man who in his day is sufficient unto himself, and so is possessed of that power of detachment, that independence, which are necessary to him who is to create the better order that is to be.

We have, however, seen that the individuality of

THE STATE AND THE INDIVIDUAL

Socrates revealed itself, as all great individuality must, in social ways. The great man is the great servant, sooner or later. And there is no other greatness than that of service, though of course it may be a service of the remote unborn future rather than of the existing present. Social service is the means of true self-realisation. Thus when the most gifted fail to put their gifts at the service of their city or country, it is not only the city and country that suffer but they themselves.

This idea comes out in a conversation already referred to which Socrates is said to have held with Charmides, who, although he showed himself possessed of superior administrative capacity, declined to put it at the disposal of the community. Socrates appealed to him to give the city the benefit of his capacities, for in doing so it would not only be the rest of the citizens, but his own friends, and not least himself, who would reap the advantage.

It is alike to the highest common interest and a condition of personal happiness that the best and the ablest men should be in the seats of the rulers; there they would enjoy a free self-determined life themselves as well as furnish it to others. But when the men second-rate or third-rate in character and ability were allowed to usurp the functions of government, it could only spell injury and disaster to those over whom they were, and disgrace to themselves.

If only to escape oppression, injustice, and all the miseries that wait upon wickedness or incompetence in high places, the noble-minded should take the reins of office in their own hands.[1]

Zeller, in his "History of Greek Philosophy," has rightly insisted on the emphasis which Socrates laid upon individuality, the absolute and unwavering deference

[1] Mem., iii. 7; ii. 1; iv. 1.

which he paid to his own private judgment and reason. He has characterised this attitude as quite opposed to Greek ideas on the subject, according to which the state is " the original and immediate object of all moral activity," and there is no " private virtue." Not only is he a bad citizen who acts against society, but also he who merely withdraws from social relations. Socrates, says Zeller, desired people to concern themselves with themselves in the first place, and only after that with the state.[1]

In support of this view he refers to Xenophon's Mem., iii. 6, and iv. 2. Neither of these passages will support such a conception or construction of Socrates' sentiments. Their purport is clearly to show that before a man rushes into politics and seeks to become a civic ruler he should equip himself with the necessary knowledge of himself and of the affairs which he will have to handle. He must educate himself before he presumes to educate and guide the state. How can he govern justly any democracy if he knows neither what justice nor what democracy is?

It was because of the appalling ignorance of social facts and principles and ends displayed by candidates for office, the utter lack of the sense of responsibility among his ambitious fellow-citizens, that Socrates felt bound to remain outside public life at Athens as far as possible, and become its uncompromising, yet friendly critic.

It was not because he thought a man could be virtuous or a full man while slipping all his social obligations, that he took up his solitary apostolic rôle, but because he saw that no greater benefactor could be given to the Athenians than a thorough, drastic and detached critic.

He was never more completely social in his motive

[1] Zeller, pt. ii. p. 96.

THE STATE AND THE INDIVIDUAL

than when he was ploughing his lonely furrow. Hence also we feel compelled, with whatever humility born of a great admiration for his painstaking, thorough research, to dissent from Karl Joël in certain features of his characterisation of Socrates. Joël is more radical and consistent than Zeller, because to all intents and purposes he scraps Xenophon in what is peculiarly Xenophontic. Grote can admit that the active practical social phase of his interest and life might exist in Socrates side by side with his detached critical and dialectical impulse, which is the view we have advocated. But all the practical is swallowed up by the dialectical in Joël's view. Socrates is the man of conviction, *not* of deed; the "autocrat" who had to come before the "Saviour." Socrates is "the analytical impulse become flesh." "He is the founder of the right of individuality, of the man over against the environment. He is the discoverer of the inner world; he cuts himself off from the existing order of society, and builds a new order out of his own inner fullness and might." "The wrecker of convention was no social enthusiast."[1]

In all this, moreover, he was simply unearthing the inborn affinity and tendency of the Greeks to individualism—a tendency which showed itself throughout the fifth century, and which came to its utmost limit and turning-point in Antisthenes and Aristippus.[2]

Neither in Xenophon nor in Plato, the author of the "Republic," can we see any ground for Joël's *denials*, though there is, of course, plenty in both for what he affirms.

Socrates was a mighty, titanic individualist,—true, —true also that his social reforms were to come not as the result, not primarily, of new social organisations,

---

[1] For all this see Der Echte und der Xenophontische Sokrates, vol. II. pt. ii. pp. 961–965.   [2] *Ibid.*, p. 958.

but as the work of better and wiser individuals. But there can hardly be any doubt that the individualism of Socrates was not of the anarchic but of the social kind; that society was always viewed as the field for its exercise and expression.

For Socrates the purpose and welfare of a society consisted in securing to all classes in it the welfare and happiness of the individuals belonging to them; but, on the other hand, that welfare and happiness were impossible in a badly ordered, badly governed state.

The fact that Antisthenes and the Cynics laid great stress on the " kingly art" of rule, together with the fact, if it were proved, that Xenophon, in writing his " Memorabilia " transcribed Cynicism and its doctrines, does not prove that Socrates did not, and could not, lay stress on the function of a city's government, nor hold similar views to Antisthenes on any other point.

Joël shows one-sidedness. He is right in what he asserts, wrong in what he denies; for in Plato as in Xenophon the reformation of individuals which Socrates labours for through his criticisms is such as will make them fitter to realise not only the ideal self, but the ideal state. In Xenophon and Plato both self and society are treated as inseparable from each other in the thought of Socrates.

The whole motive of Plato's " Republic "—the idea that justice is not merely a virtue of the individual, but at the same time a quality of the social order, embodying the mutual relation of rulers to ruled, and vice versa —is a true development of the Socratic position.

If Joël's view is the whole truth, then the full and free submission of Socrates to the Laws, as personified and articulate in that exquisite passage of the " Crito " already referred to, has no justification in history and fact, and it is hard to understand why Socrates did not take his chance and, wiping the dust of Athens from his feet, flee to Thessaly, or some other place of safety. The Cynic has no state; he "lives under the open sky, and wherever he goes, there is sun and moon and stars and communion with the gods."

But Socrates knew that out of Athens his occupation would be gone; and though he was the great "autocrat," the great "subjectivist," the great discoverer of the independent authority of the conscience within, he never denied that man is a "social being," that all these things had only the highest worth, meaning, and actuality for him within the society of the city-state. It was his city, loyal to its own laws, which, he recognised, gave him the conditions of birth, nurture, education, and a share in all the common good. He was its debtor for all he was and had,[1] and it is more to be valued, is higher and holier than father or mother.[2]

Browning said that the name of Italy would be found graven on his heart—even deeper was the name of Athens graven on the heart of its great son, Socrates. No one had more right to take the name of Athens upon his lips and say:

"Life of mine, I love thee."

In the "Crito," § 52, the Laws are by himself represented as speaking thus to Socrates:

"Of all Athenians you have been the most constant resident in the city, which, as you never leave, you may be supposed to love. For you never went out of the city either to see the games, except once when you went to the Isthmus, or to any other place unless you were on military service. Nor had you any curiosity to know other states or their laws; your affections did not go beyond us and our state; we were your special favourites; and here in this city you begat

[1] Crito, § 51. [2] Ibid.

your children, which is a proof of your satisfaction. You even pretended that you preferred death to exile."

The relation of Socrates to society, as we have tried to elucidate it, receives further illustration in his doctrine of Justice. Here also we find the presence of a positive and a negative attitude, in this case, to the actual laws of society, an attitude at once of submission and of transcendence. Socrates was no anarchist or antinomian, nor, to use a phrase of Mr. G. K. Chesterton's, did he set up a "convention of unconventionality."

In a conversation with Euthydemus [1] he quotes the Oracle at Delphi as saying that the way to please the gods is by acting according to the law of the state, and Xenophon adduces examples of his strict conformity to Athenian law when it imperilled his own safety. When the populace, under the influence of hate and passion, forgot what the laws ordained, Socrates refused to budge a jot from their enactments.

The "Crito," as already noticed, illustrates the same characteristic of his conduct, so that we cannot attribute it to mere misunderstanding of Socrates by Xenophon. We find Socrates maintaining that the just is the lawful,[2] and that the just man is the law-abiding man. Throughout the chapter he evidently treats the laws of a state as the expression and embodiment of those principles of character and conduct which are opposed to the arbitrary, the fickle, and the merely self-regarding passions and propensities of our nature.

It is of the utmost importance that the laws should be reverenced, and not played with. They stand for order against that chaos in which human life and character fall to pieces.

It is nothing to say that what man has enacted he may yet repeal, as it is no reason for playing the traitor

---

[1] Mem., iv. 3.   [2] Mem., iv. 4.

THE STATE AND THE INDIVIDUAL 169

in war to say that the war may be brought to an end and peace restored.[1] It is more important that we should obey the laws than that every law should be worthy of obedience.

If a law is wrong, it must not be broken, but put right by constitutional means. This attitude is clearly and forcibly brought out in the "Crito" of Plato, where Socrates gently but firmly puts from him the temptation to evade the death penalty passed on him in accordance with Athenian law. He feels it his duty to submit to the Laws even though he feels them to have been wrongly applied. To disobey them is to overturn the very foundations of society, for "no state can subsist and stand, in which the decisions of law have no power but are set aside and overthrown by individuals."[2]

"Our country is more to be valued, is higher and holier than father or mother or any ancestor, and more to be regarded in the eyes of the gods and of men of understanding; also to be soothed, and gently and reverently entreated when angry even more than a father, and if not persuaded, obeyed."[3]

What then of such a problem as that with which Antigone is confronted in Sophocles' play? Here is a girl who, with all the dwellers in Thebes, is interdicted by Kreon the King from scattering dust on the body of a man who is her brother, because he has died fighting against the city.

On the other hand, the welfare of that brother in the other world depended upon the pious rites of burial. Shall she obey the command of an earthly ruler, or perform the duty of a sister? Shall she reverence the unwritten laws eternal in the heavens or the enactments of man?

Antigone decided to obey the instincts and affections

[1] Mem., iv. 4.   [2] Crito, § 50.   [3] Crito, § 51.

within rather than Kreon's commands, and to face a terrible death by immurement.

We see the greatness of Sophocles in that solution, and it must have appealed to the Athenian public. But would it be Socrates' solution, in view of his teaching about the inviolability of the laws? We answer yes.

For to Socrates also, according to Xenophon, there were divine laws—laws unwritten, universal, inscribed on the hearts of all men of all lands [1]—laws, *e.g.*, which relate to marriage, to social life, to the recompensing kindness with kindness, and so on, whose sanction lies in the evil and disastrous consequences which inevitably ensue if they are broken. These are not the result of human enactment, they exist and operate, though all men were to repudiate them; they must therefore come from the gods. [2] Now the gods only lay down such laws as are just, and so the law-abiding man and the just man are one.

It will be noticed that Xenophon leaves this subject somewhat confused by failing to distinguish clearly between the human laws and the divine laws, or to recognise that they may come into conflict with each other, as in the experience of Antigone.

In such a case it seems, however, pretty clear from this chapter of the "Memorabilia" that only that is truly law and lawful which is in harmony with the deeper laws of the gods. This follows from the consideration that no human legislation could avert the natural penalties of their violation. They alone are supreme and inviolate, and hence in any case of conflict it is they which must be obeyed.

That being so, it becomes impossible to give unreasoning implicit obedience to the laws of the state, and we may accept it that Socrates was too clear headed

---

[1] Mem., iv. 4, 19.   [2] Mem., iv. 4, 24.

not to see this inference, and too clear conscienced not to draw it. He cannot possibly have rested in the confusion in which Xenophon leaves him, by his identification of human and divine legislation.

Hence we are compelled to the view that for Socrates the truly just man is the man who obeys the dictates and behests of God, as they are to be read in the soul of the individual and in the experience and history of mankind.

At the same time, we are to be pervaded by a spirit of obedience to the laws of our state. There must be a heartfelt allegiance to these, otherwise we shall have every man who has an objection to any existing law of society simply ignoring or breaking it. The inevitable outcome of such an attitude would be to reduce society to its primitive elements, and re-introduce chaos.

Pure individualism is absolute reaction, and Socrates was no reactionary of that kind. He believed in individuality, but he believed that that individuality was not possible in society.

For him the practical problem is—How can I be true to myself, without being fatal to society ? How can I reform society without destroying it ? How can I fight it without slaying it ? How can I become an idealist without becoming an anarchist ?

He challenges the state not as its enemy, but as its friend ; his attitude was that of Mr. G. K. Chesterton to the universe at large.

" Before any cosmic act of reform we must have a cosmic oath of allegiance . . . the moment we have a fixed heart we have a free hand. . . . For our Titanic purposes of faith and revolution what we need is not the cold acceptance of the world as a compromise, but some way in which we can heartily hate *and heartily love it.* . . . We have to feel the Universe at once as an ogre's castle, to be stormed, and yet as our own cottage, to which we can return at evenings."[1]

Athens was exactly that to Socrates. He stormed it out of love for it. He had that "primal loyalty" which makes the most implacable revolutionist, and always at evening he returned to sleep within its beloved walls.

Because I love man I must obey God rather than man. This paradox runs everywhere; it is the paradox of sanity. For he loves society most who does not love it just "enough to get on with it, but enough to get it on." And that is the love wherewith Socrates loved it.

[1] Orthodoxy, ch. "The Flag of the World."

CHAPTER IX

HIS ETHICS

"Wisdom is the principal thing."—PROVERBS.

(a) HIS METHOD

THE most important function of life is to pass judgment on ourselves—the next most important to pass it on others. Now when we are judging humanity and its conduct we are dealing not only with facts but with values. We say a certain reform is just, a certain action pious, a certain woman good, a certain man courageous. These terms are the current coin of our language in which society has minted its long and varied experience. But are we sure we know what we mean by them, and are we sure we mean the right thing?

It is a matter of everyday experience that what one man calls good another calls bad; what one section of society calls simple equity and justice another calls spoliation and robbery; what one school calls beautiful another calls hideous, and so on. As we have seen, this fact of continual discrepancy and conflict in our moral and aesthetic appreciations and judgments struck Socrates very much. As he reflected upon it he came to the conclusion that human welfare can never be achieved till we have thoroughly sifted, purified, and fixed these ethical conceptions by which life is guided and determined, and which represent the communion of the human mind and spirit with

Reality in its moral character. And so says Xenophon, "he would always be discussing these aspects of human experience and turning over in his mind the questions, 'what is pious and impious? what is beautiful and ugly? what is just and unjust? what is prudence and madness, courage and cowardice? what is a state, and social? what is government? who is a governor?' and the other categories involved in a free self-determined life."[1] The earlier and more "Socratic" dialogues of Plato, if we may be allowed a still generally recognised distinction, convey an impression that confirms Xenophon's statement as to the subjects which monopolised Socrates' mind and thought, for they are concerned with arguments about what really constitutes "courage," and "friendship," and "piety," though the same sort of interest pervades later dialogues of Plato, like the "Theætetus" and the "Republic," in which we have the search for the true nature of Knowledge and of Justice.

These norms or ideas are the ruling and determining things, therefore they must be the most real things; and if we want to get away from the clash and conflict, the confusion and flux of unreflective private opinion, away from all that to the stability and fixity of truth, we must clear up our conventional ideas and get to know their precise significance.

The way Socrates did it was this. He would come across, let us say, some callow youth, particularly wise in his own conceit, one who, because he did not think much, was all the more pleased to think he knew all that was to be known. He would begin by paying a few ironical compliments, if necessary, using them as a bait to attract his fish to the hook, and so get the rather reluctant wiseacre drawn into discussion. His victim states that of course he knows what right

[1] Xen., Mem., i. 1, 16.

HIS ETHICS

and wrong is, and is probably visibly irritated that anyone should be guilty of such humbug as to doubt it. Socrates then begins in earnest, with a secret chuckle and a merry twinkle in his eye, to land the silly trout wriggling and flopping out of its element, and in the sight of all beholders.

He would ask him, *e.g.*, whether lying and deceit is right or wrong. Let us call the youth E.

E. confidently replies, Wrong.

Soc. But suppose you are at war, is it wrong to lead the enemy astray and deceive it.

E. Oh no, deceit is quite right then.

Ah, Socrates would reply, you meant of course that it is wrong to deceive friends and only right to deceive enemies.

E. provided by his generous examiner with this door of retreat, flies through it, and says, yes, that is his meaning. He has, you see, already had his ideas cleared up a little with Socrates' help, and has analysed his original conception more precisely, so as to admit that it is right to deceive a foe, wrong to deceive a friend. But Socrates has him again.

Soc. Suppose, E., you have a friend who has got worried and low-spirited and wants to put an end to his life, and suppose he comes to you and asks you to lend him a knife, would you not be right in saying that you have no knife in your possession, and meanwhile communicate with his people while you pretend to be procuring one?

E. has to confess that in those circumstances a little deceit would be quite right towards a friend.

And so on Socrates would go, compelling his subject to contradict or modify one after another of his own admissions till the poor man is left quite bewildered, and has after all to concede his ignorance of what right and wrong is and the need on his part of more radical and systematic thought and reflection, in order to attain a clear definition of them.

The Socratic method of attaining knowledge involved the processes of hypotheses, classification, and definition.[1] He starts off from ordinary experience, the commonly accepted, bringing forward a number of concrete instances to which a certain category is applied, carefully classifying them according as they are judged to be of one quality or its opposite. Having thus got his collection of instances to which the term Right, say, is admittedly applicable, all others being sifted out and excluded, he proceeds to analyse them and discover the element or essence which is common to all. That gives us the " definition " of the quality.

Aristotle assigns to Socrates the honour of first using this method of definition in " Ethics." He says the Pythagoreans " had discussed the definition of a few concepts, connecting them with the theory of numbers. They asked, *e.g.*, what is opportunity, or justice, or marriage ? "

But to assign a numerical representation to such things is very different from definition in the Socratic and modern sense, and Aristotle writes in these words : " Now Socrates confined his studies to the moral virtues, and was the first to attempt universal definition in connexion with them."[2] He fixed thought for the first time on definitions.[3]

True knowledge consisted in definition, the unchanging essential common element amid all the differences and varieties and fluctuations of concrete particulars. The definition of Courage or Piety or Virtue is the isolation and statement of that which

---

[1] Aristotle, Metaphysics, M 1078, b, 28.
[2] Aristotle, Metaphysics, M 1078 a. A. E. Taylor, Aristotle on his Predecessors, p. 101. [3] *Op. cit.*, 987, b, 4.

HIS ETHICS

constitutes these things what they are. It is, if you like, the *reality* of them, something which can only be got at by the exercise of reflection and reason upon the material of experience.

This contribution of the genius, one might almost say the common-sense, of Socrates to logical method and ethical theory was to become of enormous importance in the history of philosophy, for it was the forerunner and the basis of the Platonic doctrine of Ideas, the first great idealistic theory of reality we possess. In view of the Platonic development, it is impossible to exaggerate the service which Socrates has rendered to human thought. He taught men to look for and recognise universals, and all that Plato did was to regard the universals of Socratic definition as independent things, realities of the world of thought, which is the absolute world, separate from that of sense-experience, independent of it, giving to it, indeed, any substantiality it possesses.

Plato thus turned the world upside down. Like Kant he achieved a revolution to which that of the change from the Ptolemaic to the Copernican astronomy furnishes but a feeble analogy. Common-sense regards the world we apprehend through our senses as the real world; it consists of what we call things, facts, and these are the "chiels that winna ding." And the man who impugns its reality, and the reality of things of which it consists, is told to try his theory on the nearest wall. But for Plato the world of our senses is a world of unreality, of mere shadows and images. The real world is that which we reach and apprehend by thought, the world of Ideas. The former world is ever changing, passing away, moving between entity and non-entity, nothing in it remains one and the same. What a contrast to the world of idea! Goodness is Goodness, Beauty Beauty, now and forever; they are eternal, absolute, without change ; they are not mere abstract qualities only to be found in the concrete things and inseparable from them ; there is a world in which they exist and subsist, pure, unmixed, separate, themselves by themselves. In this lower world we only get their shadows and images, all mixed up and confused, and in changing relations to one another.

" Plato," says Aristotle, " accepted Socrates' teaching, but held that it applied not to any sensible thing, but to entities of another kind—because in his view it was impossible that the common definition could be that of sensible things, which are always changing. These entities he called Ideas."

We have said that not Socrates but Plato made this particular innovation of regarding the universal quality expressed in Definition as the reality, in the sense of existing apart and independently in the world of Absolutes. In this we are in harmony with what Xenophon tells us, and are following the explicit declarations of Aristotle, whom we have just quoted. The former gives plenty of examples[2] of the pursuit of definitions of moral qualities by Socrates, but he nowhere hints anything like what we know as the " Theory of Ideas " in Plato's sense just explained. Elsewhere Aristotle declares that " Socrates did not make his universals separate things, nor yet his definitions." [3]

This is an extremely interesting and important matter, for recently in this country Professor Taylor of St. Andrews has attacked the traditional view and argued that when Plato puts the doctrine of Ideas into Socrates' mouth in his dialogues, he is only attributing to him what was in truth his own.[4]

---

[1] Aristotle, Metaphysics, A 987, b. 4, 5.
[2] Mem., iv. 6.   [3] Metaphysics, M 1078, b, 30.
[4] See, *e.g.*, Taylor, Varia Socratica, pp. 89, 266.

This view ought to be mentioned, but personally we cannot resist what appear to us the convincing arguments on the other side.

Both Xenophon and Aristotle, we may take it, knew Plato's dialogues, in which case the former as well as the latter knew of the theory of Ideas, yet Xenophon never attributes it to Socrates, and Aristotle denies it to him. Besides, in the earliest and presumably most "historical" of the Platonic dialogues we have set out before us Socrates' activity as Xenophon also represents it, *i.e.* definition-hunting, and in them the "theory of Ideas" is not mentioned at all; it is only in dialogues which embody Plato's later and more mature philosophical activity that it appears.

The traditional view seems to be much the most consistent with all the evidence, and demands less of that ingenious but forced interpretation which characterises Taylor's.

(*b*) Knowledge and Virtue

The result of Definition as Socrates pursued it is to lead us to knowledge of that in which rightness or wrongness, justice or injustice, prudence or recklessness, consists, so that we shall be able to apply these terms appropriately and rightly. And it is at once obvious that as our conduct is determined by our ideas, right ideas, and the ability to attach the right moral term and description to things, are necessary to right conduct. A man whose moral conceptions are obscure and confused is sure to go wrong, he will inevitably blunder and commit mistakes in action. Clear knowledge alone can save us from such error, and save us from all the other causes of error, *e.g.*, current custom, irrelevant circumstances, and our own prejudices. Thus to have a firm, clear grasp of the true ideas of things, as a result of the intellectual process of Definition, would mean nothing less than a moral liberation. It would result in moral freedom—freedom, that is to say, from the influence of that whose influence is only allowed to operate on us because of our ignorance; it would mean truth and truth alone as the guide of conduct, and that is freedom in the ethical sphere. Harmony with reality is the condition of liberty of the kind which alone can be called moral liberty, and which alone the illuminated and emancipated mind would desire. And Harmony with reality or with truth in our actions is what is meant by virtue. Since then it is only to be attained by knowledge or wisdom, we may say that *Virtue is knowledge.* As Emerson, in his essay on "Spiritual Laws," puts it: "Virtue is the adherence in action to the nature of things, and the nature of things makes it prevalent. It consists in a perpetual substitution of being for seeming."

That *Virtue is knowledge* is the cardinal thesis of the ethical theory of Socrates, and he made all the virtues to consist in specific kinds of "knowledge" or "science."[1] For knowledge Xenophon puts "wisdom": "He (Socrates) declared that Justice and every other virtue is *wisdom.* That is to say, things just and all things else that are done virtuously are beautiful and good; and neither would those who *know* these things prefer anything else to them, nor would those who do not know them be able to do them, but even if they set about them they would go astray. So it is the wise who do what is good and beautiful, but those who are not wise cannot, but even if they try, blunder. Well, then, seeing that just actions and all other beautiful and good actions are done

---

[1] Aristotle, Nicomachean Ethics, 1144, b, 18, 29; 1116, b, 4. Eudemian Ethics, 1216, b, 2. Magna Moralia, 1182, a, 15; 1183, b, 8.

HIS ETHICS

with virtue it is evident that justice and all other virtue is wisdom."[1]

Knowledge, prudence, wisdom, these three terms by which Socrates is said to have defined virtue, carry rather different overtones of meaning, though they are closely related, and we may take it that virtue as he understood it really comprised and involved all three. It meant that virtue as a moral fact involves experience, insight, and complete knowledge of all the elements of a situation. Men may be just by accident, good by nature, pious by custom, in a certain sense of the words, but not in the full sense of the word virtue. Indeed, to such justice and goodness and piety he would deny the name of virtue.[2] For *that* you must do the just or good or pious act because you know it to be so. It then becomes in a real sense not merely action, but *your* action, for you know exactly what you are doing. In the other cases you are more or less passive in your conduct.

The constitutive element or the characteristic element in virtue, then, being knowledge, Socrates defines the particular virtues as knowledge in particular relations and circumstances.

Thus in the "Laches," we have the virtue, Courage, defined as the knowledge of the evil and the good, of the things which create fear and hope, a definition, however, which is discarded as too general, since temperance and justice, *e.g.*, are also the knowledge of good and evil in some sense, and so the dialogue ends without the specific nature of the knowledge which constitutes Courage being cleared up.[3] In the "Protagoras," Courage is defined as the knowledge of what is, and what is not, dangerous, while ignorance of these is cowardice, that is to say, no man will be truly courageous who acts

---

[1] Mem., iii. 9, 5.   [2] Mem., iii. 9, 14.
[3] Plato, Laches, 197, 198.

stoutly in the face of dangers, without knowing they are dangers. On the other hand, it is foolhardiness and not courage to act without fear, where fear ought to be.[1]

As the "Memorabilia" puts it, "those who know how to cope with terrors and dangers well and nobly are courageous, and those who fail utterly of this are cowards, and the ability to do so involves knowledge; and those who know what ought to be done also have the power to do it."[2]

> "When duty whispers low, Thou must,
> The youth replies I can."

Courage, then, is the knowledge of what ought to be feared, and what ought not to be feared; if your ideas on that score are right, your conduct will be right; if they are wrong, your conduct will surely be wrong. Virtue is the knowledge which makes one act just the right act in those circumstances, the act which is in accordance with the real and true character of things; one might phrase it, harmony with facts, with truth and reality. It might, of course, happen to be just the act the circumstances demand, without the knowledge, though Socrates hardly contemplated this possibility; but then it would not be true virtue, it would be luck or chance. And the man who happened to be right to-day, might just as easily be wrong to-morrow, whereas, acting with knowledge, he would be right every time; his voluntary reaction would in all cases be adapted to the demand of the occasion.

On the same principle, Justice is defined as the virtue of those who know what is lawful[3] in their relations with their fellow-men, who know what they "ought" to do, how they "ought" to behave, towards them, this being identified with what the laws ordain; the

---

[1] Plato, Protagoras, 359, 360. Cp. Xen., Mem., iv. 6, 10.
[2] Mem., iv. 6, 11.   [3] Mem., iv. 4, §§ 12, 25; iv. 6, 6.

just and the lawful [1] are thus regarded as one and the same thing, and in the argument as Xenophon gives it both are connected with "treating men nobly and well" and with "refusing to do any wrong." [2]

We have already discussed the question of the relationship between law and the right. It is enough here to repeat that Socrates' meaning apparently is that Justice consists in knowing what the Divine Laws ordain as the right and proper thing to do, which is sure to work out for the good of others and of oneself.[3] So far as the actual legislation of any society does not coincide with that, it must be altered, for in such a case it is the expression of mistaken and false knowledge, and therefore one would suppose cannot be objectively and absolutely just, though it represents justice for those who live under it, and whose business is obedience.

From this point of view we can see clearly enough why Socrates considered knowledge so essential in any who aspired to the kingliest and most royal of the arts—that of ruling and administering a state. The position of ruler is one in which a man may do endless harm to others as well as to himself, hence the supreme necessity that such an one should know accurately what is right, and what is wrong. He must be above all things just and able to embody justice in social relations, and that is impossible if his moral ideas are in the state of confusion in which Adeimantus, in the "Republic," declares the conventional ideas to be, because they do not concern themselves with what Justice and Injustice are in themselves and in their effects in the soul "unseen either by gods or men," but entirely with their external consequences and fortunes. The consequence of this superficiality, this lack of penetration in thought, is that people go

[1] Mem., iv. 4, §§ 12, 13, 18; iv. 6, §§ 5, 6.
[2] Mem., iv. 4, 12.
[3] Mem., iv. 4, 19 ff.

all wrong in their sentiments about justice, and think that they can by cleverness and deceit secure, without being actually and inwardly just, all the benefits which a reputation for justice brings,[1] and they even prostitute religion [2] into the service of their injustices and immoralities, because of their lack of knowledge of the true nature of Justice and Injustice and of their inherent spiritual effects, their effects on the soul itself.

The true ruler, then, is he who has this knowledge and insight, and can make earthly laws after the pattern of the divine. He has the knowledge of what justice in its essence is, and can embody it in the laws and relations of the state, and so secure the common weal. The common weal is his aim, and he not only has the aim, but he knows the ways and means of its attainment, apart from which Justice cannot be actualised among the citizens of the state.[3]

But Socrates goes further than all this, and means more, in his dictum that Virtue is knowledge. Not only must a man *know* rightly in order to act rightly, but if he knows rightly he *will* act rightly. If conduct is wrong, then knowledge, ideas, have gone wrong. And here we arrive at the storm centre of the ethics of Socrates. He believed implicitly that " we needs must love the highest when we see it." No man errs or sins voluntarily.

This must not be taken to imply that no one ever commits an action which is not good and virtuous, for if that were so there had been no need for Socrates to stimulate and encourage his fellow-men toward Virtue. Men do the wrong thing, the bad thing, that is universally admitted. The question is why ? And Socrates answers because they don't know what they are doing, don't know fully and completely and accu-

---

[1] See Republic, ii. 363–7.   [2] *Ibid.*, 364.
[3] Cp. Döring, *op. cit.*, p. 450.

HIS ETHICS

rately; they don't see aright. This "want of insight is the one and only source of moral shortcoming."[1]

Such is the view we find expressed in several dialogues of Plato and attributed to Socrates by Aristotle:

"Then, said Socrates, if the pleasant is the good, nobody does anything under the idea or conviction that some other thing would be better and is also attainable, when he might do the better. And this inferiority of a man to himself is merely ignorance, as the superiority of a man to himself is wisdom. . . . No man voluntarily pursues evil or that which he thinks to be evil. To prefer evil to good is not in human nature."[2] "We will what is good, what is neither good nor bad we do not will, still less what is bad."[3]

Consistently with this doctrine in Plato, Aristotle tells us that Socrates would have regarded it as a terrible thing for a man to be enticed or controlled by anything other than his knowledge, for such a condition would be no better than slavery. He stood up for reason as though there were no such thing as lack of self-control, on the assumption that no one acted contrary to the best except through ignorance.[4] He held that no one would choose wrong in preference to right, and erased lack of control of the passions entirely from his psychology.[5]

Such doctrine appears to go right in the face of ordinary human experience, which is replete with instances of what seems to be the overcoming of knowledge by pleasure, and the consequent choice of the evil in preference to the good. Socrates, holding to the position that knowledge is the commanding thing[6]

---
[1] Gomperz, Greek Thinkers, ii. p. 66. (Eng. trans.)
[2] Plato, Protagoras, 358 b, c, d. (Jowett's trans.)
[3] Gorgias, 468 C.
[4] Aristotle, Nicomachean Ethics, 1145, b, 23.
[5] Arist., Magna Moralia, 1187, a, 7, 1200, b, 25.
[6] Plato, Protagoras, 352 c, d.

and that it cannot be overcome by passion or pleasure, proceeds, in the "Protagoras," to justify this view so opposed to common opinion.[1] His argument is too obviously unsatisfactory to be even specious, for it turns on the identification of the good with pleasure which has gone before. If it be said that a man prefers evil to good " because he is overcome by pleasure, it is the same as saying he prefers evil to good because he is overcome by good, which is absurd."[2] A man, however, might go wrong by making a mistake in regard to pleasures, by miscalculating their relative magnitude ; and all that is necessary to save from such miscalculation is a science of measurement. For the lack of that we are deceived and misled, which means not that we are overcome by pleasure, but that we are the victims of illusion or of the lack of accurate objective knowledge. Again it is ignorance which is at the root of evil.[3]

The particular argument of the "Protagoras" is hollow, because if some other motive than pleasure, which is assumed to be the good, had been taken, the absurdity of saying that the good is overcome by it would not have seemed so obvious. The main principle, however, that knowledge of the good determines action is not affected by the weakness of that particular line of defence. Does this principle necessitate the inference that there is really no lack of self-control in man? And did Socrates eliminate or forget the force of passion in the human heart ? The tendency of much in Plato and a great deal in Xenophon is against such a construction, and they are our first-hand authorities. The "Apology" of Plato represents him as seeking to recall the mind of his contemporaries from the things of the body, the seductions of wealth

---

[1] Protagoras, 352 b, d; 353 a.
[2] *Op. cit.*, § 355.   [3] Protagoras, 356, 357.

and bodily pleasure, to the cultivation of the soul. Xenophon's "Recollections" are full of Socrates' recognition of the dangerous power and fascination of appetite, and as we have pointed out he regarded self-control as the corner-stone of all the virtues, and also as the condition of the maximum of pleasure itself. "Since incontinency," he is made to say, "will not suffer us to resist hunger and thirst, or to hold out against sexual appetite, or want of sleep (which abstinences are the only channels to true pleasure in eating, drinking, love, and slumber, won by those who will patiently endure till each particular happiness is at the flood), it comes to this, we are cut off by incontinency from the full fruition of the more obvious and constantly recurring pleasures."[1]

Socrates knew only too well the temptations of passion, but he held, that whatever be the Good, conduct always was determined by that, and therefore in all circumstances we follow that which at the moment we estimate and know, or think we know, to give the preponderance of good. Contrary to that we cannot act, but the passions and appetites unfortunately come in to disturb and falsify our estimates and knowledge, and so lead us into error which inevitably results in wrong action; we mistake our good, subsume the contemplated action under the wrong category, and thus fail of our real end and commit evil.

It is quite a mistake, and a very obvious one, to say that "Socrates argues as if what Aristotle calls the irrational part of the soul did not exist."[2] It is not knowledge in the abstract which determines action,

---

[1] Mem., iv. 5, 9. Cp. § 6 where he says incontinency "confounds men's wits and makes them choose the worse in place of the better."
[2] Gomperz, Greek Thinkers, ii. p. 67 (Eng. trans.). Cp. Fouillée, La Philosophie de Socrate, ii. p. 4; also Joël, *op. cit.*, i. pp. 266 ff.

but our knowledge, or idea, or estimate of what we regard as the "good," and our lower or passional or "irrational" nature most assuredly comes in to affect that knowledge. It may, *e.g.*, mislead us into regarding the nearer pleasure as the greater, or cause us to forget that an immediate pleasure may leave in its consequences a balance of pain,[1] assuming, that is, with Socrates in the "Protagoras" that pleasures and pains can be totalled up and a balance struck, and in spite of some of our modern philosophers we must admit that in ordinary life something of the kind does take place.

To provide the reason with a defence against these extraneous powers which deflect the needle from the pole, Xenophon tells us Socrates insisted on the necessity of self-discipline and that exercise which keeps the passions in their right and proper place. Just as the body which is not exercised cannot perform its functions, so is it with the soul. It can't do what it should nor abstain from what it should not. Hence fathers desire their sons to go into the company of the good, for it is an exercise of virtue.[2] "Want of practice causes us to forget the words of instruction, and when we forget these and when they are forgotten the state of the soul in which we desired prudence is lost to memory. . . . Many a man who can be frugal when cool, when the passion of love seizes him, becomes reckless in expenditure and stoops to dishonourable gains. . . . To me it seems that all beautiful and noble things are the result of constant practice and training and pre-eminently the virtue of temperance. For in the same body are planted with the soul pleasures which persuade it to throw aside prudence and indulge them and the body by the quickest means."[3]

[1] Plato, Protagoras, 353.   [2] Mem., i. 2, §§ 19, 20.
[3] Mem., i. 2, §§ 21–3.

HIS ETHICS

True, accurate, knowledge of the Good, Wisdom, then, depends for its survival on the discipline of one's nature. The science of the Good demands a skill which comes only from practice and the balance so achieved of all the parts of the soul, the rational and the irrational.

Over and over again [1] Xenophon gives Recollections in which the existence of the passions is recognised and the need for their discipline inculcated if the full beauty and strength of human character is to be attained and the good life realised; the gods give none of the things that are beautiful and good to men without toil,[2] and if there was one thing more than another with regard to Socrates as a man, which impressed itself on those who associated with him, it was the thorough discipline and control which he had exercised upon himself.[3]

Socrates then by no means allowed himself to forget the existence of evil passions and inclinations, but he held that knowledge could wield an imperium over them as the tranquil moon does over unquiet seas. When the lower forces seem to have the upper hand and to get their way with us, it is only because they have first been able to produce some blindness, some warping of the mind's vision within us. Under their influence for the time the man forgets, he cannot keep the right idea and conception steady and clear before his inner eye, it becomes distorted, thrust out by the inclinations or passions, especially if his hold upon it, and its hold on him, is weak through lack of discipline and habit; knowledge is falsified and the false knowledge brings its appropriate consequences. But at the moment of acting the man glimpses the

---

[1] See, *e.g.*, Mem., iii. 9, 1-3; iii. 9, 14; ii. 1, 28; iv. 5, 1. Cp. Döring, Die Lehre des Sokrates, pp. 513-18.
[2] Mem., ii. 1, 28.   [3] Mem., iv. 5, 1.

action as his good, the counteracting ideas are at least momentarily displaced, their pull is snapped, and the deed is done. Next moment it may be repented of as wrong, foolish, mad, but that is when normal consciousness and knowledge has flooded back in again, when the man has again come to *himself*.

It may seem that there is a philosophical perversity and eccentricity about the Socratic doctrine, but even to-day it is held by men whose business is to observe human agency and analyse the workings of the mind. It is virtually the theory of Will propounded by Professor William James,[1] and it will not be out of place to quote a passage from Mr. Arnold Bennett, in which the doctrine that conduct is a matter of knowledge or intellectual perception is very uncompromisingly affirmed. We say intellectual perception, but we must remember that the whole active nature, the experience and the character of a man goes into his normal perception. What we see depends on what we are. There is no isolated faculty.

" The culture of the brain, the constant disciplinary exercise of the reasoning faculty, means the diminution of misdeeds," said Balzac in " La Cousine Bette." " A crime is in the first instance a defect of reasoning powers." In the appreciation of this truth, Marcus Aurelius was, as usual, a bit beforehand with Balzac. Marcus Aurelius said, " No soul wilfully misses truth." And Epictetus had come to the same conclusion before Marcus Aurelius, and Plato before Epictetus. All wrong-doing is done in the sincere belief that it is the best thing to do. Whatever sin a man does he does either for his own benefit or for the benefit of society. At the moment of doing it he is convinced that it is the only thing to do. He is mistaken. And he is

---

[1] Psychology, vol. ii. pp. 560 f. Talks on Psychology, pp. 186 f.

mistaken because his brain has been unequal to the task of reasoning the matter out." [1]

This passage from Bennett will show that the view that virtue is knowledge and that no one does wrong voluntarily, by no means involves the elimination of the passions or of the soul's irrational part, as Aristotle inferred.

Perhaps some native weakness of body or spirit may make it harder for the subject to see his conduct for what it is, and know just what he is doing. If he be of a timorous disposition, then the knowledge which means courage will be very difficult for him to retain in the moment of trial. He imagines things, as children in the dark imagine they see ghosts; he may normally disbelieve in the things and call himself foolish, but the knowledge he has, the belief he holds, gets displaced by the palpable suggestions of his emotional condition, or his bodily condition.

Here is someone who, as we say, sees the better and follows the worse. The Socrates of Xenophon and Plato would not have denied such happenings in a certain sense. The cause, however, he would have said, was that at the point of action the worse had taken on the semblance of the better, for this particular man. We all know that sophistry of passion which simply translates the bad into the good, the undesirable into the desirable, for the time being, a sort of hypnotism which makes us blind to some features of our act which are there, and makes us see other features which may not be there at all, and all the while there may be a latent sense that we are making a fool of ourselves, a ghostly trace of normality, and the next instant a conviction that we *have* made a fool of ourselves. But the moment of volition was the moment of a flash of false colour over our deed, in

[1] Arnold Bennett, The Human Machine.

which we saw it as our good, though it was not *the* Good. This interpretation is given in the "Meno," where Socrates says that people desire evils thinking them good, and all men are alike in this respect that they act always from their idea of what is good.[1]

Leaving the question of the theoretical soundness of this position, in which Socrates is supported by various modern philosophers, we may say that probably it suggested itself to Socrates as a result of his own inner experience. With him, undoubtedly, reason was supreme, and "when it whispered low, Thou must," he at once replied, "I will." The dust of passion lay beneath his feet and he looked always through the transparent medium of thought. Practice and self-discipline had put his soul into perfect condition for the right estimate of every alternative of conduct which presented itself. It was naked reason without the flesh-tints and rose-mists. For him to see the better, to know it, was to do it and not let slip; the vision was steady, circumstances made no difference. To him "knowledge and wisdom" were indeed the "mightiest things."[2]

Not only did Socrates puzzle people by saying that no man errs voluntarily, he amazed them by suggesting that the man who errs knowingly is really more moral than he who errs unknowingly. One can imagine the delight it gave Socrates to propound these disturbing paradoxes to the self-complacent and cock-sure bourgeoisie of Athens. He must have laughed inwardly many a time as he startled them with his audacities; we can see the merry twinkle in his eye as he turns the apparently safest moralities of Euthydemus outside in and upside down.[3] Of course it would be crude interpretation which committed Socrates to the opposite position of that which he assails in others with

---

[1] Meno, § 78. [2] Protagoras, 352. [3] Mem., iv. 2, §§ 20–3.

difficulties and objections. A man may be allowed to point out the difficulties of a particular attitude without necessarily being satisfied with the alternative attitude, for he might, if occasion arose, just as easily point out objections to *it*. But there is a very real kernel of truth in the paradox that the man who is voluntarily unrighteous is, or at any rate may be, more righteous than the man who is involuntarily unrighteous.

He argued that it was so, by help of his favourite analogy of the arts. He who misreads or misspells unconsciously is more illiterate than he who does so deliberately.[1] If we may be permitted to illustrate the point further, take the case of music. The lady who deliberately goes half a tone flat in singing, knowing that she is out of harmony, may surely be regarded as more musical than one who gets flat quite involuntarily and without any consciousness of her mistake. And in this particular the analogy of the arts holds good. To take an extreme case, a civilised man of ordinary good character commits more voluntary offences against the moral law than a primitive savage, but the savage is not on that account at a higher stage of moral development or nearer spiritual perfection than the civilised man. The most hopeless feature in the state of soul of the cannibal who eats his brethren is not the fact of his eating them, but the fact that he does not feel or know that he is doing anything wrong. That is the measure of his low estate. He would be at a higher level, he would have more morality if he did the deed with a due sense of its enormity. What exalts the publican and sinner above the pharisee himself in the spiritual scale, is that the one knows he is a publican and a sinner and the other does not know he is a pharisee. Therefore the former is nearer the kingdom of Heaven than the latter. The volun-

[1] See Mem., iv. 2, §§ 20, 21.

tary sinner may reach the stage of conviction of sin, which is the possibility of the attainment of virtue, but there is no such hope in the case of him who is so low or so hardened that he does not recognise the action as a sin. In that sense we are all familiar with the truth and ready to admit it, that voluntary wrong-doing is the mark of a higher morality than involuntary.

(c) THE GOOD

Man in his conduct always seeks some good, but what, according to Socrates, is *the* Good? What is it which gives worth to everything else, and makes it truly desirable? What are we all after when we truly know ourselves? At first sight it looks as if we were all after different things, that the standard of value varied from individual to individual. One man seems to live for success in business, another for the betterment of his fellow-men, another for pleasure, while for some

> "To mak' a happy fireside clime
>   For weans and wife,
> Is the true pathos and sublime
>   Of human life."

Can we find in all these varied and sometimes conflicting ends, some common, universal element which makes them desirable to their different devotees? Is it that they give pleasure? Is pleasure in itself a good, and nothing but a good, thing?

One might infer from the " Protagoras " that Socrates took that view, for there he holds that the pleasant and the good are one, and the painful and the evil one,[1] so that right conduct is a question of the accurate measurement and balance of alternative pleasures.

[1] § 351. Cp. § 358.

Such a doctrine is literally Hedonism, and we should know by this time that Socrates was no Hedonist. Virtue, he knew, was not the primrose path of dalliance, but a hard road; it offered not ease and pleasure but toil and difficulty. He was rather an eccentric Hedonist, who nurtured his theory and sentiments on extracts from Hesiod like the following : " Wickedness may a man take wholesale with ease, smooth is the way, and her dwelling-place is very nigh; but in front of virtue the immortal gods have placed toil and sweat; long is the path and steep that leads to her, and rugged at first, though, when the summit of the path is reached, then for all its roughness the path grows easy."[1]

His approval of Prodicus's story of the " Choice of Heracles," an approval for which Xenophon vouches,[2] reveals his mind on the subject. It was the doctrine of a preference of the hard and heroic as against the soft and pleasant. We must recollect that it would be as sound and sensible to attribute equal authority to all the speeches in the book of Job, as to regard every position for which Socrates argued with interlocutors as the expression of his own sincere convictions. He would take some hypothesis and argue from it as true in order to deduce certain consequences and enforce certain views, but the hypothesis need not represent his own fixed belief by any means. It might serve well enough for a dialectical display in which he could achieve his main end, to show the unsatisfactoriness not only of the opinions of others, but perhaps also of any position he himself had to suggest.

At the same time he held that the virtuous life was that which, on the whole, gave the largest and the securest balance of pleasure. He declared that nobody got more pleasure out of life than he did with all his abstinences and deprivations. We cannot, however,

---

[1] Mem., ii. 1, 20.   [2] Mem., ii. 1, 21 ff.

on that account, entertain the notion that pleasure was the impelling motive of Socrates' life and work. To achieve the Good must necessarily be pleasant, but that does not mean that pleasure must be the Good. There are ends and objects and duties in life for which one counts hardship and suffering cheap. "Must we not suppose that these will take their sorrows lightly, looking to such high ends? Must we not suppose that they will gaily confront existence, who have to support them, not only their conscious virtue, but the praise and admiration of the world? And once more, habits of indolence, along with the fleeting pleasures of the moment, are incapable of setting up a good habit of body or of implanting in the soul any knowledge worthy of account; whereas by painstaking endeavour in the pursuit of high and noble deeds, as good men tell us, through endurance we shall in the end attain the goal." [1]

In this passage Socrates is made to state his divergence from the ethics of Aristippus, the founder of what is known as the Cyrenaic school. Whether it is or is not reconcilable with the "Protagoras," it stands as Xenophon's conception of what Socrates' life and doctrine were, and while there are traits in this discussion with Aristippus which strike us as less characteristically Socratic than Xenophontic, yet the substance of the views expressed is true to what we otherwise know of Socrates' character and sentiments, and it is attestation of a scale of valuation in the Socratic ethics not based upon mere considerations of pleasure.

The argument in the "Protagoras" goes on the hypothesis that all pleasures as such are alike in quality, and only differ in magnitude or quantity. But such a view goes in the face of experience, as continually recognised by Socrates himself. He would not for a moment

[1] Mem., ii. 1, 19. (Dakyns' trans.)

have put the pleasure of physical enjoyment on the same plane as that of intellectual or spiritual enjoyment.

Pleasure in itself most people would admit to be a good, and pain an evil; but they never do exist in themselves, and in their relations and consequences their moral quality may be changed, according to their effect in hindering or helping in the attainment of what is the highest Good of life.

Pleasure is in exactly the same case as any other subordinate good, it is relative to the use we make of it. For example, Socrates, in another conversation with Aristippus,[1] identifies the good and the beautiful, and declares that whatever is good is in the same respect beautiful. But that does not mean that Beauty is the *summum bonum*. So is it also with health, wealth, or courage. None of these can be defined as the absolute good.[2] They are relative to something beyond themselves. This characteristic of lesser goods is also brought out in the second chapter of the fourth book of the "Memorabilia."[3] There, indeed, Socrates takes up a thoroughly radical attitude and insists that even wisdom,[4] and happiness,[5] may be a source of evil to their possessor, as well as the good things just mentioned. But this is an instance in which Socrates is not expounding his own doctrine, but simply pursuing Euthydemus from position to position in order to refute him and bring home to him a sense of his ignorance. He is playing his dialectical game.

In the "Euthydemus" of Plato again the relativity of such goods as health, wealth, beauty, and honour is brought out, and it is maintained that these things, good surely in themselves, if the abstraction be per-

---

[1] Mem., iii. 8. [2] Mem., iii. 8, §§ 2 and 3.
[3] See §§ 31 ff.   [4] *Ibid.*, § 33.   [5] *Ibid.*, § 34.

mitted, derive their moral value and worth from the use to which they are put. They may all become evils if there is not present the knowledge and wisdom which can use them rightly.[1] In the "Meno" also it is distinctly affirmed that while the Good is profitable always, every other thing which men call good, health and wealth, aye, even justice, courage, memory, the good things of the spirit, are sometimes profitable, sometimes hurtful, according as they are and are not under the guidance of Wisdom.

Thus, if Socrates is to be described as a Hedonist, he might equally be described as a "Beautyist," a "Wealthist," a "Healthist," or an "Honourist," but the evidence is overwhelming that he found the absolute good in none of them. In each case the element of knowledge and wisdom must be added to ensure that all these goods be put to a right and beneficial use. He believes in them all, in everything indeed,[2] so far as, under the control of wisdom and knowledge, it contributes to man's welfare, to his supreme Good.

The element of utility also entered into his conception of the Good. There are passages[3] in which Socrates asserts that whatever is good must be good *for something*, the good being identified with the useful. Similarly he held, in regard to beauty, that it consisted in the fact that the object suited its purpose. Everything, in so far as it fills its place in the universe, performs its function and is useful, is good and beautiful, whereas the useless, wherever it is to be found, is ugly and so far bad.[4] Socrates appears as a

[1] § 280. Cp. Mem., iv. 1, §§ 2, 4, and Œconomicus, i., §§ 8-12.
[2] Mem., iii. 8, 6. [3] Mem., iii. 8.
[4] Cp. Plato, Republic, 505 a. "The form of the Good is the highest object of science and this essence, by blending with just things and all other created objects, renders them useful and advantageous." (Davies and Vaughan.)

stout common-sense utilitarian, with no nonsense about him. A house however ornamental which was not adapted for its main purpose would neither be a good nor a beautiful house to Socrates. Failing in the very reason of its existence how could it be beautiful or good?[1] On the other hand, the meanest objects in creation, if they served the end of their being, were to him at once good and beautiful.

Here was a sympathy as wide as worth itself, a feeling of the goodness of all useful life however insignificant the use, the root of that democracy of spirit which makes Socrates' character large and broad and sane like nature's self.

Sometimes he carried the idea to whimsical lengths, for the sake of the fun, as when in a jovial hour he argued that he was more beautiful than Critobulus because with his snub nose and protruding eyes he had freer and wider vision than the other with his more regular features, and with his upturned nostrils could better catch the various odours borne on the passing breeze.[2] This pronounced utilitarian tendency is also to be found in the fact that, according to Xenophon, he advocated the study of the sciences only so far as they were necessary and useful for the ends of practical life. To that extent he was willing to waive his principle that the sciences should be left severely alone, a principle originating from the fruitlessness of their pursuits in his own experience. So far, however, as they were useful at all he was quite willing that they should be studied. In science for life's sake he believed.[3]

In accordance with this view the good and beautiful man would be he who fulfilled the end and mission of his being, realised the purpose of his existence, which

[1] Mem., iii. 10, §§ 9-15.   [2] Xen., Banquet, v. 5-8.
[3] Mem., iv. 7, §§ 2-8.

would of course vary from individual to individual. While the bad man, the ugly man, would be he who is out of his proper place, the man in a position for which he is not meant or fitted. The highest good of life, then, is attained when everyone is in the position and discharging the functions by means of which he can be of the greatest use and advantage to the community in general and himself in particular. So Socrates declared that the farmer who did his farming well, the doctor who did his doctoring well, were nearest to the heart of God.[1] In general terms he defined the highest object of man to be well-doing,[2] and he who did not do well in some particular sphere of life was useless and displeasing to God.[3]

We may say then that Man's supreme good consists in well-doing, in accomplishing the work to which he is called, and thus one of the important aspects of self-knowledge is knowledge as to what you can work at, what you have a faculty for.[4] As Carlyle said, the latest version of the gospel of self-knowledge is to " Know thy work and do it . . . know what thou canst work at, and work at it like a Hercules."[5] To be at one's wrong work is to be at the source of rivers of misery—misery alike for oneself and for others.

The question arises as to the motive which ought to operate in all our work ; is the end of it to be simply our own welfare and happiness or that of the community as a whole ? Professor Döring has ventured to state that the underlying idea of the Socratic ethics is always one's own advantage and happiness. Even in the cultivation of friendship it is our own happiness we seek.[6] " We must assume the exclusive

---

[1] Mem., iii. 9, 15.
[2] *Ibid.*, iii. 9, 14.
[3] Mem., iii. 9, 15.
[4] Mem,, iv, 2, §§ 23-31.
[5] Past and Present, bk. III. ch. xi.
[6] Döring, Die Lehre des Sokrates, p. 496.

HIS ETHICS

dominance of the egoistic motive in human nature."[1] But surely this indicates an utterly wrong understanding of Socrates' appeal to self-regarding considerations when he argues for the blessings of friendship and the duty of undertaking social responsibilities. It reveals a strange blindness to the dominant motives of Socrates' own missionary career. He drew no distinction between the good of an individual and the good of his friends or of those whom he ruled. They were identical on the plane on which Socrates' thought moved. A man naturally sought his own happiness, but the wise and good man sought it, where alone it was to be found, in the service of others, and labours which promoted their welfare and made them also happy.

On one occasion, Xenophon tells us, he met someone who had been appointed a general and minister of war—Socrates seems to have known almost everybody worth knowing in Athens from Pericles and Aspasia downwards—and he reminded this officer that Homer had called Agamemnon a "shepherd of the peoples,"[2] probably because it was his business to see to the needs of those under him, "the shepherd careth for the sheep"; while by calling him a "good king" he probably meant a king "who does not only battle well against enemies, . . . or stand up nobly for his own life alone, but one who is the cause of happiness and welfare to those whom he rules.[3] For a king is chosen not to look well after himself, but also that those who have chosen him may attain welfare by him. Men go to war in order to attain the best life, and they choose leaders to lead them to that goal, and that it is their bounden duty to do."[4] "Have no hesitation," he told a youthful cavalry officer, "but direct your

---

[1] *Op. cit.*, p. 495.
[2] Iliad, ii. 1. 243.
[3] Mem., iii. 2, 2.
[4] Mem., iii. 2, 3.

men to these matters, from which you yourself will be benefited and *all the citizens through you.*"[1] "When considering the virtue of a general he stripped everything else away and left one thing only—to make those whom he led happy."

It is perfectly clear that Socrates did not encourage men to enter into public life simply for their own advantage without regard to that of the community, or from any merely egoistic motive. I may argue with a man who refuses to undertake a position of responsibility in the state, though he has the qualifications for it, and try to persuade him by pointing out the evil consequences to himself (as well as to others) which will follow from thus timorously declining his social duties and allowing affairs to fall into the hands of less competent place-seekers. But to reason from that, that I think one's own happiness the exclusive motive either in human nature or my own, or that I enthrone it as the Highest Good, is to reason without either imagination or shrewdness and to reason wrongly. I may even admit that all men out of given possibilities choose those which they think best and most profitable for themselves, without being justifiably accused of adopting egoistic ethics. We all act from a conception of our own good, that is the form of the moral life, but it all depends on what that conception is whether I am an egoist; like Socrates himself I may interpret my own good and profit as a life of altruism and self-sacrifice for the sake of the good and the happiness of mankind as a whole.

Socrates would admit that self-satisfaction in some form, Happiness, is the motive and end of action. And this Happiness is an end in and for itself, so that it is quite superfluous and unnecessary to ask why a man aims at Happiness.[2] But even Happiness is not

---
[1] Mem., iii. 3, 15.   [2] Plato's Symposium, 241, 242.

HIS ETHICS

an Absolute Good if it is made to consist in things which are ambiguous and may turn to ill, such as Beauty, Wealth, or Honour.[1] As we have seen true Happiness, which is the Absolute Good, consists not in good fortune but in the life of well-doing, a life whose happiness includes and involves that of others, a life indeed which aims at their welfare and happiness. The people to whom his heart went out in friendship and love were those " in whom the faculties of the soul unfolded in virtue." Such natures as these " only needed to be educated to become not only happy themselves and happy administrators of their private households, but to be capable of rendering other beings as states or as individuals happy."[2] It is evident again in this sentiment that one's own happiness is contemplated as only a fraction of life's true blessedness, and that if our own is to be full and complete it must pass into the happiness of others; it must consist in the fulfilment of our duties and obligations in the state according to our capacity, in service and beneficence. Happiness will only be absolutely achieved when justice is realised in communal life, in that conception of justice which Plato elaborated later in his " Republic," that is to say, when everyone does his own proper work, fills his own proper sphere, whether that of ruler or ruled, in a life of well-doing with the view of promoting the good of all.[3]

Happiness is not a mere passive state, it is the bloom of health and intense activity, like the bloom of a flower, the delicate exhalation of all the forces which go to sustain life and growth. The career of ruler is that in which the greatest happiness is permitted because it is that which demands and necessitates the activity of the largest powers and faculties, that in

---

[1] Mem., iv. 2, 35. [2] Mem., iv. 1, 1. [3] Mem., ii. 1, 19.

which it is possible to perform the greatest service to others and to the state, and produce the maximum of happiness all round. But this noblest consummation is only possible where the ruler has knowledge, and is in touch with truth and reality and fact, in his own soul and in the world; he must know the true end of personal life and the true goal of the world—a view in which we have the suggestion which Plato was to develop into his doctrine that all will be right with the world only when the philosophers are on the throne, when the rulers are men who, as it is said in the "Theætetus," know the "essence or nature of man as man,"[1] whose eyes see through the murk and mist of opinion and sense and accident to the "Ideas," the eternal Laws, the Absolute Good, that sun[2] in whose light alone can man or state be safely guided through the seas of life and the shoals of time.

Whatever definition be given of the Good, whether it be called Pleasure, Happiness, or Well-doing, there will always remain differences in men's power to identify it rightly in concrete cases. In practical life what authoritative means have we for deciding as between various judgments, perhaps conflicting judgments, upon any particular course of conduct? Whose view is to be authoritative in the last resort, or can we get no further than to say that each man must be judge for himself? We are not left in doubt as to what Socrates' position was on this point. Not the multitude, not the majority, but the wise man, the man of knowledge and insight, must be final arbiter. There can be no hesitation in accepting the teaching of the "Theætetus" as genuinely Socratic on this particular matter, and in it the doctrine that each particular man must be his own authority and standard on questions of opinion and judgment is repudiated.

[1] Theætetus, 174 b. [2] Cp. Repub., 508, 515 ff.

Soc. Shall I tell you, Theodorus, what amazes me in your acquaintance, Protagoras.

Theod. What is that?

Soc. I am charmed with his doctrine that what *appears* to each one, that for him *is*. But I have wondered that he did not begin his work on Truth with the thesis that a pig or a dog-faced baboon or some other yet stranger monster which has sensation is the measure of all things; then when we were reverencing him as a god, he might have condescended to inform us that he was no wiser than a tadpole, not to speak of his fellow-men—would not this have produced an overpowering effect? For if truth is only sensation, and one man's discernment is as good as another's, and no man has any superior right to determine whether the opinion of another is true or false, but each man is to himself the sole judge, and everything that he judges is true and right, why should Protagoras be preferred to the place of wisdom and instruction, and deserve to be well paid, and we poor ignoramuses have to go to him if each one of us is the measure of wisdom to himself? I say nothing of the ridiculous predicament in which my own midwifery and the whole art of dialectic is placed; for the attempt to supervise or refute the notions or opinions of others would be a tedious and enormous piece of folly, if those of each man are equally right.[1]

Precisely the same attitude is insisted upon in the " Crito," where Socrates argues with his dear old friend that in all the ordinary affairs of life, and in the arts, we abide by the opinion of the trained expert [2] and not by that of the unskilled multitude, and so ought we also in questions of ethics. " In questions of just and unjust, fair and foul, good and evil also ought we to

[1] Theætetus, 161 C-E. (Jowett's trans. slightly altered.)
[2] Crito, 47 A-C.

follow the opinion of the many and to fear them; or the opinion of the one man who has understanding? Ought we not to fear and reverence him more than all the rest of the world: and if we desert him shall we not destroy and injure that principle in us which may be assumed to be improved by justice and deteriorated by injustice?[1]

The same appeal to wisdom and the wise man, the same deference to him, while those who are on the lower plane of life and character are ruled out of court as too inconsiderable, runs through Xenophon's "Memorabilia." The only difference in the testimony is an added touch of bitterness in the Platonic language, taking the place of a certain sympathetic piety in that of Xenophon.

"What is the distinction, Euthydemus, between a man devoid of self-control and the dullest of brute beasts? A man who forgoes all height of aim, who gives up searching for the best and strives only to gratify his sense of pleasure, is he better than the silliest of cattle? But to the self-controlled alone it is given to discover the hid treasures. . . . These choose deliberately the good and avoid the evil. Thus it is that a man reaches the zenith, as it were, of goodness and happiness, thus it is that he becomes most capable of reasoning and discussion."[2] Such is the man who attains wisdom,[3] and it is obvious that such is the man for whom alone Socrates has any reverence and to whose judgment he will pay any respect. He is the man who has the capacity for dialectic and consequently for right ethical discrimination and judgment.

Summing it up it simply means that morality and the Good are not merely relative things, that each man is not the law for himself, but that the nearer a human

---

[1] Crito, *ibid.*, c, d. Cp. 48 a, and Repub., 493 c, d.
[2] Mem., iv. 5, §§ 11 and 12.   [3] *Ibid.*, § 6.

being comes to realising the essential thing in his nature, the more developed the rational, which for Socrates is also the divine, in him, the more clearly and authoritatively does he apprehend the supreme good, the more does he approximate to the absolute standard of human conduct.

CHAPTER X

HIS RELIGION

" It is well said in every sense that a man's Religion is the chief fact with regard to him."—THOMAS CARLYLE.

(a) THE WORLD

THE strength of Socrates' character, the motive power of his life, sprang from piety of mind and heart. A belief in the overruling [1] and inworking of God in the universe was the very atmosphere in which he lived. His character and his aims were through and through religious. The background of his thought was God, and hence the calm subsisting at the heart of every agitation within his soul. The radiance of the Unseen and Spiritual lay across his life, and filled the world for him with good, so that Duty always had its sweetness and work its song. He felt all through that he was not his own, that he had a mission to fulfil, and he was straitened till it should be done; yet his task was not a slavery, but that service which is perfect freedom. His was a self-dedicated life to a call from on high, to which his attitude was one of grateful acceptance and welcome.

Xenophon relates a conversation which he heard [2] between Socrates and Aristodemus,[3] the latter of whom took up rather a superior attitude to religious senti-

---

[1] Cp. Plato, Phædo, 62, 63.   [2] Mem., i. 4, 2.
[2] See Plato, Symposium, 173 B.

ments, in which the master made use of his characteristic methods. He seeks to lead him to the sense of the wisdom and greatness and goodness of the Mind which has fashioned all things, and to show him, or make him realise, that all this beneficent and harmonious scheme of things cannot be the product of mere chance, but demands the belief in " a wise artificer who loves life." [1]

Everywhere throughout the Cosmos we trace the presence of design. Particularly in the case of our own body is it evident. And if one is justified in admiring the artistic products of a Homer or a Sophocles, or a Zeuxis or a Polycleitus, what reverence and honour are due to Him whose artistry produces living beings, every part of whose bodily organism shows that it has been created designedly to produce the best life of the whole! Neither chance nor blind force will account for the exquisite fitness of eye and ear and mouth and hand for their functions as ministers to man's life. There one sees the special benevolence of God to our race. For He has also given us members and functions not granted to the lower animals.[2] He has conferred upon us the noblest kind of soul, " which can rise to the apprehension of the gods who have constructed the greatest and most beautiful things." [3] He has given us superiority in nature, body, and spirit. We alone can serve the gods, and we alone live like gods. Our organisation, status, and privileges, then, as human beings, so lofty and divine, seem to Socrates to prove that behind all are the design and the working of a beneficent Deity.

To-day the scientist would give another and different explanation of these facts which so impressed Socrates. He would attribute them to Evolution under the law of Survival of the Fittest. But if by that is meant

[1] Mem., i. 4, § 7.   [2] Ibid., § 11, 12, 13.   [3] Ibid., § 12.

that all the adaptation and harmony and organisation in living beings is the result of the action and reaction of merely mechanical forces, then the theory has been found wanting by modern thinkers of various schools. Martineau held that behind all the blind forces must have been some designing and directing Power.[1] The Hegelians have felt the need to postulate an Absolute Spirit as the inner reality of the world and its movements. And more recently Bergson has had to assume, in addition to the merely physical factors of development, a Spiritual Reality, which he calls Life, and which is possessed of an inherent tendency to ever fuller expression, ever higher development, a Life not otiose or stagnant but tidal, flowing into all the nooks and crannies of matter, which it shapes into an increasingly perfect medium of its own growing impulse and expression. The highest manifestation of this immanent force is consciousness, and if it does not operate by design in the ordinary sense, it is only because its activity is as much above design, as it is above our finite spirits.

The important point, however, is that in advocating the recognition of that which is ultra and supraphysical, of Mind, in the Universe, Socrates is supported by all modern idealistic philosophy, as well as by the representatives of religion.

He had other arguments by which he substantiated his position. It is recognised that our body is made up of small quantities of elements, which exist in enormous quantities in the world; it is only because they are in the world that they have been available for our bodies. But we also have mind, and where has *it* come from, if not in the same way from the great store of mind in the world? Man's mind must be a *particula mentis divinæ*.

---

[1] Study of Religion; chapter, Teleology.

Again, on the analogy of our own personality, there is the argument, indicated by Xenophon,[1] and more fully articulated in the " Phædo " of Plato, that just as the actions and movements of our physical body are directed and controlled and determined by the mind within, so is it with the whole world and its phenomena; these are only explicable, only intelligible to us, as the operation of Cosmic Mind, which by the very nature of mind must act for the best, from an end which is the Good.[2] That being so, we are compelled to regard all the forces of the world as different but ultimately harmonious expressions of one Reason or Will, directed toward the Good. For Socrates, indeed, and Plato, as for modern philosophers like T. H. Green, Reason and Will towards the Good are but two expressions of the one fact. And because all is under the lordship and control of Mind, the process of the world is toward an end or goal, and that in the case of the Mind of the universe can be no other than the Highest, the Absolute Good.

Religion is thus for Socrates well fitted to be the ground of an insuperable optimism, the spring of a quenchless hope and faith:

" God's in His heaven;
All's right with the world."

" Ah, my good sir, lay to heart and understand that even as your own mind within you can turn and dispose of your body as it lists, so ought we to think that the wisdom which abides within the universal frame does so dispose of all things as is pleasing to it; and it cannot be that your eye can range over many a mile, and the eye of God be unable to see all things at once; or that your soul can think of what is near it and also of what is distant, while the thought of God is in-

[1] Mem., i. 4, § 9. [2] Cp. Phædo, 97 c-99.

competent to embrace everything at the same time. If only you will try by serving the gods whether they are willing to give their guidance to men in dark places, you will know that such is Godhead in its nature and greatness that the gods can see all at a glance, can hear all, are present everywhere, and care for all at one and the same time." [1]

So Socrates states his faith in the omniscience, omnipresence, and providence of the Godhead.

There is one other attribute of God emphasized by the Platonic Socrates, both in the "Theætetus" and the "Republic," which there can be no mistake in including in the conception of God held by the historical Socrates, and that is His Goodness [2] or Righteousness. As Spirit or Mind the creature and controlling Divinity of the world must, as we have suggested, seek the Absolute Good, and He can neither be evil nor the cause of evil. From the point of view of His Omniscience also we can infer, on Socratic principles, that God will neither err nor commit wrong or evil. Hence also, the irreconcilable antagonism of Good and Evil which we meet with in the "Theætetus" and "Republic" must have been part of Plato's inheritance from Socrates, though it is very doubtful whether the element of pessimism in Plato, and his assertion that evil must always exist is compatible with Socrates' thesis that evil is ignorance.

"Evils, Theodorus, can never pass away; for there must always be something which is antagonist to good. Having no place among the gods, of necessity they hover round the earthly nature and this sphere. Wherefore we ought to try to escape to the other world as quick as possible. And this escape is the becoming like God as far as is in our power; and likeness to

---

[1] Mem., i. 4, §§ 18, 19. Cp. Phædo, 62 b.
[2] Cp. Phædo, 62 d, 63 a.

Him means to become just and holy and wise. But, my dear fellow, it is by no means easy to convince mankind that it should pursue virtue and avoid vice, not in order that a man may seem to be good, which is the reason given by the world, and in my judgment is only the repetition of an old wives' fable. Whereas the truth is God is never unrighteous at all—He is perfect righteousness; and he of us who is the most righteous is the most like Him." [1]

In the "Republic" it is argued that God is good in reality, and as such is the cause of no evil because "that which is good is not the cause of all things but only of what is as it should be, being guiltless of originating evil." [2] He can only be responsible for that which is good and beneficial in human life, and according to Plato, that is the lesser part. [3]

This doctrine of God as the Creator and Source of all good, in His nature perfect righteousness, able to keep all men and created things within His view and to hear their cry, to whose perfections it is the duty of mankind to approach as nearly as possible, is a doctrine not unworthy of the best in Christendom itself, and illustrates the height in theological thought and speculation which it was given to Socrates and Plato to attain. It was a theology whose foundations were laid in reason and moral experience, and which in its loftiest upsoaring never tried to cut itself off from its base. All through it was a *moral* theology, and at its crown and summit, a God who was a moral God. There was a sweet reasonableness about it which many ages of Christianity might envy.

(*b*) It may have occurred to some readers to remark that it was characteristic of Greeks as of Romans to believe in gods, not in God—that they were polytheists.

---

[1] Theætetus, 176 a, b; trans. (after Jowett).
[2] Repub., ii. 379 b.   [3] *Ibid.*, 379 c.

The Socrates of Xenophon and Plato seems to use the singular and the plural almost indifferently. Such a circumstance shows that the polytheistic mode of thought was a wavering one, and that the arithmetical aspect of Godhead was a very vague, subordinate and unimportant one. Such trace of discrimination in the use as there may be in Socrates will be referred to subsequently. What we must recognise here is that among the great Greek philosophers and poets, a marked leaning to a view of the universe akin to Monotheism was prevalent. As the idea developed that the world was not a chaos, nor yet a pluralism of mutually independent and co-ordinate powers or wills, but partook rather of the nature of a unity or system, rational and moral, it was only natural that the gods should come to be conceived as having their arbitrary powers limited by some supreme Power or Will, and so there gradually rose above the horizons of thought and imagination, like a peak to dominate the lower range of hills, the conception of Necessity or Fate.[1] It marked the recognition of law and order in the physical and especially in the moral world.

The question then became one of reconciling such an idea with that of Zeus, who even in Homer is recognised as supreme, "the Father of gods and men," the term Father connoting not necessarily physical generation, but dignity, as in the Christian application of it to God. In the "Iliad" and "Odyssey," Fate and the Will of Zeus are made practically synonymous. And later one of the cult names of Zeus was "Leader of Fate."[2]

But in a great interpreter of the drama of human and divine experience like Æschylus, the identifica-

---
[1] Pfleiderer, Philosophy of Religion, vol. iii. p. 91.
[2] Farnell, The Cults of Greece, i. p. 79.

tion is not so easily or so consistently made. In that titanic and sublime tragedy, "The Prometheus Bound," the hero-martyr, pinned to the lonely gorge, sustains his defiance of the despotic and tyrannical will of Zeus by faith in the ultimate supremacy of a higher power than even that of Zeus, viz. Fate, the Moral Order, which will overthrow all injustice and wrong whether of men or gods. So, too, in Herodotus the gods cannot escape Destiny.[1]

Usually, however, Æschylus is less audacious in his departure from the dominant Greek mode of thought, for which the nod of Zeus moves the world and his will fixes its destinies.[2] Sophocles and Euripides could be quoted to the same effect.

Even in Aristotle, Zeus incorporates into himself the principle of Fate,[3] but by this time Zeus and God were interchangeable terms, and the Conception of God had become exalted and purified till all that could be regarded as morally unworthy was excluded from it, and Deity could do no evil. There could be no such antagonism between Zeus and the Moral Order as emerged in the "Prometheus."

In literature and philosophy, then, there was a distinct tendency towards the recognition of one will behind all events, the will of Zeus supreme, and he was worshipped under appropriate titles as the God with whom men had to do in various spheres and circumstances of life.[4]

The striking point, however, is that the monotheistic tendency of the higher Greek thought did not interfere to any extent with the polytheism of the popular cults. The lower gods still retained reverence

---

[1] Farnell, *op cit.*, p. 81.
[2] See Campbell, Religion in Greek Literature, p. 273.
[3] De Mundo; Farnell, *op. cit.*, p. 81.
[4] See Farnell, *op cit.*, pp. 44 ff.

and worship within their own sphere, one reason doubtless being that later suggested by Apuleius,[1] that men could more readily realise intimacy with lesser deities, not so universalised nor exalted above human tribes and emotions [2] as Zeus. In this respect their functions would answer in the popular religious experience of the Greeks to those of Christ in Protestantism and of the Virgin Mary and the Saints in Roman Catholicism, for we must not forget that even Christianity has failed to maintain a strict and pure monotheism in the intercourse between its devotees and its God. Zeus, like the Christian God, appears to have been too high and lifted up, too universal in his attributes and functions, to meet fully the wants of ordinary human beings. Though he was assigned various functions and gathered unto himself the different ideals and aspects of character which men desiderate in their deities, there yet continued to flourish under the shadow of that Olympus on whose brow he sat, the cult of other minor gods.

What was Socrates' position? The only conclusion we can come to on all the evidence we have considered is that the question between "God" and "gods" was to him a subordinate and comparatively unimportant one. Number really matters extremely little. Not the arithmetic, but the morality and spirituality of your Godhead is the point. Nor must this be counted to him for pagan blindness. He was at least no less advanced and enlightened than the late William James on this point, and James was unworthy neither of the era nor of the society in which he lived. We are so apt to be horrified at things in a society outside the traditions and sympathies of our own, religiously, things which in our own society we can

---

[1] De Deo Socratis, p. 116; opera edited by Hildebrand, vol. ii.
[2] *Op. cit.*, pp. 140, 141.

contemplate and tolerate without turning a hair. We may quake at the Spectre of the Brocken seen through the dividing mists, and find when we approach it closer and see it clearer that it is only an old familiar friend of our own.

Socrates appears to us to have had considerable sympathy with the conventional worship even while predominantly influenced by the philosophical view. His speculative activity undoubtedly drew him on to a monotheistic conception of the universe, but he did not utterly cast off the gods and modes of worship of the common men and women among whom he had been born and among whom he lived. The Religion of his people had wound itself about his heart with the clutch of many tender sentiments. He was a believer in Reason, but he was not a disembodied Rationalist. Writers like Joël present him to our imagination as a rickle of logical bones stalking about the graveyards in which he has buried the flesh and blood of ordinary human experience. Not so can we picture him. He was not the pure intellectualist who keeps himself unspotted from the emotions and sentiments of the world. He was a man who stood between the old and the new; he was amphibious, and breathed the air of two worlds, the world that was aging and the world just to be born.

He reminds us of the image Plato gives us of Glaucon rising out of the sea, with the stones and shells and greenweed of the lower, denser, element clinging and dripping about him. He was an Athenian, though he was also very much more; he was a spectator of all time, and existence, but he looked out upon it from the market-place of the city whose stones and people were dear to him as life. You might compare him—*magna comparare parvis*—to some Scotch Presbyterian professor in the grip of Hegel, or to an Anglican Broad

Churchman. He indulges in heretical orthodoxy. He can use the orthodox nomenclature, do the orthodox things, but the inner idea is changed, there is a new vintage in the old bottles.

Thus he continued to speak of " the gods " and to perform sacrifices to them ; he even taught that men should worship according to the prescribed rites of their city or state and not make a fuss about their New Theology. The forms, or the absence of forms, is not the vital thing. It is all a matter of spirit. And so he gives the impression of waving away the discussion of rites and ceremonies as rather trivial for a philosopher to bother himself about one way or another, and gives a genial patronage to the beliefs and faith of the " weaker brethren." His attitude seems very like that described in mellow tints and inculcated with soft grace by Mr. A. C. Benson in his essays " From a College Window " :

" The true concern of the believer is to be his own attitude to life, his relations with the circle, small or great, in which he finds himself. . . . He need not trouble himself about traditional ordinances, elaborate ceremonials, subtle doctrines, metaphysical definitions. He must concern himself with far different things ; let him be sure that he is patient, and just, and tender-hearted, and sincere ; let him be sure that no sin is allowed to lurk unresisted in the depths of his spirit. . . . Let him be quiet and peaceable ; let him take freely the comforts of the holy influences which Churches, for all their complex fabric of traditions and ceremony, still hold out to the spirit ; . . . the Churches themselves have gained by age and gentle associations, and artistic perception, a large treasure of things that are full of beauty,—that are only hurtful when held to be special and peculiar channels of holiness and sweetness, when they are supposed to have a definite sanctification which is opposed to the sanctification of the beauty exterior to them. Let the Christian be grateful for the beauty they hold, and use it freely and simply. . . . Let him not even seek to go outside of the persuasion, as it is so strangely called, in which he was born," &c.

Socrates spoke of the oracle of Delphi as having authoritatively pronounced the conformist attitude as the one to be adopted. Prof. A. E. Taylor has called him "the first non-conformist of history," but the phrase seems singularly infelicitous, for Socrates, in common with many more cultured and critical spirits of the time, was a conformist. At heart he is an Independent, but externally he won't be a Separatist. He makes you feel he can quite easily do without all the mythology and all the religious ritual about him, that the "Inner Light" is sufficient for him, but he prefers to walk in the old paths so far as they do not lead away from that Light. We have not understood Socrates, nor, perhaps, got a true inkling of his greatness, till we see that he was not only a man of robust reason, but of hardly less strong sentiment. His emotions were deep, if his intellect was lofty, and the combination produced a sweet reasonableness and toleration in his religious judgments.

Xenophon represents him as a man of deep piety, who paid due and regular court to the city's gods, by prayer and sacrifice, openly and in the sight of all. And we find nothing to controvert this in Platonic allusions in which we expect fidelity to Socrates, viz., little artistic details. Thus in the "Symposium" it is said, "Socrates took his place on the couch and supped with the rest [evidently he did not taboo flesh-food]; and then libations were offered and after a hymn had been sung to the gods and there had been the usual ceremonies," &c.[1] Of course we must be careful of laying too much stress on every reference by Socrates to the gods. Thus, his last words in dying were that he owed a cock to Asclepius, and that Crito must see the debt paid.[2] It would never do to infer from such an incident Socrates' serious belief in Asclepius the god of healing. It is a joke on Socrates' part as the *rigor mortis* is about to creep over his heart, a stroke of humour, not with one foot but literally with both feet in the grave, in which he expresses his dying conviction that death is not for him an evil but a deliverance, an emancipation, a blessing. Just previous to drinking the poison-cup, he had asked the jailor if he might pour a libation, but as this is not permitted he simply replies, " I understand, but it is permitted and one must pray to the gods that one's journey to that other world be prosperous. This I pray, and so may it be."[3]—a recognition of the unseen divine Powers in whose hands is man's future destiny, and without any sense of need for distinction or clear division among them.

The charge brought against him was that he did *not* recognise the city's gods, but strange deities—so it was formulated in court by Meletus. But in the account of his defence given by Plato, he merely evades the point of the charge, by trapping Meletus into self-contradiction. He gets the accuser to say that what he means is that Socrates is an out and out atheist and disbeliever in the gods, but as the strange divinities whom he is declared to worship must be sons of the gods, it follows that he *must* be a believer in the gods too.[4] Meletus can't have it both ways.

He is further accused of teaching that the sun and moon are mere stones and not gods, to which Socrates

[1] Symposium, 176 a.
[2] Phædo, 118.
[3] Phædo, 117 b, c.
[4] Apology, 27 c, d.

contents himself by replying that it is Anaxagoras who teaches this, and he himself cannot claim any originality in this respect. The impression on our minds is that he is merely playing with Meletus and his charges, and it is doubtful whether he does or does not mean it to be inferred that he worships the sun and moon. It depends on how one interprets the question, " Oh, don't I even worship sun and moon ? " Grote takes it as an assertion of his belief in them as gods,[1] and this view does certainly derive support from the reminiscence of Alcibiades that during the campaign at Potidæa, after a remarkable fit of mental abstraction, Socrates offered a prayer to the sun and went his way.[2] But it must be remembered that Socrates was at Potidæa thirty-two years before the end of his life, and a man's beliefs and adorations may change more than once in that interval.

Moreover, it is not inconceivable that Alcibiades could be mistaken about the real object to whom Socrates' prayer was uttered, if the latter simply made use of the term " Sun " in invocation as a metaphor. It is the commonest thing imaginable in prayer for Christians to address God as " a Sun and Shield," or as " Sun of my soul," &c. Plato himself used it in speaking of the Supreme Idea of the Good, because the Idea in the world of realities takes the same place and function as the Sun in the physical world, the world of appearances.

The evidence of Aristophanes' " Clouds " is to the effect that Socrates and his associates adopted the Anaxagorean view of the sun as a red-hot stone, but we shall find later that Aristophanes is not to be taken as law and gospel on Socrates' religion. We leave the question undecided, then, for lack of conclusive data, as far as the deity of the sun is concerned.

[1] Plato, vol. i. p. 413.   [2] Symposium, 220.

Personally we incline to the opinion that Socrates did believe in the existence of lesser divinities and spirits. There is the statement in the "Symposium" that God does not take to do directly and immediately with men, but communes with them through such intermediaries.[1] The doctrine is put into the mouth of Diotima, and is only repeated from her by Socrates, perhaps in order to suggest that Socrates has no reason or proof to give of it, but accepts it as a revelation, beyond the sphere of dialectic. "Love," repeats Socrates, "is no god but a great spirit, one of the beings who occupy a middle place between God and man; for God himself does not hold intercourse with man, and all the fellowship which exists between gods and men takes place through this intermediate order, whose function is that of interpreter and go-between."[2]

Now all this world of religious imagination peopled with dim forms of divinities and spirits, conjured up before the mystic vision not only here but also in the "Phædrus"[3] and "Timæus,"[4] may be held to spring more appropriately from Plato's gorgeous mind than from Socrates' more simple and rational imagination, but there seems to be no evidence for denying that the background of his mind was haunted by the dim shapes of gods which were left undisturbed by the exorcism of an exclusive Rationalism. Only he never strove to formulate a clear articulate doctrine regarding them, and on the dim horizons of his soul they seemed continually to be emerging and melting again into the identity of one godhead. This divine world lay beyond the sphere in which his dialectic had application, and hence he was not inclined to dogmatise about it or to deny it, though probably he would not

---

[1] See Symposium, 202 d, e; 203 a ff.
[2] *Ibid.*, 202 d, e (paraphrase).   [3] 246 e.   [4] 41.

have acquiesced so self-consciously in the genealogies of the gods of Greek mythology as Plato did, unless we read a dash of irony and impatience into his meaning when he declared, "It is impossible to doubt what we have learned from witnesses, who declared themselves to be the offspring of the gods, and who must of course have known their own family affairs." Still there was undoubtedly much in his constitution and character (something of that modesty and reverence which was the instinct of Athenians), which would incline him to endorse Plato's dictum with regard to the divine world which transcends human knowledge: "We must obey the law, and believe." To adopt a characterisation of George Eliot's, which strikes us as extremely true of Socrates, we may say " he had that mental combination which is at once humble in the region of mystery and keen in the region of knowledge," a combination in which he bears a strong likeness to a Tyndall or a Huxley, in modern times.

Socrates had given up all personal devotion to physical research as prosecuted in the various sciences, though that does not necessarily connote entire indifference to the work of others along these lines, and he had given it up because he was more concerned to know himself and solve the problems of human experience which lay nearer the needs of life; and for the same reason, if we assume that the true Socrates speaks in the " Phædrus," he also turned away from the mass of Greek theology as embodied in the legends. When a man began with that sort of thing, there was no logical end to it, and to Socrates it was all vain and profitless. He had no time to spend on these elaborate constructions, so he just accepted them to be going on with, in common with his fellows, in a genial off-hand, uninterested sort of way, devoting himself, as he put it, to the serious study "not of fables but of myself, that I may see whether I am really a more complicated and more furious monster than Typhon, or a creature of a gentler and simpler sort, the born heir of a divine and tranquil nature." [1] The sentiment smacks of the quaint Socrates, as salt air smacks of the sea.

The same attitude is expressed in the "Euthyphro," one of the early "Socratic" dialogues, and thus receives strong confirmation. When Socrates has it quoted to him in justification of human conduct that Kronos and Zeus acted in a particular way, his reply is that he can hardly accept these tales about the quarrels and fights of the gods. If people dogmatise and declare them true, then, he says with a touch of irony, he must abide by their superior wisdom, but as for himself such matters lie beyond the range of his knowledge. Euthyphro hints that he can tell him a good deal about these gods and their ways, but Socrates has not time for that sort of thing at present. His attitude is one of bored scepticism, of detachment and practical indifference. He would rather learn from Euthyphro what the practical human virtue of piety is.[2] It is the strain of common sense and the saving tendency toward utilitarianism coming out again.

The position is very similar to that of plenty of devout Christians to-day toward many of the Old Testament stories, to doctrines of angels, and to large parts of the Apocalypse. These things have simply lost all relation to the inner life and become void of all appeal to large numbers of Christians, who simply leave them aside, neither accepting in any effective way, nor yet explicitly rejecting them. There they are in the authentic books, but they form no part of the real faith of cultured Christians, bear no relation to the spiritual motives by which they live.

[1] Plato, Phædrus, 230 a.   [2] Euthyphro, 6.

And we have to remember that in standing partially on the outside of the popular religious tradition Socrates was by no means alone: he was simply one in whom the more cultured spirit of the age was mirrored, a spirit which took the gods with a grain of salt, having lost the firm belief in their vivid individual reality as persons. " The Olympians," says Prof. Gilbert Murray, " are artists' dreams, ideals, allegories; they are symbols of something beyond themselves. They are gods of a half-rejected tradition, of unconscious make-believe, of aspiration. They are gods to whom the doubtful philosophers can pray, with all a philosopher's due caution, as to so many radiant and heart-searching hypotheses. They are not gods in whom any one believes as a hard fact. . . . Something like this, I take it, was the character of the Olympian Religion in the higher minds of later Greece. Its gods could awaken man's worship and strengthen his higher aspirations; but at heart they knew themselves to be only metaphors. As the most beautiful image carved by man was not the god but only a symbol to help towards conceiving the gods, so the god himself when conceived was not the reality but only a symbol to help towards conceiving the reality." [1]

One wonders what sort of reverence and belief in their deities a people could have, who permitted their introduction upon the comic stage as objects for the broadest farce and the most rollicking laughter? On the assumption that Aristophanes ever posed as a serious defender of orthodox religion and the gods against the scepticism of philosophers and sophists, one can only be amazed at the wholly irreverent way in which he handles them on his stage.

In the " Knights," Nicias suggests to Demosthenes

[1] Four Stages of Greek Religion, pp. 97, 98.

that they had better go to the shrine of some god and pray for mercy:

"DEM. Shrines! Shrines! Why, sure, you don't believe in the gods?

"NIC. Yes I do.

"DEM. But what's your argument? Where's your proof?

"NIC. Because I feel they persecute me and hate me in spite of everything I try to do to please 'em.

"DEM. Well, well, that's true, you're right enough in that."[1]

In the "Birds" Peisthetairus suggests that the birds should build a Babylon in mid-air, and in order to bring the gods into due submission to them, they should starve them out by intercepting the supplies of sacrificial smoke; they should also send an envoy to Zeus and demand his abdication, and to forbid him and the other gods in heaven:

> "To trespass on our atmospheric domain
> With scandalous journeys to visit a list
> Of Alcmenas, and Semeles; if they persist,
> We warn them that means will be taken, moreover,
> To stop their gallanting and acting the lover."[2]

The birds will be a good substitute for Delphic Dodona, and for Zeus himself,

> "We'll not keep away, scornful and proud, a-top of a cloud."
> In Jupiter's way, but attend every day
> To prosper and bless."

But comedy went beyond these comparatively decent limits. "The innumerable adulteries of Zeus, his disguises, his prodigious amours, as many scenes with enticing details as would make the audience

---

[1] Frere's Trans. Works, vol. ii. p. 70.
[2] Frere, *op. cit.*, p. 162.

HIS RELIGION

split their sides with laughter," were held up before the public.[1]

So Charon, Æacus, and Pluto, solemn figures of the underworld, are treated as amusing old bogies and hell a theatre fittingly made to frighten the simple.

" The Poseidon of Aristophanes is a blockhead." [2]

In the Frogs we have Æacus scolding Dionysius like a fish-wife, calling him a wretch, a shameless, a triple rogue, "who stole my dog Cerberus and escaped, &c.[3]

Heracles fairs very badly at the hands of Athenian Comedy, being represented as a giant, with small head and overhanging belly, a sensual voracious rake who can easily be bought through any of his appetites.[4]

It is quite evident that there must have been a public at Athens that thought the popular traditions and conceptions as fit only for farce, and who regarded no satire upon the unspiritual and immoral elements of the legends of the gods as too vitriolic and scathing.

Xenophanes in the sixth century had set a philosophical fashion in theological criticism when he said that there was one God above all gods and men, and that Homer and Hesiod had ascribed to the gods " all things that are a disgrace among men, thefts, adulterers, deception of each other." [5]

In Euripides and Plato alike we see emerge with a bold and unmistakable clearness the thought that the traditional gods are no gods, that there cannot be two systems of morality, one for gods and another for men, the latter far higher and purer. The godhead

---

[1] Couat, Aristophane, p. 239.
[2] Couat, *op. cit.*, p. 237 ; Birds, 1565 ff.
[3] See Frogs, 465 ff.
[4] Birds, 1603, 62 ff. ; Frogs, 503 ff. See Couat, *op. cit.*, 232–5.
[5] See Burnet, Early Greek Philosophy, 1st edit., p. 115, or Adam, Religious Teachers of Greece, p. 200, for fragments of Xenophanes.

therefore must be purged of evil and baseness and immorality.

Euripides, *e.g.*, referring to the old myth that the slaying of Neoptolemus at Delphi was a divine retribution because his father had insulted Apollo, compares such an action on the part of a god to the sleepless grudge of a base-minded man.[1]

There are moments when the poet, looking beyond the moral confusions of the old theology, and through the painful mystery of the world, catches glimpses of some better order lying at the heart of changes and working on this earth of ours.

> "O earth's upholder that on earth dost dwell,
> Whate'er thy name, hard to be understood,
> Zeus, or necessity of Nature's course,
> Or mind of mortals—before thee I bow;
> For on thy noiseless pathway thou dost guide
> As righteousness commands, all human things."[2]

These words are the words of Hecuba, but the voice is surely the voice of Euripides.

In Plato's "Republic" we have Adeimantus setting forth the plain blunt doctrines of the time-honoured theology, according to which the just spend their time in the next world, "reclining on couches, wine-bibbing, the fairest rewards of virtue being, in their estimation, an everlasting carousal.[3] . . . If the gods do exist and concern themselves with us, we have heard nothing of them from any other quarter than the current traditions and genealogies of poets, and they say that the gods are wrought upon and diverted from their purpose by sacrifices and supplications and offerings. If we are to believe them, we will act unjustly and offer sacrifices from the proceeds of our crimes."[4]

---

[1] For his treatment of the gods, &c., see Verrall's Euripides the Rationalist.

[2] Campbell, Religion in Greek Literature, p. 313.

[3] Republic, 363 c. [4] *Ibid.*, 365 e.

The depraving effect on conduct, then, of such views did not escape the notice of those who were given to reflection, and was, of course, clearly recognised by Plato himself, who declared that the gods were not deceitful [1] nor feeble,[2] nor licentious,[3] nor purchasable,[4] and that it was sacrilege to attribute such vices to them.

This we may take to be Socrates' doctrine also, for nothing else is consistent with the figure alike of the "Memorabilia" and the "Dialogues of Plato." He was not concerned to deny the existence of these gods; it was not worth while; but if they are to be retained, they must at least be freed from all that is unworthy; while the arithmetical constitution of the invisible Godhead is a very subordinate consideration, but the lofty moral character of it must be upheld and vindicated. The moral law must control the Godhead, not the Godhead the moral law. This is the conviction which Plato makes him express in the "Euthyphro," where Socrates argues that a thing is not holy because the gods love it, but that they love it because it is holy.[5]

This is to approve a change in men's estimates and valuations which is of far-reaching import. It is to put morality at the very heart of religion, and to place goodness above any arbitrary and conventional means of pleasing the gods. It is at once to humanise and moralise theology, to bring it back to the simplicity of goodness, truth, and righteousness from the artificialities of any system based on the arbitrary prerogatives and preferences of its gods. We shall see the ethical character of his religion brought out more fully in his discussion of the nature of Piety. In addition to this what we have tried to indicate in the

[1] Rep., 382.   [2] Ibid., 388 c, 389 a.   [3] Ibid., 390 b, c.
[4] Ibid., 390 d, e; cp. 391.   [5] Euthyphro, 10.

foregoing is that Socrates had no clear and definite system of the gods in his mind, with the spheres and functions of each clearly separated and defined. Such an articulate polytheism had been eclipsed by the cardinal thought of Deity or Godhead as such in the various phases of its activity and relationship with mortals. It was immaterial therefore whether one spoke of God or gods, and any attempt to discuss and define the point by human reason Socrates would probably have treated as presumptuous and futile, believing that it transcended human knowledge and was among those divine things that we ought not to pry into and which don't concern us. If there is any maintainable distinction, it is that "God" is the term preferred when the world and providence is being considered, "gods" when it is a matter of divine dealings with men.[1]

Enough for him that he believed the divine powers to be interested in men and to take care of them.[2] "There is no good thing which they do not give us,"[3] and all the blessings we enjoy in life and all that is needful for our terrestrial existence come of their grace; they send the seasons with their pleasant vicissitudes and the fruits of the earth; from them are fire and water. The animals too are given by them to be helpers and fellow-workers with man. So also to the gods we owe those senses by which we apprehend and enjoy the world without, and the inner faculties of memory and reason by which civilisation is built up.[4]

"It seems to me," says Socrates in the "Phædo," "to be well said that gods look after us and that we men are the possessions of the gods."[5]

---

[1] Joël, *op. cit.*, i. p. 135. [2] Mem., I. i. 19.
[3] Euthyphro, 15 a. [4] Xen., Mem., iv. 3.
[5] Phædo, 62 b; cp. Plato, Laws, 906 a.

And yet though they are the authors of all this good, they themselves remain invisible. God who orders and sustains the whole visible fabric of things abides unseen by mortal eye, like the soul, which governs and controls our body.[1] And yet, as already said, they are everywhere, and nothing that we plan or say or do escapes their all-seeing eye.[2]

The Socratic conception differs in no very material way from that of Christ, who believed in the existence of legions of angels under the supreme command of one who was both Creator of all and his own Father. The same essential attributes are assigned to the Deity, and there emerges the same trustful faith in the guardian care of God over men, who are His own flock, the sheep of His pasture, His " possessions."

Christendom has not always maintained inviolate such a high and hopeful doctrine.

(c) Socratic Piety

So far we have been dealing with what the Deity is to man, now the question arises, How does man come into touch with the Deity, how can he please God? To answer that question involves the consideration of what Socrates understood by Piety, and we shall find that while adopting the recognised forms and ritual, he put a fresh content into them. He refined and spiritualised what he accepted, like the later Hebrew prophets and like Jesus himself, who, as far as one can learn, did not directly attack the Jewish sacrificial system as such, but declared that in itself it was not enough, that morality and a right attitude of heart and soul must go with it.

" If thou art offering thy gift at the altar, and there rememberest that thy brother hath aught against

---

[1] *Mem.*, iv. 3.   [2] *Ibid.*, I. i. 19.

thee, leave there thy gift before the altar, and go thy way, first be reconciled to thy brother, and then come and offer thy gift."[1] The Law with its ritual is not impugned, but it is to be fulfilled in a new spirit.

> "The heart's aye the part aye
> That makes us right or wrang."

The problem of what constitutes piety is discussed in Plato's dialogue Euthyphro, and also in some reminiscences of Xenophon's. In the former Socrates leads on Euthyphro from one definition to another, showing him that none of them are satisfactory or self-consistent. First of all piety is stated to consist in just such conduct as Euthyphro is engaged in with such apparent zeal and self-complacency, viz. prosecuting anyone guilty of sacrilege or crime. But Socrates does not want merely examples of pious action, but the true definition, a statement of the quality whose presence it is in all examples of piety that makes them pious. Euthyphro takes another shot: "Piety is that which is dear to the gods, and Impiety is that which is not dear to them."[2] Whereupon Socrates points out that with gods who quarrel and differ with each other, loving and hating different things (as in the orthodox theology they do), the same action would on this definition turn out to be both pious and impious at the same time. Moreover he goes on to show that to define piety as that which is loved by God, is to substitute one fact about the thing for the thing itself, for, it is admitted, a thing is not holy because it is loved by God, but is beloved by God because it is holy.[3]

Still further on Socrates gets Euthyphro to admit that piety is a part of justice, *i.e.* there may be justice where there is no piety, but there can never be piety where there is not justice.[4] Asked to specify what

---
[1] Matt. v. 23.   [2] Euthyphro, 6.   [3] *Ibid.*, 10.   [4] *Ibid.*, 12.

part of justice piety and holiness are, Euthyphro answers, that part which "attends to the gods." Being pressed by the insistent dialectician as to the precise meaning of the phrase "attention to the gods," Euthyphro gets a trifle impatient and bored, and declares he understands by piety "pleasing the gods in word and deed, by prayers and sacrifices; that is piety, and it is the salvation of families and states, just as its opposite, which is unpleasing to the gods, is their ruin and destruction."

Socrates translates this definition into the bald language of economics, as a nice little commercial transaction between gods and men, in which you give them gifts in sacrifice and ask back gifts in prayer;[1] in more vulgar parlance, a case of scratching their back that they may scratch yours.

Euthyphro, being only human, is nettled by the underlying facetiousness of his solemn cross-examiner, and after an unsatisfactory weak piece of argument, by which Socrates leads him into the ditch again, Euthyphro says he is in a hurry and must be off, and so Socrates is left lamenting that he does not yet know what piety and holiness are, and must continue at the mercy of Meletus and his charge of impiety, whereas "I might have proved that I had been converted by Euthyphro, and had done with rash innovations and speculations in which I had indulged through ignorance, and that I was going to lead a better life in future." The dialogue thus ends with a characteristic bit of jesting irony levelled at his accusers, as well as at Euthyphro, who was so sure that he knew what piety was, and that his conduct was all right.

The dialogue, however, suggests the points insisted on in the discussion of the same subject with Euthydemus in the "Memorabilia,"[2] viz. that if our piety is to

---

[1] Euthyphro, 15.   [2] Mem., iv. 6.

be secure from error and mistake, it must be based on knowledge. Tradition and convention and dogmatism won't do. Piety means honouring the gods in the proper form, or according to the law, and to do this we must know the proper form, or the law, a knowledge which will inevitably be followed by corresponding conduct, for who that honours the gods at all would do it otherwise than in what he knew to be the proper form ?

(*d*) We have noted the sly depreciatory suggestion of Socrates about sacrifice and prayer as too commonly practised, though of course Euthyphro repudiates the idea that it is a piece of business on the level with the market, wherein gods and men buy each others' commodities at mutually advantageous prices.

Socrates at any rate did not hold the vulgar commercial theory of sacrifice and prayer. Deity has need of nothing,[1] as even the ordinary religious man knows when he comes to reflect.[2] What, then, is its meaning and purpose ? If Xenophon be right, the Socratic doctrine is that it is a way of showing gratitude to the gods.[3] But how can one do that in any way that is at all adequate ? It seems impossible. Socrates, however, takes a genial view of the Godhead, and falls back on the Delphian oracle [4] with its dictum that we must show this gratitude according to the law of the State, *i.e.* by means of sacrifices in proportion to our means. We do not show the gods honour by offering them less than it is in our power to give ; but, having done our best, we can rest in the hope of their highest blessing.[5] And that best is impossible apart from obedience to them.

It is not at all a question of the amount or the costliness of our gifts, but entirely of the right spirit. The

---

[1] Mem., i. 6, 10. [2] Euthyphro, 14 e. [3] Mem., iv. 3, 16.
[4] Ibid. [5] *Ibid.*, iv. 3, 17.

thing that gives worth to all our giving to the gods is the heart of humble obedience to them.[1] The little offerings of the poor man are as precious in their eyes as the large offerings of the wealthy, otherwise the offerings of bad men would be more acceptable often than those of the good.[2] And if that were so, human life would not be worth living,[3] for its moral foundations would be overthrown, and its moral value dismissed in the courts above. Socrates held the conviction that the satisfaction and joy of the gods in our gifts is in direct proportion to the piety and holiness of the giver.[4]

He was not the first to hold such views. Pythagoras was credited in Cynic schools with having inculcated that in sacrifice the purity of the soul was of more value than the costliness of the offerings.[5] How far Socrates was influenced by Pythagorean teaching is a very debatable point, and it is not of much importance that we should assess the exact measure of his originality. What is worth insisting on is that the whole temper of his mind and tone of his thought was such as naturally to lead him to lay stress on the inner and spiritual as against the outer and mechanical, and to let the latter rest as it was, so long as the former could be made right and pure. Attend to the spirit and motive of your religion, and the forms may be allowed to look after themselves. He stood for the supremacy of character and morality in rite and ceremony, and for the inner and spiritual over against the merely external, in man's quest for reconciliation and peace with God.[6]

It must be confessed that a right sense of values

---

[1] Mem., iv. 3, 17.
[2] Ibid., i. 3, 3.
[3] Ibid.
[4] Ibid.
[5] Joël, *op. cit.*, vol. ii. pt. i. p. 209.
[6] Cp. Adam, Religious Teachers of Greece, p. 351.

in these matters was becoming more and more necessary in Greece, and the necessity was winning recognition among thoughtful people, for the elaborate sacrificial system was leading to abuses, as voiced by Adeimantus in the " Republic " of Plato, and to priestly hypocrisy and worldliness as satirised by Aristophanes. The doctrine sedulously diffused and commonly accepted that men could escape the penalties of their sins, and win the personal favour of the gods, apart from inward repentance and virtue, could not but corrupt character and undermine morals.

" There are quacks and soothsayers," says Adeimantus, " who flock to the rich man's doors and try to persuade him that they have a power at command, which they procure from heaven, and which enables them by sacrifices and incantations, performed amid feasting and indulgence, to make amends for any crime committed either by the individual or by his ancestors ; and that should he desire to do a mischief to anyone, it may be done at a trifling expense ; for they profess that by certain invocations and spells they can prevail upon the gods to do their bidding."[1] Indeed, Adeimantus also attacks the Mysteries associated with the name of Orpheus on precisely the same grounds—that they hold out to men a prospect of " being absolved and purified from " wrong and vice by the offering of sacrifices and the participation in what he calls " pleasurable amusements," thus encouraging men to think that they will be able to escape the consequences of their injustice.[2]

Here, then, was a system which lent itself to success without goodness, welfare without virtue, and which could be readily enough perverted into the false doctrine that the gods could be bought over to one's selfish ends by paying the necessary price.

[1] Republic, 364; Davies and Vaughan's trans. [2] Republic, 365 a.

Aristophanes points out the utterly self-interested and unspiritual character of such a religion in his " Knights,"[1] where Agoracrite, the sausage-seller, and Cleon his rival are represented as offering sacrifice to the gods for the most palpably selfish ends. It is not submission of the will to God, but submission of God to one's will, which becomes the object of such a cult. In his " Plutus " he satirises the insincerity, unspirituality, and materialism which characterises its devotees,[2] and even its priestly officials. When the high priest of Zeus contemplates his shrine without worshippers, it is not the decline of the faith which most distresses him, but the diminution of the takings, and he resolves that he will become an acolyte of Plutus, a position that promises more profits.[3] In the same play we have a scene in the temple of Asclepius by night, whither Carion the slave has conducted the blind Plutus for treatment. The lights have been snuffed, and the sick put to bed, but Carion can't sleep, and happening to open his eyes, what does he see but the priest quietly cleaning the holy table of the dry figs and cakes offered by the good souls. He steals round the altars, and quickly empties what is on them into the bag he carries, thus appropriating them to his own use.[4]

The corruptions and tendencies to abuse of ceremonial religion were thus making themselves felt as a problem for the moralist and thinker, and the higher ethics of Socrates, the stress he laid upon soul and conduct, grew out of the deeper needs of the times, and was in harmony with them. He was just the teacher and exemplar that the religious situation demanded —one who, while treating the established order with all due reverence, yet placed the main emphasis on the state and attitude of the soul within, with the conduct

[1] 424 b, c.   [2] Plutus, ll. 1172 ff,
[3] *Ibid.*, ll, 1186 ff,   [4] *Ibid.*, ll, 665 ff.

which issues therefrom, was of opinion that the gods were more pleased with the deference of those who were holy,[1] and gave them the fullest obedience,[2] and went so far as to say that they were the men best and most beloved of the gods who in the ordinary duties of everyday life performed their tasks well.[3]

His position was the result of that solid common-sense and quiet sanity which characterised all his relations, secular and sacred, and which were the embodiment and expression of the faculty of Reason, constructed and enriched by wide reading, large experience, and assiduous thought upon the many problems of human conduct.

(e) The impression of well-balanced moral health and sound spiritual insight in matters of religion, which Socrates gives, is further strengthened by what we are told of his attitude regarding prayer. A man's inmost thinking may be judged pretty well by his praying. The real character will flit out and in, and appear round corners, amid any number of conventional artificialities of petition and phrasing.

Aristophanes gives us an idea of the character of a good deal of the praying that was in vogue in his day. It had a fair quantity of superstition, and a keen eye for the main chance in it, just like the sacrificing. It aimed too often at getting the gods over to one's own side, and winning their favour for one's own ambitions, in this respect resembling the notorious prayer of Holy Willie, who was by no means a purely imaginary character in Christendom.

> "But, Lord, remember me and mine
>   Wi' mercies temp'ral and divine;
> That I for fear and grace may shine,
>   Excelled by nane,
> And a' the glory shall be thine,
>   Amen, Amen!"[4]

---

[1] Mem., i. 3, 3.   [2] Mem., iv. 3, 16.
[3] Mem., iii. 9, 15.   [4] Cp. Aristophanes, Plutus, ll. 134 ff.

HIS RELIGION

People would enumerate as many of the gods as possible in their invocation, so as to conciliate the good-will of all of them, a feature which the comic poet parodies in the "Knights,"[1] and in reference to which Couat wittily remarks that "the most solid piety was that which had the best memory."[2]

The prayers of Socrates were short and simple; he could cast himself in full trust upon the wisdom and goodness of the Godhead. In this respect he was ahead of Christianity in some of its Scotch forms, in which the Almighty would be informed beyond any possibility of mistake just what was wanted of Him, as in the case of the minister of a rural parish where the crops had been laid by rain, who is said to have prayed that a wind should be sent: "O Lord, we pray Thee to send us wind; no a rantin, tantin, tearin' wind, but a noohin', soughin', winnin' wind."

In Socrates' eyes it was an absurdity, as well as an irreverence, to try to instruct and coax the Deity. Better to have faith that the gods know best what things are good, and pray that they may give us these.

"His formula of prayer was simple: 'Give me the things that are good,' for, said he, the gods know best what good things are—to pray for gold, or silver, or despotic power were no better than to make some particular throw at dice, or stake in battle or any such thing the subject of prayer, of which the future consequences are manifestly uncertain."[3]

> "We ignorant of ourselves
> Beg often our own harms, which the wise powers
> Deny us for our good; so find we profit
> By losing of our prayers."[4]

In the dialogue, "Alcibiades II," Socrates is made to

---

[1] ll. 865 ff.
[2] Couat, Aristophane, p. 253.
[3] Mem., i. 3, 2.
[4] Shakespeare in Antony and Cleopatra.

quote admiringly the prayer of some poet for his friends :

> " O Zeus, grant us blessings, prayed for or not,
> And defend us from evils even that we pray for."[1]

" In its perfect faith and self-suppression," remarks Prof. Adam, " the Socratic formula of prayer is more Christian than Greek."[2] But it was not entirely unique and solitary. Pythagoras was said to have taught his disciples that the wise ought simply to pray to the gods for blessings,[3] and Xenophanes, a philosopher of the sixth century[4] before Christ, who had severely criticised the traditional conceptions of the gods, was content that prayer should be summed up in the petition for " power to do that which is right." It brings out the fact that paganism so called did not wander about in utter darkness, without God or hope ; there were many who believed in the goodness of the gods above them, and who could rest in the faith of the old Roman poet :

> " Aptissma quaeque dabunt Dî
> Carior est illis homo quam sibi."
>
> " The gods will grant what is best for us,
> For man is not so dear to himself as to them."

This humble childlike faith was the very core of the personality of Socrates ; it was the very acra of his character. His life was one of absolute trust in the transcendent divine goodness ; this was its keynote, a note of strength and joy ; with such trust he could face either life or death ; for everything works together for good to him who thus knows God.

He always had the sense that the divine will was operating above and through life, guiding everything to its destined goal of good, and that it was man's privilege to be a helper of the gods, co-operating with them, and sharing their purpose. It is, therefore, in perfect

---

[1] Alcibiades, ii. 143 a.
[2] Adam, *op. cit.*, p. 352.
[3] Joël, *op. cit.*, vol. ii. pt i. p. 209.
[4] Born *circa* 570 B.C.

HIS RELIGION

consistency with Socrates' mind and character, especially as he laid so much store by work done well and done with all one's might, that he should tell Critobulus, as he does in Xenophon's "Œconomicus," that the exhortation to endeavour to begin all work with heaven's help, commands his entire assent.[1]

There is one other prayer, put upon Socrates' lips by Plato, and it grows and blossoms from them with the beauty of a rose in its natural place. It seems to give us the very essence and peculiarity of the soul of the great sage, in its spirituality, and a certain quaint abruptness in thought. It comes at the close of the "Phædrus." Socrates and his companion rise to leave the beautiful little spot, with its grass and spring and spreading plane-tree, where they have been together in high discourse of the soul. The entire natural and spontaneous religious feeling of the sage suggests a fitting expression for itself in prayer, and he prays:

"Beloved Pan, and all ye other gods, who haunt this place, give me beauty in the inward soul; and may the outward and the inward man be one. May I judge the wise to be the wealthy, and may I have such wealth as only the wise could bear and carry."[2] "Give me beauty in the inward soul, and may the outward and the inward man be one,"—what more perfect blossom can be culled from all the liturgies in which man has ever sought to build into words his high desire and unalienable aspiration. In it prayer has become a lyric, and all the poetry of religion has crushed its sweetness into fragrant speech.

We have been accustomed in certain religious circles to hear indiscriminate references to paganism and all its works, in the supposed interests of the religion of Jesus, and to the supposed glory of God. It is needless to say that ordinarily the people who stoop to such

---

[1] Œconomicus, ch. vi. 1. [2] Phædrus, 279 b, c.

wholesale superficial depreciation of other religious systems and spiritual cults are ignorant of their finer products, and have but little sympathy with the catholicity of their God, whose light breaks through the many-sided prism of human thought and experience in varied colours, to give light to them that walk in darkness, and so lead them into communion with Himself. The highest reverence for God is the reverence for all He has made. If He has looked and seen that it was all very good, it is not for His professed worshippers to look and see that nearly all of it was very bad. That is to show such a pathetic lack of moral and spiritual appreciation, linked to such a vulgar expression of it, as can only alienate the humble and devout and sincere seeker after those things of beauty, good, and truth which anywhere and everywhere the Creative Spirit of the Most High has scattered over the many pathways of man's pilgrimage here below.

Let us love the highest religion in a Socrates as well as in a Paul. "To summarise the whole matter, Piety, according to Socrates, consists, on the one hand, in the free observance of religious ceremonies after the custom of the state, in the presenting of offerings according to one's means, in prayer for the Good in general, and, on the other hand, in the achieving of the good and the avoidance of the evil from awe of the disfavour and punishment of the gods." [1]

We quarrel with this summary of Prof. Döring's only in the last suggestion, that for Socrates the motive of well-doing is the fear of the gods' punishment. No doubt the approbation of the gods was a strong factor with Socrates, but he would surely have said, with F. W. Robertson, that "if there be no God, no future state, yet even then it is better to be generous than selfish, better to be chaste than licentious, better

[1] Döring, Lehre des Sokrates, pp. 448, 449.

HIS RELIGION

to be true than false, better to be brave than to be a coward." Plato was not above him in this.[1]

(*f*) It is in prayer that most religious people realise the closest intercourse and communion of the soul with its God. But Socrates was among that smaller number who believe themselves to have special visitations of the Divine, and to be the recipients of direct intimations from it. Such impressions and convictions, arising out of one's inner experience, have a way of authenticating themselves beyond all doubt to those who have them, and they are generally confined to men and women with an unusually intense realisation of religious realities. It is not surprising that it is out of this class there come the great spiritual prophets of the world's history. And wherever we find such experience in some form, we may be sure that we are in the neighbourhood of strong prophetic and religious affinities.

Socrates was a man whose intellect and reason could never be at rest; he must have clearness and consistency on all subjects which are vitally important to us. All the more impressive, therefore, to find that he believed himself in contact with that spirit world, of which another great intellectual wrote:

> "Die Geister-welt ist nicht geschlossen
> Dein herz ist todt, dein sinn ist Zu."[2]

We have already seen that in the Platonic dialogues we are taught to realise that there is more in heaven and earth than any merely rationalistic philosophy can dream of—that there is room in them for strange creations of poetry and imagination. The universe is peopled with dim forms and phantom shapes beyond our ken.

No other view is really so reasonable as that. The

---

[1] Rep. 358 d, and 367 e. Life and Letters, i. p. 104.
[2] Goethe, Faust.

belief in higher spiritual beings than ourselves is one to which common sense would lead us.

It was a belief congenial, of course, to the Greek, and Socrates shared it. But he had no dogmatic theory about such worlds unrealised. It was enough for him to accept it so far as it seemed to enter his experience, and in one matter of the guidance of his life he believed it did enter.

There was something of the mystic as well as of the rationalist in the rich soul of this prophet and truth-seeker. He had experiences of rapt contemplation, such as we hear of in the case of the Christian saints and mystics. And any account of him which denudes this aspect of his character of significance is partial and insufficient. It is leaving the Prince of Denmark out of *Hamlet*. For to our mind it is not more in the Socratic dialectic than in the Socratic experience of religion that we most truly find the man.

The whole character includes both sides, of course, but the tendency of recent philosophical commentators is to shift all the significance of the revelation of Socrates to his achievements in logic. It was certainly a mighty birth of genius whose issue was to be Plato, in which philosophy opened its eyes on a whole new world, but when we are dealing with the personality of Socrates, it represents only one part of a larger and richer whole. Socrates was essentially a philosophic mind, but he was also, and no less essentially, a religious spirit. And to him religion was not simply a matter of ideas and beliefs, but even more of feeling and inner experience.

There was a tremendous mental intensity about Socrates, but whether that of itself would account for those occasions of absorption when he became lost to the world about him, whether he was like a piece of machinery that "sleeps" when it is going at top speed, or whether we must assume some psychical abnormality, such as would relate him on one side to the religious devotee like George Fox, it is difficult to decide. We think the evidence points to an explanation which must involve both characteristics.

There were times when, perhaps without any warning to those around him, Socrates would suddenly relapse into a fit of profound abstraction, and this must have been sufficiently well known, in the Socratic circle at least, to make it possible for Plato to weave it into his artistic portraiture of the master. For example, in the "Symposium,"[1] it is related that he was just approaching the house of Agathon, who had won the prize for his first tragedy. Aristodemus was along with him. The latter, however, on entering, became aware that he was by himself. A servant was sent out to fetch Socrates, but brought back the message that he had retired to the portico of a neighbouring house; "there he is standing, and when I call he will not come."[2]

Aristodemus, to prevent Socrates being further disturbed, excuses him by saying, "This is a habit of his. He withdraws, and stands absorbed just where he happens to be." Socrates was accordingly left alone, and came in when the feast was about half over, "not having been absorbed a long time, as was his wont."[3]

The language definitely suggests that these periods of rapt contemplation were fairly frequent in Socrates' experience. And Alcibiades tells the story of one such occasion when Socrates had a "spell of this self-concentration in thought from dawn till noon." By that time he attracted the curiosity of the others, but still he remained lost to the outside world, and in that condition he remained standing through all the follow-

[1] Symposium, p. 174.   [2] Ibid., 175 a.   [3] Ibid., 175 c.

ing night, till the sun rose next morning, when he addressed an invocation to the sun and went away.[1]

"We are reminded," says Gomperz, "of Newton, who, late one morning, was found sitting half-dressed in bed, sunk in meditation; and on another occasion remained for a long time in his cellar, where a train of thought had taken possession of him, while in the act of fetching a bottle of wine for his guests."[2]

We are not, however, definitely informed of the precise state of Socrates' mind in these conditions. Was it always the solution of some intellectual problem of the philosopher? Had it nothing in it of the rapt emotion or beatific vision of the saint? Was it not an experience like that of the Indian philosopher and mystic, to which Mr. W. B. Yeats has referred in his introduction to the beautiful book of "Song Offerings," by Rabindranath Tagore? Of Mr. Tagore, he says, it was told him by an eyewitness that "every morning at three, he sits immovable in contemplation, and for two hours does not awake from his reverie upon the nature of God. His father, the Maha Rishi, would sometimes sit there all through the next day: once upon a river he fell into contemplation because of the beauty of the landscape, and the rowers waited for eight hours before they could continue their journey."[3] We must not fail to remember the complexity of Socrates' mind and temperament, nor forget that he is represented to us as subject not only to these fits of abstraction, but also to hearing a divine voice, and to seeing visions. Macaulay came fresh to the reading of Plato from other fields where he had gathered wide knowledge of human nature, and the impression which the personality of Socrates made on his mind is not to be put aside without more ado, although it is always marred by a certain

---

[1] Symposium, 220 c, d.   [2] Greek Thinkers, ii. p. 47.
[3] Song Offerings, Introd., pp. x, xi.

lack of sympathy, which we should hardly have expected in a deeply pious man, and a historian of power. He says in his diary of July 1853, this, among other things :

"The stories of the oracle, the divine monitor, and the dream are absurd. I imagine that, with all his skill in Logomachy, Socrates was a strange, fanciful, superstitious old fellow. Extreme credulity has often gone with extreme logical subtlety. Witness some of the Schoolmen ; witness John Wesley."[1]

It is something as inclusive as this view, though corrected by a recognition of the sane moral and intellectual vision of Socrates, which we have been forced to adopt.[2] Socrates showed no "extreme credulity" or "superstition" in his attitude towards the religious mythologies and rites of his times. All the more impressive and startling, therefore, his experience and acceptance of the more intimate and personal intercourse of the Divine with his own soul. Whether or no we choose to dismiss these experiences as credulity and superstition—and on the objective aspect of them we refrain from passing a judgment—at any rate the admission of their subjective reality throws clearly up before our minds the intensely religious temperament of Socrates. It was really this inner personal and individual experience of, and intercourse with, the powers of the upper spiritual world, deeper and more intimate than ritual conformity with the established religion of the state, which was the most powerful influence in Socrates' life. His temperament was not of the ecclesiastical, but of the mystical order ; the true centre of his religion was not the temple but the soul.

There are several instances in Plato of Socrates

[1] Life and Letters, by Trevelyan, ch. xiii.
[2] Cp. Plutarch's Moralia : De Genio Socratis, ch. 9.

referring to visions, as a means by which the gods revealed their will.[1] In the "Apology" he declares that discussion with others was a duty imposed on him by Apollo, and he was confirmed in it " by oracles, visions, and in every way in which the will of the divine power was ever signified to anyone."[2] According to the "Crito," he had a vision in the night, while he lay in prison awaiting the day of death, in which there seemed to come to him a lovely and beautiful woman, clad in white garments, who called him, and said: "O Socrates, the third day hence to Phthia shalt thou go."[3]

It was quite clear to Socrates what the vision meant, and the fact appears to have turned out accordingly.

In the "Phædo," we are told that while in prison he busied himself in turning some fables of Æsop into verse, and composed a hymn to Apollo, because of a dream that had often come to him, sometimes appearing in one form and sometimes in another, but always saying the same words:

"Socrates, cultivate the muse."[4]

It does not seem to us that these passages are to be taken as examples of Socrates' ironical and humorous way of speaking, unless, indeed, we are prepared to interpret the "divine voice" also in that way, and treat it as a mere figure of speech, and that is not possible, for it was not for a figure of speech that Socrates was accused and condemned. We are compelled to admit that with all his intellectualist and rationalising

[1] Cp. the Apostle Paul, Acts ch. 22, vv. 17 and 18; Tertullian, "The majority of men, almost learn God from visions"; Inge, "Christian Mysticism," p. 16, "They played a much more important part in the life of the early Church than many ecclesiastical historians are willing to admit."

[2] Apol., 33 c. The sentiment of the "Republic" is against these visions and divinations and soothsayings, see 382 e.

[3] Crito, 44 a, b.   [4] Phædo, 60 d–61 b.

HIS RELIGION

passion, he continued to believe in the direct intercourse of the Deity with the individual through visions and oracles, and that he himself was so constituted as to be the conscious recipient of these supernatural revelations and admonitions. On this side of his nature he recalls George Fox, the founder of the sect called Quakers, who, on one occasion, we are told, fell into a trance which lasted fourteen days, and out of which he came as though he were another man,[1] and who also, at various times in his life, heard voices. Like Socrates with the vision and command about cultivating the muse, Fox also had his doubts and hesitations about the exact meaning of a "voice."[2]

There were, of course, important differences between Socrates and Fox as regards culture and intellectual power and development; but the similarity as regards these peculiar experiences, however we may interpret them, points to a similar religious temperament in the case of Socrates as in that of Fox, a temperament intense in its emotions and convictions, so intense as to demand a personal contact with, and an original experience of, the higher spiritual world, and not to be satisfied with a conventional religion of external rites and forms. Its religion must be a religion of the Inner Light.

It was common accepted belief in the time of Socrates that the gods revealed their will to men by the voices of thunder or of birds in the external world,[3] and according to Xenophon, Socrates was in favour of recourse to divination,[4] in the case of affairs and enterprises whose issue lay outside the sphere of purely human control and knowledge; but the characteristic feature of his own experience was that the gods' will was de-

---

[1] Life of George Fox, by Bickley, p. 23. [2] *Op. cit.*, p. 23.
[3] Xen., Mem., i. 1, 3, and Xen., Apol., 13.
[4] See *e.g.* Mem., iv. 7, 10; cp. iv. 3, 12; i. 4, 15.

clared to him directly and apart from the usual external media. The form which the supernatural communication took with him was most distinctively not dream or vision, but a voice, unaccompanied by any visual appearance. And it must be definitely recognised that in his own apprehension and interpretation of this phenomenon, it was not merely the sudden and emphatic registration in consciousness of the decision of any natural instinct or insight or endowment, but truly and authentically an intervention on the part of Deity through the medium of some sort of spirit or divine sign.

The evidence of both Plato and Xenophon is conclusive on that point. Socrates was convinced that the gods of their own free grace did stoop to guide mortals in their ordinary lives with regard to events of doubtful issue,[1] and he had experience of it in intimations or signs within his own soul.

"You have often heard me say that a sort of divine thing, a spirit agency (daimonion), comes into my experience, the point indeed which Meletus, surely in jest, has made matter of indictment. Ever since my boyhood I have had experience of a certain voice, which, when it comes to me, always forbids me to do something which I am going to do, but never commands me to do anything; it is this which opposes my following a political career."[2]

It was in view of the dictates of this voice that he refrained from preparing any set defence when on trial.[3]

Socrates placed implicit confidence in its admoni-

---

[1] Xen., Apol., 13; Mem., i. 1, 2.
[2] Plato, Apol., 31 d; cp. Theages, 128 d; Euthydemus, 272 e; Phædrus, 242; Repub., 496 c; Euthyphro, 3 b; Apuleius, De Deo Socratis, ch. 19; Xen., Mem., i. 1, §§ 2 and 4; iv. 8, §§ 1 and 5.
[3] Xen., Mem., iv. 8, 5.

HIS RELIGION 251

tions, and, if we may credit Xenophon on this point, he claimed never to have been deceived by it, and never to have misled friends by any advice he gave on the strength of it.[1] It was quite a constant and familiar monitor, and spoke its warning even in affairs of but slight importance.[2] But when Plutarch[3] relates the story that it once saved him from a scuffle with a herd of pigs by warning him to turn back from a certain road, while those who went on got splashed with mud among the hogs, we feel that the supernatural has taken a turn toward the ridiculous, a fate which is apt to befall it in the hands of credulous and enthusiastic devotees.

Another point in regard to the sign mentioned by Plato is that it was of such a peculiar and abnormal nature, that he can claim that to only an odd one, if to any at all, had it ever before been granted,[4] and this ought to prevent us from identifying it simply with the voice of conscience.

We may lay it down at once, if we are to accept our authorities at all, that it was no ordinary and common human faculty or gift. The one feature in regard to it in which Xenophon appears to be in explicit contradiction with Plato, is that while the latter always speaks of it as warning Socrates against doing certain things it is not to his best interest to do, the former states that it also exhorted him to things he should do.[5] But, as Zeller has argued, the contradiction is more apparent than real, for if the divine sign did not forbid him to take any particular course, he could therefrom assume its approbation of it, although one would infer

---

[1] Mem., i. 1, 4.
[2] Plato, Apol., 40 a; 1st Alcibaides, 103 a.
[3] Plutarch's Moralia, De Genio Socratis, ch. 10.
[4] Repub. 496 c; cp. Mem., iv. 3, 12.
[5] Mem., iv. 8, 1; iv. 3, 12; i. 4, 15.

from Xenophon that it definitely enlightened him as to what things he ought to do.

To Socrates, then, the " daimon " or " sign " was no other than the voice of Deity, and was the expression of his sense of direct supernatural communion, without the intervention of external phenomena. God not only speaks through the wind, and fire and thunder, but also through the still small voice within. That being so, this communion is quite independent of time and place, and the usual means of divination. It becomes not a physical, but a spiritual phenomenon, in this respect marking a great advance on the state religion of the time. Moreover, it renders void the theory that the gods' intercourse with men is confined to certain definite ceremonies or sacred occasions. Socrates felt personally and inwardly in touch with the supernatural through all the affairs of his life. It is true religion touched life at many points for the ordinary Greek, but even so, it seemed to be more a statutory, official, hereditary affair, its sanctions being invoked on recognised social occasions, but with Socrates it comes to have an intimate and private value and meaning concerned with everyday life and conduct. The divine makes its presence felt in the mysterious depth of the soul, and this characteristic makes Socrates' experience an important contribution to the development of spiritual religion. Socrates put the most implicit faith in the " sign," and rendered it unquestioning obedience. It was under its direction that he shaped his life in its larger as well as in its lesser aspects. It was guided by its monition that he abstained from the career of politics to which every Athenian of mature years was devoted, and gave himself up to his mission of recalling his fellow-countrymen to the paramount interests of the soul, and of quickening in them a sense of the need of knowledge or science as a condition of the welfare of the individual and society. His was a life sainted and set apart by the express ordination of the Deity, transmitted not through priest or hierarch, but sealed by the immediate impression of the divine call on the spiritual sense.

The Sign

Its Interpretation

It is needless to say that commentators and writers have tried to give a less supernatural explanation of the Socratic " voice."

Whether one can accept Socrates' own belief about it depends largely on one's conception of God and the world.

A religious man might well hold that it was the right interpretation, and that we have no right to go behind the immediate self-consciousness and experience of Socrates in the matter.

And certainly if Christian testimony is to rest secure against criticism on the basis of the soul's experience, as is often claimed to-day, so also must that of Socrates. We have no logical or just right to accept the immediacy of experience in one case, and reject it in another. The man who judges of such things by the accident of the particular religious traditions in which he happens to have been brought up, is at once out of court as an impartial judge of religious phenomena. From a quite different point of view, Joël labours to deprive the " sign " of its extraordinary and peculiar character as an unique religious experience.

" It is more," he says, " than an individual, partly physiological, partly psychological abnormality";[1] and he proceeds to ask if Socrates were so little of a

---

[1] *Op. cit.*, vol. i. p. 71.

philosopher as to bring such a well-attested phenomenon among the mysteries of the purely personal.[1]

That representation of the case he holds to be due to Xenophon's pronounced supernatural leanings.

"The path from divination in general to the 'sign' (divinity) of Socrates is no private footpath for him alone; it is the path of the Socratic philosophy in its general significance, the path of the spiritual progress of humanity from externality to inwardness, from superstitious awe of the alien Power of Fate, to the individual's sense of *personal responsibility*."[2]

No doubt the Socratic "voice," when reflected on, means the change from externality to inwardness, and no doubt all that enters into its great value for humanity in its spiritual progress, but it is going against the simple facts, as they appear to us, to denude the phenomenon of its private and mystical element.

It is Joël's theory that to Socrates man was an intellectual, the "knowing," being; but that over and above this element there remained an insoluble residuum, "which made itself felt, in the exercise of the faculty of choice as individual tact, as conscience, as intuition, as an unerring instinct and feeling for the intellectual or moral occasion. This undefined psychical power, whose working Socrates must have recognised, but which he could not explain, this strange inner faculty, he called 'a divinity' ($\delta\alpha\iota\mu\acute{o}\nu\iota o\nu$). It was the revenge of the emotional part of the soul (Aristotle) that it allowed itself to be pushed by this rationalist into the furthest distant corner of his being, and then from that obscurity exercised so decisive an influence upon him."[3]

Now from a general consideration of Socrates' use of religious language, it is by no means impossible that

---

[1] Joël, *op. cit.*, p. 71.　　[2] *Ibid.*, i. p. 73.
[3] *Ibid.*, i. p. 75.

he should use the term divinity in a loose, popular way, or "ironically," and signify by it whatever was inexplicable and *outré* in his experience, but, if we are right in what we have said, it was not so in this case. Nor can it be maintained on the evidence that he gave the name "divinity" to what he himself believed to be a natural faculty present, more or less, in men generally, and rightly definable as mere "tact" or "intuition," or an unerring instinct for the occasion—the *savoir faire* of a diplomatist, who knows just the right thing to do without being able to give detailed reasons for its rightness.

Socrates was profoundly convinced of the limitations of human knowledge in comparison with the field of human action; he was deeply conscious of the mystery which, for man, wraps the world and the issue of human conduct. "The God alone is wise, and his oracle declares human wisdom to be worth little or nothing, employing the name of Socrates as an example. He is the wisest of men who, like Socrates, knows well that he is in truth worthless so far as wisdom is concerned. The really disgraceful ignorance is to think that you know what you really do not know."[1] Hence his profound sense of that dependence upon God in which Schleiermacher found the eternal essence of religion.

The opinion of the great German historian of Greek philosophy, Zeller, on the Socratic "voice" is very much the same as that of Joêl. He calls it an "inner oracle"[2] and describes it as "a premonitory *sense* [*vorgefühl*] of the character of certain actions as advantageous or injurious; it is the inner voice of personal tact which without reflection becomes the motive of action to the faithful and incorruptible observer of the

[1] Plato, Apol., 23 a, 29 b.
[2] Geschichte d. Griechischen Philosophie, vol. ii. p. 30.

world of human life." It is an inner voice to be explained partly from the wide knowledge of life and acute insight of the Attic sage and partly from this self-knowledge and consciousness of what was appropriate to his own character. Its psychical origin, however, was not at the moment recognised by Socrates, and so, in accordance with the spirit of the time, he transformed it into an immediate divine revelation.[1]

Zeller distinguishes it from the voice of conscience,[2] which has to do with the moral tone of actions, not with their consequences in detail, and he also distinguishes it from the divine call to the philosophic life, which Socrates always attributes to "the god."[3] To our mind, however, a reference to the passages in the "Apology," where Socrates speaks of his call to be a spiritual prophet to Athens suggests a very close connexion between "the god" at whose behest he enters on his mission, and the "voice" which restrains him from a political life, participation in which would have exposed him to antipathies which would soon have terminated his higher work; and Piat is, in our view, nearer to the feelings in Socrates' mind when he identifies the "voice" with the "god."[4] Neither can we follow Zeller when he says that the voice betokens the same withdrawal of the deepening spirit into itself—the same wrestling with an idea not brought to full consciousness, as on other occasions plunged Socrates into trance-like meditation.[5] It was the very lack of the sense of personal activity which made the voice seem to come from a higher source, as in the experience of other mystics.[6]

[1] Zeller, *op. cit.*, p. 23. [2] Cp. Piat, Socrate, p. 219.
[3] Apol., 29 d, 30 a, 31 d; Theætetus, 150 c, f; Rep., 496 c.
[4] Piat, Socrate, p. 211. [5] Zeller, *op. cit.*, p. 34.
[6] See Underhill, Mysticism, pp. 78, 79.

Fouillée[1] is so far nearer the subjective facts when he likens the voice to reminiscence and intuition, emphasizing the moment of spontaneity in the total mental state, and comparing it to the unusually heightened and clarified state of consciousness which love produces. One may call it an "inspiration." The voice for Socrates was certainly no idea to be elucidated or problem to be solved, it was an impression to be received. Fouillée in his further characterisation of it goes on to say that the hearing of it as a voice must be due to hallucination.[2] The divinity must not be construed as a positive and distinct being.[3] "It is only a vague, interior voice, a sign, a presentiment, something indefinable, which is attributed to a divine cause, but without personifying this cause into a divinity in the literal sense of the words."[4] Socrates himself never defined it clearly, nor attributed it to any particular god,[5] which may be true enough, seeing that Socrates was altogether vague about the persons of the Godhead generally, but we do not think there is any room for doubt that Socrates believed it to be an objective voice within him uttering God's will.

Piat says: "For him it was the word of the great God, God invisible, omnipotent, who made and governs the world." "It was the inward personal expression which the Providence of the world took for Socrates."[6]

It is going beyond the meagre data to assign thus definitely the God to whom Socrates referred the voice, and to distinguish Him so sharply from the other gods of mythology. We are not inclined, in view of our previous discussion, to agree that Socrates attributed the divine sign directly to the Supreme Deity; on the

[1] La Philosophie de Socrate, vol. ii. pp. 309-14.
[2] Ibid., p. 313.   [3] Ibid., p. 314.   [4] Ibid., p. 314.
[5] Ibid., p. 314.   [6] Piat, Socrate, p. 220.

whole, it is likelier that at any rate he would conceive God to speak through some intermediate spirit or guardian deity. But it must be admitted that Socrates did not, so far as our data go, critically analyse the experience he had, and was content with believing it a divine sign, without trying to identify its exact source.

Piat's verdict upon the phenomenon as a whole is expressed with a reserve that admirably suits the incomplete state of our present knowledge. He is inclined to regard it as a psychical hallucination, but recognises that it would be rash to dogmatise. "If God is anything personal, if He is nearer to us than we to ourselves—and the contrary is far from demonstrated—why should He not have had mysterious conversations which the ears of the soul alone can hear?"[1]

It is simply a cult of mediocrity, or a prejudice of naturalism, to lump abnormal experiences like those of Socrates with psychopathic phenomena, as is sometimes done. It is not far from a conceit of the commonplace to cite some of the greatest religious personalities of history, men whose influence over average humanity has been extraordinary and far reaching, as the subjects of mental disease, because their experience has not been in accordance with ordinary rule.[2] Average humanity is not in possession and use of every human faculty and sense. It may be only the child in the womb, waiting to be born into worlds beyond its present ken, through the opening of senses yet closed; and here and there may appear a soul of finer endowment, in whom one of these senses is to be found, though still imperfect. There is nothing more natural on strict evolutionary principles than that man's spiritual sense may undergo spontaneous variations in the case of certain members of the race, bringing them into touch,

[1] Socrate, p. 221.
[2] Cp. Underhill, Mysticism, pp. 61–75.

in special ways, with the unseen environment of the soul. And Socrates may well have been one of these elect and privileged spirits, in whom a certain chord is keyed to vibrate to the voice of God, and to become vocal with His message however transmitted.

One may, of course, look to the modern theory of the subliminal self to afford the explanation of the peculiar features of the "daimon" of Socrates, but in the meantime that would only be seeking the explanation of the obscure in the mysterious. That theory can throw no illumination on our psychological problem. To have recourse to it would be like accounting for a light by the dark lantern in which it burns.

The subliminal self, says Professor James, " contains, *e.g.*, such things as all our momentarily inactive memories, and it harbours the springs of all our obscurely motived passions, impulses, likes, dislikes, and prejudices. Our intuitions, hypotheses, fancies, superstitions, persuasions, convictions, and, in general, all our non-rational operations, come from it. It is the source of our dreams, and apparently they may return to it. In it arise whatever mystical experiences we may have, and our automatisms, sensory or motor; our life in hypnotic and 'hypnoid' conditions, if we are subjects to such conditions; our delusions, fixed ideas, and hysterical accidents, if we are hysteric subjects; our supra-normal cognitions, if such there be, if we are telepathic subjects. It is also the fountain-head of much that feeds our religion. In persons deep in the religious life, as we have now abundantly seen—and this is my conclusion—the door into this region seems unusually wide open; at any rate, experiences making their entrance through that door have had emphatic influence in shaping religious history."[1]

But the region in which certain phenomena lie does

[1] Varieties of Religious Experience, pp. 483, 484.

not explain these phenomena and their varying characters, nor does it determine their worth and value. Moreover, to take the bull by the horns, what conceivable mental phenomenon does not enter through the subliminal consciousness into our experience, and carry upon it some colour of the medium through which it has come? There is not much help in this hypothesis.

The wisest plan, we repeat, seems to be to rest where Socrates himself rested. He admitted its mysteriousness, and defined it in terms of his immediate sense of its character and value as a "something divine." Here at any rate we cannot go further without grave risk of going astray. In a world in which, as Carlyle insisted, everything is in the last analysis supernatural, and, as Mr, Chesterton has said, the most ordinary thing miraculous, it appears to us like straining at a gnat while we swallow a camel, to deny that in his peculiar experience of the sign Socrates could be in immediate and peculiar touch with the divine agencies whose activity sustains all that has life and being, and out of whose consciousness our own has been hewn.

The only difference between such experiences and those which we regard as normal and accept without question, is merely one of frequency and value, and not of inherent credibility. The history of the Christian religion has furnished numbers of parallels to the Socratic voice. Many of them will hardly stand criticism, and are due to hallucination, but that is no ground for discrediting their authenticity in the case of men of admittedly high or concentrated religious sensibility. No amount of spurious imitative experience affects those cases where the condition of genuine and original experience existed.

There is the voice at Christ's baptism. There is Saul on the way to Damascus hearing a voice from heaven, so real to him, apart altogether from the question of his interpretation of it, that it revolutionises his life. There is St. Augustine in the garden hearing the distinct command, "Tolle et lege." John Bunyan, busy with a game of cat on Sunday, all at once hears the distinct question as from above, "Wilt thou leave thy sins and go to heaven, or have thy sins and go to hell?" George Fox, the founder of the society called Quakers, heard "voices" on various occasions.[1]

One must admit the difficulty in distinguishing between the cases where nerve conditions or psychical conditions, as, *e.g.*, of predisposition and expectation, will themselves account for the hearing of these voices; the subjective history of the individual will, in a proportion of the cases, afford sufficient explanation, and it is impossible to set up any infallible criterion. The subject is exceedingly obscure and delicate. But unless we are prepared to characterise as illusory and mistaken the ordinary exercises of the religious man, wherein he claims to have direct communion with the transcendent Deity, we see no logical and consistent ground for scepticism in regard to all phenomena of the nature of the divine sign of Socrates.

And now we turn to indicate the general significance of this inner experience of Socrates in the history of man's spiritual progress. Athenian comedy and the drama of Euripides, as well as the teaching of the philosophers and Sophists, nearly contemporary with Socrates, show that the traditional and official religion was breaking down at the touch of reflection; and the cult of the Mysteries points to the need that was being felt in Greece for a more individual and personal religion to satisfy the needs of the soul. In these respects Socrates seems to mirror the age. The "Divine Voice" represents in the religious sphere that for which the doctrine of Reason stands in the sphere of Truth and

[1] See, *e.g.*, Life by Bickley, pp. 14, 23, 26, 29, 68, 283.

social relationships, viz., the principle of inwardness and the right of individuality, though we do not claim that Socrates rose to the abstract conception of such principle and right. It signifies a private and personal communion of God with, or relation of God to, the individual soul, and that not through any external state-established rites and ceremonies, but spiritually and directly. It is God in the soul, God making His grace felt and His will known, inwardly to the individual in an unmistakable way. Constituting, as it does, a break away from the established religion, it is not altogether strange that the orthodox Athenian should regard it as a dangerous innovation. It struck him as an attempt at getting *entrée* to the divine presence otherwise than by the recognised statutory way. In that respect it was claiming divine respect for the individual as such and apart from state sanctions. There was no saying to what nonconformities it might lead, if the private citizen once got free of the grip of the state upon his religious experiences. It would certainly tend to disturb the old position of equilibrium between the individual and society when the former was entirely relative or subordinate to the latter. As Professor Joël has put it, emphasizing, as is the purpose of his work, the Cynic features of the picture of Socrates which has come down to us: "The peculiar cult of the divine voice is Cynic; it typifies the apotheosis of subjectivity; Socrates made the Cynic a subjectivist. It was subjectivity that he proclaimed.[1] . . . If there is anything historical in the divine sign at all it affirms that to a man of strong individual instincts like Socrates the voice of one's own being, wonderfully strange and inexplicable, yet seemed worthy of reverence."[2]

We must not, however, be supposed to suggest that Socrates proclaimed independence as a principle, either

[1] *Op. cit.*, vol. II. pt. ii. p. 961.   [2] *Ibid.*

in society or religion, for he had a very deep reverence for duly constituted authority, and spoke as if the law of the land were always to be taken as the guide of conduct and the norm of religion. His attitude was analogous to that of St. Paul to the Law and the Prophets and Jewish religion. He frequented the synagogues, accepted and believed the Old Testament, yet he inculcated a higher and more spiritual and catholic principle. The old loyalties remained, while he proclaimed a new idea.[1]

He was not conscious, really, of the full meaning and tendency of the forces which found expression through his personality; he was instrument as much as agent in the great spiritual movement which his life and work symbolised; he was building larger than he knew, as it is the prerogative of the genius and the inspired man to do. He is an illustration of Emerson's aphorism that "Character teaches above the will." For with all his teaching about conformity to law, the principle of individuality and independence was always breaking out in him through character. His whole personality in its various experiences and activities was of itself a direct challenge to authority in thought, politics, and religion. It was not so much that he advocated independence, but that he *was* independent. Men looking at him could not fail to see the principle embodied and be influenced by it either in the direction of approval or opposition. He was a germinal personality, rooted in the old, and bursting into flower and fruit which carries the seeds of the new.

There is one further question of great interest with regard to Socrates as a religious man, to which, in conclusion, we would refer. Did the inwardness of his religious views and the spirituality of his temperament lead him into association with any of the contemporary

[1] See Acts xxiv. 11-16; Romans iii. 21, 22, 28; Galatians *passim*.

societies and cults which existed to meet just these intenser personal needs of the soul which he felt?

Sorel, a French writer, has expressed the opinion that Socrates posed as a hierophant and sacred teacher, adducing as the ground of his views the representation given by Aristophanes in the "Clouds," where Socrates is presented as the chief priest of a little semi-religious, semi-scientific community, which, badly housed, unwashed, and caring nothing for the amenities or elegances of ordinary life, devotes itself to searching into the mysteries of heaven and earth, and to the cultivation of a dangerous dialectic.[1] The candidate for admission to the brotherhood has to undergo certain rites of initiation suggested in Aristophanes' caricature, where Strepsiades is admitted as a student to the Notion-den.

Professor A. E. Taylor[2] has argued for a similar view. He believes Socrates to have been one of a little band of Pythagoreans leading an ascetic life, engaging in mystic rites, and constituting a small dissenting community or sect in the Athenian state. The conception of Socrates as the leading spirit of such an esoteric circle, as broadly sketched in the "Clouds," might perhaps be supported from Xenophon's "Banquet," where Hermogenes, one of the Socratic elect, speaks of his enjoyment of a more intimate intercourse with the gods, and of especial signs of their grace, similar to those vouchsafed to Socrates himself. He does not require to have recourse to oracles, for the gods are so interested in him as never to lose him from view night or day; and knowing all things, as they do, they advise and guide him by sending to him as their messengers, voices, dreams, and auguries, thus enlightening him as to what he ought and ought not to do.[3] To this, how-

---

[1] Sorel, Le Procès de Socrate, p. 137.
[2] Varia Socratica, 1st series, pp. 17 ff, 148.
[3] Xenophon, Banquet, ch. iv. § 47.

ever, Socrates replies—in a rather detached way, and not as one who has revealed this more intimate converse with the gods to Hermogenes—that he finds nothing incredible in it, and that he learns with pleasure by what services Hermogenes binds his friends to him—a somewhat irrelevant consideration.

In this connexion one may be permitted to quote, for what it is worth, a tradition preserved in Diogenes Laertius, regarding the meeting of Socrates and Xenophon, which has the ring of the religious master-and-disciple relation about it. Xenophon, a young man, meeting Socrates, asks him: "Where is the market of life?" "Where does one mould men to virtue?" interprets Socrates. "Follow me, and I will teach you."

Such evidence, however, from Aristophanes and Xenophon is too ambiguous, precarious, and slender to be much of a support to the theory of Socrates we are considering, and it has to stand against the force of the plain meaning of Socrates' statement in the "Apology": "I have no regular disciples, but if anyone likes to come to hear me while I am pursuing my mission (of cross-examination), whether he be young or old, he may freely come."[1]

This denial, excluding as it does the suggestion that Socrates drew to himself a band of religious inquirers, who in any way formed what could be called a cult, on the basis of membership ratified by a solemn ritual and an esoteric doctrine, together with the absence of all reference to such a society in the Trial, leads us again to the conclusion that, without any definite or open break with, or repudiation of, the official religion in vogue, Socrates found it possible to cultivate and nourish that more spiritual conception of true religion which was the distinctive thing about him.

[1] Plato, Apol., 33 a.

(g) The Soul and the Hereafter

It has already been pointed out that in Socrates' view the true dignity and superlative excellence of man lies in the soul, the soul as the seat of that Reason and Intelligence which link man with Deity. It is the soul and not the body which constitutes the real self,[1] and is the thing of paramount importance. The body is merely its instrument and subordinate, there to carry out its dictates and commands.[2] He held, so we have maintained, that man's full and perfect life was to be realised, not by annihilating all bodily desires and impulses, but by regulating them and giving them their proper place, which is a secondary one, in life's rational and spiritual order. The body when kept in good condition will prove to be instrumental to the soul's purposes, and will not interfere with its apprehensions and functions, as will happen if it be neglected or abused.

At the same time the difference between the soul and the body is strongly emphasized, and it is in virtue of the former that man transcends the rest of the animal creation, and is brought into communion with Deity. It is because of it that man can rise to the height of knowing and adoring the gods,[3] for it makes him kin with them. The soul partakes in the Divine;[4] it resembles the Divine in its faculty of intelligence, memory, and foresight.[5] Hence the reverence in which Socrates always held it, and his assertion that to neglect it and its interests is of all follies the most foolish. "I do nothing but go about persuading you all, old and young alike, not to take thought

---

[1] 1st Alcibiades, 130 C. Cp. Plato, Apol., 30 a.
[2] 1st Alcibiades, 130 C. Cp. Mem., i. 4.   [3] Mem., i. 3.
[4] Mem., i. 4. Cp. Phædrus, 253 a.
[5] Mem., iv. 3. Cp. Phædrus, 246.

for your bodies and property, but first and foremost to care about the greatest improvement of the soul."[1]

The soul again is the cause of life and motion and revival in the body; it is that principle in virtue of which anything lives; its very nature is to produce life and movement.[2] And this characteristic is, in the "Phaedo," made the basis of one of the arguments for the soul's immortality.[3]

It is not surprising that with his lofty view of the soul, its dignity, its divinity, its inherent vitality, Socrates should be predisposed to the belief in its immortality. And Fouillée argues that he held that belief,[4] a view which could be profusely supported if it were permissible to attribute the doctrines of the "Phædo" and "Phædrus" and "Republic" to the historical Socrates. But those who are prepared to do so will have on their hands the task of reconciling the conviction of immortality which these dialogues manifest with the less committal attitude of those other and earlier dialogues which are usually admitted to be more direct and objective in their portraiture, the "Apology" and "Crito." All we can gather from *them* is that Socrates entertained at the best good hope of immortality, while clearly conscious that the subject was one which did not admit of positive proof and reasoned knowledge.

His attitude towards the hereafter is one of agnosticism. He does not know what happens subsequent to death, but he is an optimist, and through that final mystery his faith shines radiant and beautiful. Whatever death brings he is convinced that it cannot be an

[1] Plato, Apol., 30 a.
[2] Mem., iv. 3. Cp. Phædo, 105 d; Cratylus, 399, d, e.
[3] Cp. argument in Cratylus, 245 C.
[4] La Philosophie de Socrate, ii. p. 157.

evil, otherwise the divine voice would have warned him to avoid it. " There is great reason to hope that death is a good."[1] Death came before Socrates in two possible forms, either of which he was prepared to defend as being a happier state than life on earth.

(a) It may be a dreamless sleep that knows no waking, a complete cessation of consciousness.[2] Even so it will be a " wonderful gain,"[3] for there are few days and nights of life probably better or more pleasant than dreamless slumber—an impressive statement, which seems to point to a deep vein of melancholy in Socrates (or in Plato), and rather strange on the lips of one who held that with all his restraints and self-denials he had lived a life which for sheer happiness he would not exchange with the life of any other man. Can it be that it was the verdict of reflection, in which the many lights and shadows of experience blended into grey, as one looked back at them for a moment in the presence of the last mystery ? It was at any rate a very characteristically Greek sentiment. "Such death, says Socrates, I call gain."[4]

On the other hand, " if what is said is true, and death is but a 'covered way,' a journey to another place where the dead abide, what, O Judges, could be a greater good than that?[5] If one will meet there with just judges, with Minos and Rhadamanthus," as it is said, " with Æacus and Triptolemus, and all the other divine spirits who were good in their life here, then the journey will be a trifle ; and to associate with Musæus and Hesiod and Homer, what price would you put on that ? I am ready to die again and again if that is true."[6] What a time he will be able to have there meeting Palamedes and Ajax and Telamon, and all who have

[1] Plato, Apol., 40 c. [2] Apol., 40 d. [3] 40 d.
[4] Ibid., 40 E. [5] Ibid., 40 E. [6] Apol., 41 a.

died an unjust death, comparing his sufferings with theirs. Above all, won't he be able to question and cross-examine the great and wise of old like Odysseus, and all the other men and women. What boundless happiness! And they won't be able to kill him there, for all are beyond the power of death, if what is said is true!"[1]

"Wherefore, O Judges, be of good cheer about death, and know of a certainty that no evil can happen to a good man either in life or after death, nor are his affairs neglected by the gods."[2] As he had said on another occasion: "I believe that the gods are our guardians, and that we are a possession of the gods." "And now it is time to depart, I to die, ye to live; but which of us goes to the better lot is hidden from all but God." These are the concluding words of Plato's "Apology," and surely they breathe the very spirit of the Socrates we have learned to know and admire and love.

Where he does not know, and cannot know, he falls back upon a faith and trust in God, which enabled him to confront every mystery of life and death with a triumphant resignation, confidence, and joy. Be it the sleep that knows no waking, or the waking that knows no sleep, it is equally for the best, for it is all ordered by Him in whose hands we all are.

We venture to surmise that you will search the records of humanity in vain for a single nobler example of spiritual faith in God and trust for the unseen. In the glimpse which he permits himself of a possible heaven beyond, radiant with his superlative humour, too exquisite to be irreverent, there is not a touch or suggestion of that sensual and corpulent grossness which has too often disfigured Christian symbolism and anticipation; nothing of that dogmatism which, in the case of Christian piety, has sometimes disturbed

[1] 41 b, c.   [2] 41 c.

the fullness of trust in God's will, and almost presumed to dictate the conditions of His wise appointment; there is nothing of that terrible shadow of endless punishment, the very thought of which makes one shudder with the fear that there may be a God.

Contrast with Socrates' entire submission to God's will these outbursts of a well-known Christian preacher, and a great Christian poet, which are only saved from startling impiety by their evident sincerity and earnestness:

"I do declare it seems to me that the world had better be wiped out altogether, incontinently, unless there is a world beyond, where a man shall use the force which here he has made his own." [1]

> "Truly there needs another life to come!
> If this be all—(I must tell Festus that)
> And other life awaits us not—for one
> I say, 'tis a poor cheat, a stupid bungle,
> A wretched failure. I for one protest
> Against it, and I hurl it back with scorn." [2]

We do not think that the average experience of humanity will confirm such a tragic estimate of the present world, nor in any case is it necessarily the only expedient, to bring in a new world to redress the balance of the old. What God has made is good, and if what man has made is so very bad, he must remake and make better. If we will only all act according to the knowledge we have and the right we discern, the sorrow and suffering of life will melt like snow and happiness will blossom forth like summer. And we will look as God once looked upon this mysterious, wonderful, miraculous phantasm we call the world, and see that it is good. And the better it is, doubtless the more of it we

---
[1] Dr. MacLaren of Manchester.
[2] Browning, Paracelsus.

shall want, and not suffering but happiness will doubtless then be made the ground of a demand for immortality. Man must desire, we cannot say whether God must grant. But either way life seems great enough and high enough for enterprise, devotion, and praise.

In some respects the theology of Socrates is different from the Christian, and can never supplant it, because it represents the transition from a lower stage of religious development than does New Testament theology; but these are subordinate points, and when one turns to consider what it was in and for Socrates, one sees it as the light, the inspiration, and the strength of a truly noble and independent spiritual life, a life lived always for the higher as he understood it and saw it. It was the theology of a man who was of the company of the great, and whose thought, conduct, and influence co-operated in leading men to better things; a man whose spirit and aspiration might be finely expressed in the words of Wordsworth :

> " Give unto me made lowly wise
> The spirit of self-sacrifice;
> The confidence of reason give ;
> And in the light of truth thy bondman let me live."

CHAPTER XI

THE "CLOUDS" OF ARISTOPHANES

"TRUTH has superior rights," says Amiel. "The world must adapt itself to Truth not Truth to the world." That is the conviction which has kept the thinker, the prophet, and the reformer true to their own idea in all ages of the world's history. They have had the vision of the Eternal Idea high and clear like the sun above the fluctuating seas and the confused moving phantasmagorias of time and sense. They have lived by its illumination and felt its irresistible power, and they have taken their own soul to be God's prophecy of the world. In Maeterlinck's phrase, they have not so much possessed the Truth as been possessed by it.

Socrates was one of the comparatively few who have so been possessed by the vision of the True and the Good as to become partakers of Fate and makers of History.

The man, however, who lives by the future for the future is always to some extent at war with the past, and unpopular in the present. Often he hardly understands himself, and others do not understand him at all or misunderstand. Emerson has gone the length of asserting that "to be great is to be misunderstood." That certainly was the lot of Socrates. In his case it was all the more inevitable in that not only had he a clearer and purer soul than the average Athenian citizen, but he was much cleverer and more brilliant. And if there is anything more hateful than spiritual genius to the conservative bourgeoisie, it is intellectual cleverness.

Socrates played and flashed about the comparatively dull, heavy-eyed commonalty of his day like a rapid scimitar, threatening a dangerous cut anywhere, which it could not be alert and quick enough to parry. A reformer is grievous, but a clever reformer, having an intellect tipped with irony, is scarcely tolerable in any society.

"I am the gadfly," Plato makes him say in the "Apology," "which God has given the state, and am always fastening on you, arousing, persuading, and reproaching you."

He performed the function with a persistence and importunity which makes us wonder why he was not brought to his punishment at an earlier age than something over seventy years.

Socrates himself was convinced, according to Plato, that for such a long apostolate in the service of Truth and public righteousness and the higher life as he was permitted to exercise, he had to thank the fact that he had kept out of party politics, for no one would have been allowed to live who, amid the embroilments of a public career, struggled against iniquities in conduct and illegalities in procedure, on behalf of the cause of Justice, as he had felt himself compelled to do.[1]

As it was, a quarter of a century before his trial he had become a marked man at Athens, the butt of various comic poets,[2] especially the greatest of them, Aristophanes. These exponents of public opinion, who could be experts in playing to the gallery, would introduce him on the stage in the character of a man engaged

---
[1] Apology, 31 E, 32 A.
[2] On the attitude of Comedy to Philosophy, see Couat's Aristophane, ch. vii.

18

in constant amours with young men.[1] Doubtless the travesty arose from the fact that it was among young men that Socrates won his most ardent pupils and admirers, and prejudice may have been only too quick to interpret these relations of a "free-thinker" in accordance with practices common among Athenians at that time. Anybody who recollects the gross stories which became current in Rome in regard to the practices of the Christians in their religious assemblies, will realise to what lengths slander and misrepresentation can go, where heretics are involved. Perhaps, too, it was one of the "hits" of comic perversity thus to work up the circumstance that Socrates was in the habit of speaking of himself as a midwife, whose profession was to deliver young men of the ideas they had conceived.

Anyhow, we have seen how far from truth such a representation is,[2] for had not Socrates made it part of his mission to pour a finer and purer wine into the unclean bottles? The adulterated vintage, however, brought the laugh—and the laugh's the thing in Athenian comedy.

Aristophanes, the greatest of Greek comic writers, made Socrates the subject of his " Clouds," a play first produced in 423 B.C. There is no denying that the work is in its farcical way very clever and irresistibly funny, and one is sure that Socrates himself must have guffawed heartily over it, though, in accordance with the genius of Greek comedy, it was very crude and rough characterisation. Aristophanes cannot have intended it for anything but farcical banter, while as for the crowd that hated Socrates they would enjoy it after their own kind.

[1] See Life of Isocrates in " Oratores Attici," edited by Müller and Hunziker, vol. ii. p. 481.
[2] See p. 92 ff.

Socrates' life-mission began after it was borne in on him that the proper interest of mankind is man, that it would be a waste of time to try to solve the riddle of the universe before we have solved the riddle of ourselves, and that the soul is the key to the world. Then he was still comparatively young, but Aristophanes presents him in 423 B.C., when over forty-six years of age, as still burrowing into things beneath the earth and above the earth—a *verfluchtes dumpfes Mauerloch*, as Faust called himself—gnawing away at geometry, geography, and astronomy in the stuffy atmosphere of his "Notion-den."

Indeed one can adduce various features of the representation which effectually dispose of it as anything more than a mirror of the contorted Socrates of the popular and orthodox mind, although some modern writers, like Sorel,[1] and Professor A. E. Taylor have sought to vindicate it, as, in important respects, a reliable source of information, an authority indeed of the first importance, on Socrates. In the "Clouds," Socrates appears as devoted to the same pursuits as that class of teachers of science and rhetoric which is known as the Sophists. He comes before us as an arch-Sophist. Now, as a matter of fact, he was popularly regarded as belonging to that class, as not only the "Clouds" shows, but also at a later day a reference to him by Æschines, the orator, as "Socrates, the Sophist."[2] The identification is, in some points, very inaccurate and unjust; Socrates had considerable respect for the greater Sophists, like Prodicus and Gorgias and Hippias; he thinks they are justified in charging fees for their instruction; and though some of them are engaged in the teaching of science, a subject

[1] Le Procès de Socrate.
[2] Against Timarchus, § 71 (345 B.C.). For similarities between Socrates and Sophists, see Zeller, *op. cit.*, p. 375 (edit. 1844).

he himself has abandoned, he does not on that account despise them and their work.[1] But, taking the Sophist class as a whole, Socrates, having weighed them in balances of his own dialectic, found them sadly wanting; they were of those whose knowledge was unexamined, and their aims shallow, and they included men who, teaching rhetoric for rhetoric's sake, could only earn Socrates' contempt, as well as the old-fashioned Athenian's suspicion.

Nevertheless the confusion was not without some sound justification. Socrates had at least this in common with a class who differed very much among themselves, that he belonged to the "new school," or had deep sympathies with it; that is to say, to the school of the intellectualists, the men of ideas. However far removed from many of them in sentiment and spirit, he rowed in the same galley with them. Now the intellectualist is very apt to appear as an a-moralist, or an anti-moralist, as one may judge from the opinions held by the bulk of respectable members of society to-day about Bernard Shaw or H. G. Wells, and men of that type. Shaw seems to turn the world of sentiment and ideas topsy-turvy by his cleverness and dialectical skill. He has the agility of an acrobat, and we notice that he can prove anything he likes, however apparently ridiculous and opposed to our established notions. And our bourgeosie would feel little hesitation in describing his drama and social propaganda as an attempt to make the worse appear the better reason, and in predicting, as its inevitable consequence, the corruption of the youth tainted thereby. Many regard him as counsel-in-chief to the devil, a man of mephistophelian dexterity and mephistophelian intention. And yet the truth is that he is a man puritanically fastidious in temperament and pro-

[1] Plato, Apol., § 19, c, e.

foundly moral in aim. His crime is ideas. It was in a similar light Socrates appeared to Athenian orthodoxy, and Aristophanes hit off and stereotyped in laughter for all future generations the popular view—a view in which his character and pursuits were traduced, travestied, and misrepresented. We are not at all sure that in this Aristophanes' motive was an inimical one. The laughter of the play seems to us to be boisterous, good-natured laughter all through. The Socrates of the "Clouds" is a far-away, other-worldly, erratic, fanciful, and harmless creature. There is nothing in the play which suggests that its author really believed Socrates to be the sketch he painted, any more than he believed Zeus, Heracles, and Dionysus to be the rakes and bon-vivants he put on the stage. To the hearers of any critical acumen and any knowledge of Socrates, the play would at every turn suggest the absurdities of these popular conceptions of the great Athenian which it set forth, and end by drowning the whole business, with the furore and fuss it was creating, in a cascade of irrepressible farce. We are tempted to ask, How could anyone treat this eccentric heretic and his notorious notion-hunting with elephantine gravity and seriousness, after seeing the "Clouds," where the worst heresies and charges against him are brought out as a piece of inimitable fun, at which people have to laugh and laugh again, even in spite of themselves. What other tendency could the play have, if it was to be successful comedy, and it *is* successful comedy, than to make Socrates and his pursuits a subject of amusement instead of hatred? Aristophanes saw the humorous side of Socrates, and of the new movement about him; he also saw the humorous side of the flutter in the orthodox dove-cotes, and hence the "Clouds" as we have it.

Irresistible fun is poked at his irrepressible dialectical

zeal and subtlety, at his tireless, but to others very tiring, accuracy in the use of words, and at his method of logical division. It is all thin air, pedantic futility, hair-splitting as an art of wasting time and trying patience.[1] Aristophanes possibly enough agreed with the man in the street in this verdict, but it is not necessary for a humorist to be the enemy of an enthusiastic philosopher in order to find him a bore and solemn trifler.

Apart from the question of motive, very different opinions have been taken of the objective truth and fidelity of the " Clouds " as portraiture. Sorel regards it as, on the whole, justified; Fouillée says of it that it is "neither faithful witness nor sincere criticism."[2] We would say that it is about as far from faithful witness as the North Pole from the South, that in parts Aristophanes has his heart in the criticism, but that, taken as a whole, the key to it is to be found in the dictum of Couat about Athenian comedy in general, that "it is from the popular point of view that it observes life."[3] But we are by no means of the opinion that one is justified in assuming that Aristophanes in the " Clouds " endorses and approves the popular point of view. As it stands, the production is ninety per cent. of pure caricature.

Socrates is presented as the high-priest of a sceptical scientific coterie; he initiates his new pupil, Strepsiades, into the circle, using a pallet-bed,[4] in place of the sacred tripod on which the victim of sacrifice was wont to be placed, so that the stupid old rustic cries out in terror lest he is going to be offered up; in the meanwhile

---

[1] See, *e.g.*, ll. 145 ff., 225 ff., 740, &c. Cp. the Syracusan's opinion of it all in Xenophon's Banquet, ch. 6.
[2] La Philosophie de Socrate, ii. p. 354.
[3] Couat, Aristophane, p. 360.
[4] ll. 254 ff.

his upper garment is quietly spirited away[1] and confiscated to the needs of the school, a touch which surely, by its very ridiculousness as applied to Socrates, would, while sending the audience into fits of laughter, make them feel that they were not getting serious truth in this play, but a good hale joke. Again Socrates is dexterous enough to steal some meat from the table of the wrestling school by means of a pair of compasses made from a skewer, with which he is supposed to be making geometrical diagrams.[2] Deliberate nonsense, of course, but the echo of a question which must often have been asked: How does Socrates manage to live?

It is also suggested that he takes pay[3] for the lessons he gives both in the art of debate, which means a strife for triumph more than truth, and in scientific subjects like geometry, astronomy, geology, and geography, all comprised in the curriculum of his dingy den. There is here an identification of him with the Sophists, which is further hinted at when it is stated that his gods the Clouds, nourish a lot of Sophists, diviners of Thurii, medicine-men, &c., with their flowing locks and fingers adorned with rings.[4]

Now Socrates at his trial could emphatically declare that he never had disciples or pupils in the regular sense of the word, never took any fees,[5] since he did not profess to be a teacher[6] or anything more than an inquirer, and did not prosecute research in these sciences.[7]

Indeed, in the course of his defence, as set forth by

[1] ll. 499, 1498.
[2] ll. 175 ff. Cp. Eupolis, Fr. 361, by whom he is made to steal a wine jar when out dining.
[3] ll. 98, 99.
[4] ll. 331 ff.
[5] Plato, Apol., 19 d, e; cp. Mem., i. 6; Diogenes Laertius, ii. 5, 27.
[6] Plato, Apol., *loc. cit.*
[7] *Op. cit.*, 19 c.

Plato, he definitely refers to the "Clouds," and the picture there given of him as engrossed in scientific subjects, only to deny that he has given himself to such studies, and to challenge any to say that they have heard him discussing the matters alluded to in the "Clouds."[1] Aristophanes himself indicates how seriously these occupations of the Socratics in their den, and his own caricature of them are to be taken, by the scene he presents of them at work, when Strepsiades arrives, on the calculation of how many times the length of its own feet a fly has just jumped. He would make the audience see these researches as excruciatingly innocent and amusing.

These minor points show that in the Comedy we are not dealing with an objective treatment of Socrates, and this judgment is further strengthened by the presentation of more important aspects of the subject.

Socrates is put up as a scientific materialist, and an out-and-out atheist, for whom "Zeus is no longer current coin";[2] his Trinity is "the Clouds, Chaos, and the Tongue";[3] to talk about Zeus he regards as mere drivel.[4] The Clouds, not Zeus, it is, who send rain and thunder or lightning, in accordance with mere mechanical laws.[5] For him and his retinue of "minute philosophers" heaven is an oven, and men and women merely coals.[6] Imagine the Socratics, as Aristophanes described them, a dirty, unwashed lot,[7] and their doctrine of men and women as coals must have been a most comical hit! They would look it.

All this is really as wide of the mark as can be, as the preceding study of Socrates' development and religion abundantly shows. These charges of inquiring into things above and things under the earth, the study of

---

[1] Apol., 19 b, c. d.　　[2] l. 247; cp. 1477.　　[3] ll. 424, 365.
[4] l. 367.　　[5] ll. 380 ff.　　[6] ll. 95, 96.
[7] See, e.g., ll. 504, 835.

astronomy and geology as we should now say, of not recognising the gods, and of transvaluating recognised moral values, and making the worse out to be the better, were the usual charges brought against all who went in for philosophical speculation,[1] but they were, at any rate in his case, largely unjustifiable. He transvaluated values only in the sense of seeking to bring people to a sense of the true values and proportion of life. He was not a scientist, and did not pursue scientific speculation. So he declares in the "Apology."[2] " You have spent your whole life in investigating such questions " (*i.e.* what Justice is) " and such alone," says Adeimantus to him in the " Republic."[3] The evidence of Xenophon is to the same effect,[4] and so also is that of Aristotle.[5]

As for materialism, notoriously he was dissatisfied with it. His disappointment with Anaxagoras rose out of the fact that that philosopher, in spite of his conception of Mind in the universe, continued to speak of " air, ether, water, and other irrelevancies, as the cause of things,"[6] and forgot about Mind. Nor could he find rest in the " whirl " theory of the earth's equilibrium, as put forth by Empedocles, nor in the view that it is supported and sustained by air[7] which it breathes in, in accordance with the speculation of Anaximenes. It was the cardinal contribution of Socrates to the development of Greek philosophy that he felt the impossibility of explaining the world on materialistic principles, and saw the necessity for introducing the idealistic or spiritual principle into theories of the world.

Caricature does not end there. Socrates' school is

---

[1] Plato, Apol., 23 d. [2] Apol., 18 b, 19.
[3] Rep., 367. [4] Mem., i. 1, 11 ; iv. 7, 6.
[5] Metaphysics, i. 6, p. 987 b ; A. E. Taylor, " Aristotle on his Predecessors," p. 100.
[6] Phædo, 98 c. [7] Phædo, 99 b, c.

the place to which people who want to escape their debts otherwise than by the right means of paying them, can turn to get their wits sharpened for the venture. The Notion-den, or "Reflectory," keeps two qualities of goods to suit the needs of its patrons—the Just and the Unjust Argument. These two arguments are contrary the one to the other, and under Socratic tuition in the art of handling them skilfully, one can make the Unjust triumph over the Just.[1]

It is this Unjust Argument, " the Argument which pays nothing,"[1] which old Strepsiades comes to learn, burdened as he is with the debts of his sporting and extravagant son, Pheidippides. The clod-pated old fellow, who is a sore trial to Socrates' patience, proves too dense to become a successful logical acrobat, but he learns enough to laugh at Zeus and perjury and to stand up to his son's creditors with amusing effrontery, meeting their demands with the most irrelevant and impertinent considerations. Poor old Strepsiades has had all his morality rubbed off, but he cuts the most inoffensively comical figure without it. Why should he pay his debt to Amyntas, a man who knows nothing of astronomy?[2] And why should interest accrue on a debt at all, when the sea gets no bigger though streams flow into it?[3]

Aristophanes may be getting a stroke in at Socrates' fondness for analogies. Anyhow the Athenian sage is the head and front of a movement in education to instruct people in dishonesty and humbug.

But he is held up to the audience, not only as a corrupter of the honesty and good sense and God-fearing character of the old, but also of the piety and modesty of the young. He is classed with the representatives of a new system of education, whose product is contrasted very unfavourably with that of the good old

[1] l. 117. [2] ll. 1283, 1284. [3] ll. 1290 ff.

system, on which the Just Argument descants in the following lines : [1]

"Now first you must know, in the days long ago, how we brought up our youngsters and schooled them;
When to argument just 'twas the fashion to trust, and when Virtue and Modesty ruled them.
Little boys—'twas averred—must be seen and not heard; and to school they must go all together,
Unprotected by coats, or by wraps for their throats, in the coldest and snowiest weather;
Where they learnt to repeat, in a posture discreet, all the ancient respectable ditties,
Such as 'Sound of the war that is borne from afar,' or 'Pallas, the sacker of cities';
And to render with care the traditional air, without any new-fangled vagary:
If you played the buffoon, or the simple old tune if you tried to embellish or vary,
And to show off your skill in a shake or a trill, or in modern fantastical ruses—
All you got by your trick was a touch of the stick, for the outrage you did to the Muses."

It was a favourite subject for Aristophanes' humour. In the "Acharnians" we have the chorus of old Marathon veterans making loud lament : [2]

"We whose only 'Safe Poseidon' is the staff we lean upon,
There we stand decayed and muttering hard beside the court-house stone,
Nought discerning all around us safe the darkness of our case;
Comes the youngster who has compassed for himself the accuser's place,
Slings his light and nipping phrases, tackling us with legal scraps,
Pulls us up and cross-examines, setting little verbal traps,
Rends and rattles old Tithonus, till the man is dazed and blind;
Till with toothless gums he mumbles, then departs condemned and fined;
Sobbing, weeping, as he passes, to his friends he murmurs low,
'All I've saved to buy a coffin, now to pay the fine must go.'"

[1] Trans. from Godley's Socrates and Athenian Society, p. 173.
[2] ll. 682 ff. (Rogers' trans.) Cp. Xen., Banquet, ch. iii.

In the "Knights"[1] he refers to the change coming over the youth of Athens, from the robust, sturdy, hunt-loving type, to the effeminate intellectual.

> *Demus:* "I mean these striplings in the perfume mart,
> Who sit them down and chatter stuff like this—
> 'Sharp fellow Phæax: wonderful defence:
> Concise speaker: most inclusive speaker:
> Effective: argumentative: incisive:
> Superlative against the combative.
> *S.S.:* You're quite derisive of these talkatives.
> *Demus:* I'll make them all give up their politics,
> And go a hunting with their hounds instead."[2]

The new education strikes at the roots of those admirations and traditions in which the austere greatness of Athens in the past depends. It produces a self-conceited, *nil-admirari*, devil-may-care type of youth, who has no more reverence for his father or mother than a fighting cock.

Pheidippides after a course in the "Notion-den" is not above giving his father a good beating, on the ground that it is for his good, the same ground as that on which the father claims to be justified in beating the son.[3]

Pheidippides even goes so far as to declare that, on occasion shown, he is ready to do as much to his mother. This is the last straw that breaks the camel's back. Strepsiades can stand it no longer. He is thoroughly convinced of the practical dangerousness of such revolutionary ideas; he sees home and state reeling like a whirligig to destruction; he wakes up to the realisation of what a madman he was to throw away the gods at Socrates' bidding, and rushes out in a fury, gets one of his slaves on to the roof of the Notion-den or "Reflectory," to tear it up and fling it at the amazed rogues, its inmates, below, and

---

[1] ll. 1375 ff.   [2] Rogers' trans.   [3] ll. 1410 ff.

ends by setting the whole place on fire. Socrates shouts to know what he is doing on the roof, to which Strepsiades coolly replies, in the phraseology he had learned from Socrates, so adding insult to injury: "I am treading the air, and thinking about the sun."

Socrates gasps that he will be suffocated; and Chærophon, one of the students, that he will be burnt up. Strepsiades, only concerned with conscience and repentance, regards the blaze as an atonement for the offence he has done to the gods in having denied them! It is the melodramatic climax of the play and must have sent the spectators away in roars of laughter.

Was there anything about Socrates and his doctrines to give the slightest colour of verisimilitude to the farcical scenes between Strepsiades and his young blood of a son, Pheidippides? Xenophon has told us that Socrates instilled the principles of filial piety and reverence for elders into his own children; he was very far removed from the flippant and irresponsible anarchist, and had a great esteem for social law and order. But he certainly did teach that if welfare and happiness are to be secured in the state, power and authority must not be based on any considerations but those of knowledge, proficiency, and skill. Not the measure of our years but the measure of our acquirements and abilities must be the point that determines selection to the ruling offices, and it is easily conceivable and only too natural that the ardent youths whom he filled with his ideas and in whom he created an enthusiasm to the point of "Schwärmerei," should often repeat these doctrines, and perhaps give themselves superior airs on the strength of them, though conceit was no failing of their master. Moreover, we must again insist that his position, teaching, and influence were generally identified with those of the Sophists and teachers who were classed as the "new-school," and regarded as a dangerous lot, and undoubtedly in his rationalism and criticism of conventions he incorporated the new spirit.[1]

There was just enough point in these allusions for Aristophanes to create the laugh. It has usually been assumed that Aristophanes' intention in the "Clouds" was hostile to Socrates and the new learning, but there appears to us to be no reason for such an assumption. It was simply that he found in the philosopher with his eccentricities, who was one of the most familiar figures in Athens, a rich and fertile subject for his art. As already hinted his portraiture of the gods of mythology shows anything but the piety and reverence of sincere belief in them. He was more than half converted to the scepticism whose practical effects in Strepsiades and his son he coins into farce. "He was one of those who attack in another a principle to which they themselves are committed without understanding it," says Zeller[2] with insight. It is not even necessary to suppose he did not understand it. With the shrewdness of the man of humour he may have seen, and seen rightly enough, the laxities and evils to which intellectual enlightenment may lead the populace who are touched by it. It is legitimate to fear that the loosing of old anchorages, and the losing of ancient landmarks, may set the more ignorant and undisciplined elements in a community adrift into moral evils. One may deplore such results without belonging

---

[1] Zeller has remarked that Socrates did not create the new and most individualistic spirit; it was there. But he accepted it and embodied it in himself.—Phil. der Griechen, ii., 4th edit., p. 229.

[2] Philosophie der Griechen, 2nd part, 4th edit. (1889), p. 208.

THE "CLOUDS" OF ARISTOPHANES

to the party of reaction or being hostile to the leaders of revolt.

Even a friend, given an irresistible sense of humour, might have written the "Clouds," if he had his qualms about some of the consequences of Socrates' teaching on the popular mind. A humorist among friends is like a bull in a china shop; you never know what wreckage he will make for the sheer fun of the thing. Aristophanes would know well enough that the Socrates of his piece was a lot of rot; many of his hearers, all of them who knew anything of Socrates, must have known it too. Really, it might be a parody on the ridiculousness of the popular tales current about the master's views and character.

Did not Socrates smile at the "Clouds" as he is said to have done at the "Lysis" of Plato, saying, "What a lot of lies the fellow is telling about me"?

It is also significant that Plato in the "Symposium" represents Socrates and Aristophanes as dining together at the house of Agathon like good friends, and when Alcibiades breaks in on the scene and utters his eulogium of Socrates he turns to Aristophanes and quotes a phrase from the "Clouds" as giving a glimpse of Socrates exactly as he had seen him. Now if the "Clouds" had been a painful book to Socrates and his friends, the diatribe of an enemy and written with a hostile intention, the reference to its words by Alcibiades on this occasion must have created very uncomfortable feelings in Socrates and Aristophanes, and stirred the most unpleasant recollections. It would be an artistic *faux pas*. Was Plato likely to go to a hostile play to find a description of Socrates' demeanour to quote with effect? We hardly think so. He would have hated the "Clouds" too much thus to bring it in if he had regarded it as a virulent anti-Socratic broadside. Nor if it had been one of the contributing causes to the feeling against Socrates and a factor leading to his trial and condemnation nearly a quarter of a century later, would Plato have been likely to immortalise the relations of good-fellowship between the poet and the philosopher. Fouillée's opinion is that the two had later become reconciled to each other, which is of course a perfectly possible view of the case, but the need for such a reconciliation has been assumed rather than proved, because it seems to have been forgotten that Aristophanes was first and foremost a comic poet in his Comedy.

What the "Clouds" does do is to show us the sort of opinions and judgments which were current about Socrates, and the sort of feeling with which he was regarded in unenlightened circles. It is a first-rate authority not on Socrates but on the Athenians, and so contributes more vividly than any other book, even than the "Apology," to our knowledge of the state of mind in Athens to which the great teacher finally fell a victim.

CHAPTER XII

THE TRIAL: ITS CAUSES

FROM the "Clouds" we learn that Socrates had become an object of suspicion and antipathy as a sophist and scientific student, as an unusually clever heretic who undermined the foundations of belief in the gods by his teaching, exercised a bad influence on the young by weakening the hold of the ancient conventions and pieties on their mind, and encouraging in them an intellectual conceit and sharp practice which were the antithesis of that modesty and honesty which were regarded as the ancient pillars of human welfare and social stability. He belonged to the new school of innovators in thought, who under the generic name of sophist were a synonym for all that was dangerous to the established system in thought and religion.

The Apology of Plato confirms the fact that one of the causes of the process against him lay in the opinion—the false opinion—that he "speculated about the heaven above, and inquired into the earth beneath, and practised the art of making the worse appear the better," [1] and such speculation had become identified with religious scepticism owing to the materialism which had characterised the teaching of preceding or contemporary philosophers who prosecuted physical studies.

Another cause operating against him was the hatred

[1] Apol., 23 d, e.

he roused in the breasts of all classes by his work of cross-examination and its result in revealing the general ignorance which prevailed where the pretension to knowledge was fondly cherished. Poets, politicians, artisans, he discovered to be living in a fool's paradise of dogma and make-believe—the appearance without the reality of knowledge. Now there is plenty of evidence that the Athenians were a people who enjoyed flattery and detested criticism and rebuke. Aristophanes pillories this weakness of his fellow-citizens in the humours of the "Knights," and opens out the demoralisation and danger to which it leads. Plato was thoroughly imbued with the conviction that democracy is a beast which demands that its whims and caprices be humoured and satisfied. At a somewhat later day Aristotle can still say that what the populace love is the flatterer, and Isocrates that their ire is roused by those who dare to reprove and rebuke them.

Socrates found it true in his own experience. The career in which he showed up to people the hollowness of their own mind did not prove popular with any of the classes in society. It was like the sowing of dragon's teeth from which sprang up a host of personal enemies [1] whose *amour propre* he had mortally offended. It is not pleasant to be proved an ignoramus and a fool. Socrates might try to do it very gently, he might even administer local anæsthetics during the operation, with that subtle skill which was characteristic of him, but it was still the process of drawing rotten teeth and it hurt: it left an aching void in the patient's self-esteem. Thus he had a number of private enemies who nourished resentments and who would be only too ready to seize any favourable

[1] Plato, Apol., 23 c; Theætetus, 151. Cp. Diogenes Laertius, ii. 5, 38.

opportunity of striking a blow at him, and the most prominent among them was a citizen named Anytus.

It may be that the Athenians are deserving of a little sympathy. None of us like our illusions destroyed. Schleiermacher and Gomperz have expressed the opinion that the Socrates of Xenophon's "Recollections" must have been a terrible bore, and Macaulay once wrote in his diary that "if he had treated him as he is said to have treated Protagoras, Hippias, and Gorgias, I should never have forgiven him." But Macaulay must have failed to appreciate the dry humour of Socrates in his dealings with these noted humanists.

Other factors contributed to deepen the ill-odour that hung about Socrates' name, from his classification with the new school of scientists and sophists in Athens. They were the set whom Aspasia the celebrated mistress of Pericles, the greatest statesman of the age, gathered about her, and Socrates, to whom distinctions of class were nothing at all, and who cultivated the society of all sorts and conditions, had also had access to and conversations with her. Now Aspasia represented a type of woman quite contrary to the orthodox Athenian conventions. She belonged to a class which was not respectable in Athens; she was a brilliant woman, a woman of ideas, a blue-stocking, but also the paramour [1] of Pericles, and a foreigner from Asia. The Athenians regarded her influence as immoral, and stories were told, mere gossip and scandal, of her practices more suited to the sensuality of the life of Asia Minor than of Athens.[2] Moreover,

---

[1] On this class, see Becker, Charicles, pp. 241 ff., with references.

[2] Aristophanes, Acharnians, 527, 530–9. See on Aspasia Plutarch's Life of Pericles; Sorel, Le Procès de Socrate, p. 161; Couat, Aristophane, pp. 134, 135; vindication of Aspasia—Mahaffy, Social Life in Greece, pp. 213–16.

during the period of the Peloponnesian War, secret cults of Asiatic origin and character were introduced into the city, whose influence was not salutary, and these tendencies were identified with the revolutionary movement in ideas and the new cosmopolitanism, of which Socrates was taken as the most familiar and picturesque representative, as Voltaire and Rousseau epitomised respectively the rationalism and emotionalism of France in the eighteenth century.

Again, Pericles himself, as the initiator and champion of the war policy, fell into eclipse in the admiration of the Athenians, and became an object of widespread hostility, owing to the disasters and hardships which the military operations brought in their train. Attempts were made to strike at him and his court through the prosecution of his heterodox philosophical friends, *e.g.* Anaxagoras, the feeling of the people towards whom was likely to be aggravated by the reaction towards orthodoxy which is known usually to accompany disasters in national life.

But these factors were in operation for a quarter of a century, and more in some cases, before Socrates was actually summoned to trial. Why was the fatal blow not struck till 399 B.C., when he was over seventy years of age?

The fact is that it was not merely his religious and moral doctrines, his relations to the intellectual and sceptical movement of his time, but also his political views and relationships which singled him out as a man to be got rid of. Socrates, like Carlyle, was a critic of democracy and an advocate of the aristocracy of talent. Now in 403 B.C. the oligarchical government of the Thirty came to an end, and Democracy took its place. The latter engaged the strong passions of the people, in whose memory rankled misdeeds and tyrannies, and there is no passion so headlong as political passion, unless it be the passion of religion. And for Socrates to stand up and in a calm and measured way point out the defects and stupidity of certain democratic forms, was rather more than would have been tolerated even in any Christian community we know, where feeling is running very high. To the democrats and their adherents it must have seemed like defending the hateful system they had cast out.

It was brought against him [1] that his views of the ludicrousness of appointing the leaders of the State by lot, led and could not but lead his youthful associates to despise the democratic constitution. In fact, there were those who so far misunderstood Socrates as to think that he despised the poor and mediocre commoner altogether. There was a passage from Homer often on his lips, in which we are told Odysseus used words of gentle persuasion with the best, but

"the worst whose spirits brake out in noise
He cudgelled with his sceptre, chid and said, 'Stay, wretch, be still,
And hear thy betters: thou art base and both in power and skill
Poor and unworthy, without name in Counsel or in war.
We must not all be Kings.'"

On the strength of his love of these lines, it was said he regarded the weak and ignorant as only fit for the rule of compulsion, though, as Xenophon points out, in that case he must have regarded force as the fit argument for himself. "On the contrary," however, says Xenophon, "Socrates was plainly a lover of the people, and indeed of all mankind"—violence of any kind was alien from his nature.[2]

The opinion that he was at heart an oligarch was

---

[1] Mem., i. 2, 9.   [2] Ibid., i. 2, 10.

not weakened by the fact that one of the most notorious of the hated gang of tyrants known to Greek history as the Thirty, Critias by name, as well as others of that ilk, had been of those who associated with Socrates. In the restored Democracy these connections were not forgotten and were a source of renewed hatred toward Socrates. The orator Æschines indeed declares that the Athenians put him to death as the teacher of Critias.[1]

Xenophon describes Critias, who by the way was maternal uncle of Plato, as a man of overtowering ambition who would only have been satisfied with the concentration of complete power in his own hands.[2] He brought on his return from exile (*i.e.* in 404 B.C., on fall of Athens at end of Peloponnesian War), not merely an unmeasured and unprincipled lust of power, but a rancorous impulse toward spoliation and bloodshed."[3] He was thus particularly obnoxious to the democrats. If this was the type of man and politician the teaching of Socrates had helped to produce, then he was a danger and pest to democracy and deserved some punishment. It is not difficult to understand the feelings of those leaders of the people who had been thrust into banishment by the Thirty, and among the judges who came to sit in trial upon Socrates were those who had thus suffered exile.[4] We cannot with Æschines say that Socrates was tried and put to death because of Critias alone, but these oligarchic connections were an important factor in the situation.[5]

It would be wrong, however, to suppose that the Socratic circle was drawn wholly from any one social

---

[1] Against Timarchus, § 71 (345 B.C.); Zeller, *op. cit.*, 2nd part, p. 210.
[2] Mem., i. 2, 12.
[3] Hellenica, ii. 2; cp. Grote, History of Greece, vol. viii. ch. 55.
[4] Plato, Apol., 21 a.
[5] Cp. Adam, Religious Teachers of Greece, p. 354.

THE TRIAL: ITS CAUSES 295

class or political party.[1] He was not the man to give up to party what was meant for mankind, and over against the names of Critias, Charmides, and Plato can be set those of men whose sympathies and relations were with the democratic caucus, men like Chærephon, Crito, and Lysias.[2] There was one in particular, the well-known Alcibiades, who played a peculiar rôle in public life, being a demagogue with the ambitions of a despot, and whose career threw a sinister colour over the teaching and influence of Socrates, in the mind of the Athenians.

Romance hovers with elusive wing over the story of Socrates and Alcibiades. The latter was a youth of remarkable beauty and great promise, corrupted by the evil unisexual practices of the time, and swayed by the most immoderate ambition. Xenophon calls him "the most undisciplined, overbearing, and violent member of the democracy."[3] In youth he was spoiled by the flatteries of men who lost their head over him and desired to be the object of his special regard. But there was only one man who had the power and the magnetism of personality to completely subdue Alcibiades, a man, too, of quite different spirit and ambitions from himself, and that was no other than Socrates.[4] Alcibiades would have liked to have won Socrates to love him after the flesh, but the great good man proved absolutely uncorruptible. The Symposium of Plato gives the strongest and most definite testimony through Alcibiades' own lips, that the usual uncleanness never tainted Socrates' relations with him. And that is enough. As Plutarch puts it, Alcibiades discovered to his chagrin "that this man

---

[1] Cp. Zeller, *op. cit.*, p. 223.
[2] Sorel, *op. cit.*, pp. 226, 227; Diog. Laert., ii. 5, 38.
[3] Mem., i. 2, 12; and see also Plutarch's Life of Alcibiades, *passim*.
[4] See Plato, 1st Alcibiades.

did not wish to caress and admire him, but to expose his ignorance, search out his faults, and bring down his vain unreasoning conceit. . . . Thus learning to despise himself and to admire his friend, Alcibiades, charmed with his good nature and full of reverence for his virtues, became insensibly in love with him not as the world loveth."[1]

The association with and influence of Socrates upon him was, however, temporary only, and he began to develop the characteristics which later made his career a byword for dastardliness.

Here, then, was a case to hand to the Athenians, who on other grounds suspected the dangerousness of Socrates' teachings and hated him, to illustrate his evil influence. Was Alcibiades not a glaring example and epitome of some of the very vices Aristophanes had burnt in fast colours into Socrates' teaching? Here was youthful braggadocio and insolence, irreverence for elders and superiors, contempt of religion, its gods and its symbols, here was a man who was a law unto himself, who played fast and loose with his country, cosmopolitan if you like, void of morality and patriotism, with plenty of rhetorical ability and always ready to make the worse appear the better reason to suit his own ends.[2]

In the case alike of Alcibiades and Critias, Xenophon has pointed out that the example of Socrates was altogether against their spirit and aims and ways. His humility, his contentment with his own meagre estate, his self-discipline, were obvious to all his associates. They courted his society not because they were of his spirit or partook of it, but because they wanted something of the secret of his unrivalled

---

[1] Life of Alcibiades, Steward and Long's trans. See Paul, Epistle to Romans, ch. 1, v. 27.
[2] See Plutarch's Life; Grote's History, vol. viii. ch. 66.

dialectical skill. When they got all that was likely to serve their own ambitions, they left and walked no more with him. So long as they were near him, they were kept in restraint, and their appetites were checked; it was afterwards, away from his wholesome touch and influence, that they fell a prey to their unscrupulous lusts and ambitions.

Socrates had dealt straight and fair with them. He had once tried to sting Critias out of an impure passion for Euthydemus, stigmatising it as a "swinish affection," but he only won as his reward the enmity of Critias, who in after life became a declared enemy of his previous master, and when in power sought, along with Charicles, to bridle his mouth and put a stop to his career as teacher at large.[1]

Nevertheless it was not likely that the Athenian demos, determined to strike at the new influences, which they held to be fraught with danger alike to home and city, to law and religion, would inquire too meticulously into the right or wrong of branding Socrates with blame for the character and deeds of these two men, whom they knew to have been friends of Socrates at one time. The Athenian democracy was not a very judicial body, and was readily swayed by its passions and feelings.[2]

[1] Mem., i. ch. 2. Cp. Grote, Hist., vol. viii. ch. 55.
[2] Aristophanes, Plato, and the Orators attest this. Cp. Whibley, Companion to Greek Studies, § 406.

CHAPTER XIII

THE TRIAL

AT length, under the regime of the restored democracy, the train of circumstances was fired and the explosion took place. Socrates was arraigned before the Athenian judges. "The pent-up forces of deep ill-will and sullen distrust which had long been accumulating in the breasts of his fellow-citizens now found vent in an explosion which led to one of the most tragic events which have darkened the annals of human civilisation."[1] It was in the spring of 399 B.C. that Socrates, now a man of over seventy,[2] stood before the court of the Heliastai, composed, in numbers which varied,[3] of citizens over thirty years of age. There may have been 557 or 501 of these jurors drawn from the available 5000 and assigned to this case by lot, as was the Athenian custom. "A few hundred sailors," says Fouillée, were to be arbiters in the greatest case debated in ancient times. It was before them Socrates the metaphysician had to make his defence."[4]

They were bound by oath to judge according to the laws and decrees of the Athenian people, to hear impartially both sides, and give their verdict solely

---

[1] Gomperz, Greek Thinkers, ii. p. 92.
[2] Plato's Apol., § 17 d.
[3] Grote, Hist. of Greece, vol. viii. p. 281. Gomperz, Greek Thinkers, ii. p. 98, says 501 jurors, Archon's Court. Zeller, 4th edit., p. 198 *n.*; Fouillée, Socrate, ii. p. 413, 414.
[4] Fouillée, *op. cit.*, ii. p. 415.

on the point at issue, and without fear or favour.[1] The King Archon was President of the Court. Before him all the preliminaries must previously have been gone through, such as the summoning of the accused, with the handing in by plaintiff of the plea of justification, also the hearing of statements by the accused. The Archon decided as to relevancy of the charges, and if satisfied fixed the day of trial.[1] In Court he was supported by clerks, heralds, and police, to secure that all proceeded in due and orderly course. The parties themselves must in person conduct their own case, no professional advocates being allowed as in our present day courts, although prepared speeches could be bought. The jurors were each provided with a pair of counters, one with a hole in it, the other with a thick axle, the former to be placed in an urn for the purpose, and denoting acquittal, the latter condemnation. They were provided with seats on long benches, while opposite and facing them, on adjacent platforms, stood the plaintiffs and the defendants.

On this memorable occasion the accusers were three in number, representing different sections of the community, Meletus for the poets, Anytus for the artisans and politicians, and Lycus for the orators.[2] The two former were well known and influential adherents of the democracy. The law under which the charge was brought was a decree which had been introduced by Diopeithes in order to strike a blow at Anaxagoras and Pericles, and which declared that proceedings should be instituted against all persons "who did not

---

[1] For legal proceedings, see Whibley, *op. cit.*, § 405; and cp. Tucker, Life in Ancient Athens, ch. xiv.
[2] Plato, Apol., 23 e; Diogenes Laertius, ii. 5, 38.

believe in the gods or who taught theories about things celestial."[1]

The actual charge presented against Socrates was in these terms: "Socrates is guilty of the offence of not recognising the gods of the city and of introducing other strange deities; he is also guilty of corrupting the youth. Penalty, Death."[2]

How far these charges are to be regarded as justified will be gathered from what we have already set forth in this book. We have two records, both written after Socrates' death, of how he dealt with the accusations before his judges, one known as the Apology of Xenophon, whose authorship, however, is regarded as doubtful,[3] though Dakyns, whose translation of the works of Xenophon is a thorough and painstaking piece of craftsmanship, inclines to think the "Apology" deserves the benefit of the doubt.

The other record is that which is given in the classic "Apology of Plato," which Schleiermacher, Zeller, Grote, Fouillée,[4] and more recently Gomperz (with limitations),[5] and Prof. Taylor[6] believe to give what is in the main a faithful account of Socrates' defence.

Socrates would appear to have let this crisis in his career lie very lightly on his mind. He had a presentiment that his hour was come, that at over seventy years of age it was hardly worth his while to stoop to

---

[1] Plutarch, Life of Pericles, ch. 32 (Eng. trans. Stewart and Long).
[2] See Plato, Apol., 24 b; Mem., i. 1, 1; Diogenes Laertius, ii. 5, 40.
[3] Dakyns, vol. iii. Introd., pp. 46, 47. Zeller, Sokrates and Plato (4th edit.), p. 195 *n*., is sure it is not genuine.
[4] See *op. cit.*, vol. ii. p. 417.
[5] See Greek Thinkers, ii. pp. 100, 101, and 105-8.
[6] Varia Socratica, series I, ch. 1; also Zeller, Sok. and Plato, 4th edit., 196 *n*.

THE TRIAL

defend his doctrine and character from the aspersions cast upon them, and that it were better to leave his reputation to the argument of his whole past life and the arbitrament of a future which could see him steadily and see him whole.

To the suggestion of a friend, Hermogenes,[1] that some attention to the preparation of an apology before his judges might make all the difference between condemnation and acquittal, Socrates replied that his life was his best apology, and that, in any case, his "divinity" had opposed his attempts to prepare a formal defence.[2]

Socrates had never had reason to distrust this supernatural sign, and to him it was like an indication that probably the fullness of the time had come to lay his commission at the feet of Him who had given it.

If so, God's time was the best time. Hermogenes could not quite see it in that light, and the thought that God could take away Socrates then for the best, puzzled him.

The master's reply, as given by Xenophon,[3] is one of the noblest things in literature. Never has the deep root of religion, fixed in the divine by the filaments of faith and trust, grown to the light in more beautiful resignation, repose, and dignity of soul.

"Do you find it strange," he continued, "that to the Godhead it should appear better for me to close my life at once? Do you not know that up to the present moment there is no man whom I can admit to have spent a better and happier life than mine. Since theirs I regard as the best of lives who study best to

---

[1] Xenophon, Apology, §§ 1–7; cp. Mem., iv. 8.
[2] Cp. Plato's Apol., 17 c.
[3] Taking Mem., iv. 8, as genuine, with Dakyns, why should Xenophon not have reproduced from the Apology, assuming it also genuine.

become as good as may be, and theirs the happiest who have the liveliest sense of growth in goodness; and such, hitherto, is the happy fortune which I perceive to have fallen to my lot. . . . But, if I am destined to prolong my days, maybe I shall be enforced to pay in full the penalties of old age—to see and hear less keenly, to fail in intellectual force, and to leave school, as it were, more of a dunce than when I came, less learned and more forgetful—in a word, I shall fall from my high estate, and daily grow worse in that wherein I aforetime excelled. . . . But indeed, if it is reserved for me to die unjustly, then on those who unjustly slay me lies the shame (since, given injustice is base, how can any unjust action whatsoever fail of baseness?). But for me what disgrace is it that others should fail of a just decision and right acts concerning me? . . . I see before me a long line of predecessors on this road, and I mark the reputation also among posterity which they have left. I note how it varies according as they did or suffered wrong, and for myself I know that I too, although I die to-day, shall obtain from mankind a consideration far different from that which will be accorded to those who put me to death. I know that undying witness will be borne to me to this effect, that I never at any time did wrong to any man, or made him a worse man, but ever tried to make those better who were with me."[1]

Such was the frame of mind in which Socrates stood before his accusers and judges.

In Xenophon's account he deals more directly and straightly with the definite charges against him than in Plato's. (1) On the charge of not reverencing the city's gods, he reminds his audience that it has been his habit publicly to frequent the city's altars and

[1] Mem., iv. 8, §§ 6-10; Dakyns' trans.

THE TRIAL

festivals. (2) Nor can the fact of his belief in his own divinity with its inward "Voice" be rightly interpreted as the introduction of new and strange gods, since already the Athenian people believe that the gods speak to them in the voice of thunder, of birds, and of soothsayers.[1]

He has never taken oath by any other than the recognised deities, nor named them.

(3) In reply to the charge of corrupting the youth, he asks how such a baneful effect could come from schooling them to manliness and frugality, and self-control. He appeals to his own life, well known to all, a life of freedom from appetite, of independence of spirit, and of search after whatsoever things are good —a life which has attracted to it many of those who made virtue their pursuit. He challenges them to produce examples of the youths whose religion or moderation or industry has been undermined and destroyed by his society.[2]

"Bless my soul," exclaims Meletus, "I know those whom you have persuaded to obey yourself rather than their own fathers."

This was a charge brought against Socrates which he could not and did not try to rebut. But it involves no crime, he reminds Meletus, any more than it is a crime for a doctor to take preference of one's father, when one is ill.

There are circumstances when the doctor is naturally superior in authority to the father, and so when it comes to argument and education, the superior talent of Socrates is admitted by the sons, and they turn to him. In that there is no ground of accusation.

When we turn to the defence as rendered by Plato, we find considerable differences, and in judging as to

[1] Dakyns' Works, iii. p. 188.   [2] Dakyns, p. 190.

which to prefer it must be taken into consideration that while Plato was present at the trial, Xenophon was not,[1] being in exile.

In Plato's account Socrates makes no reference to frequent attendance at the public altars and sacrifices, nor to the similarity between his divine Voice and the voice of birds and thunder and soothsayers, though one must be careful to deduce nothing from silence. Socrates may quite well have mentioned these considerations, and Plato quite well have omitted them to feed his zest on the more dialectical discomfiture of Meletus, whom Socrates corners by the process of first of all drawing him into making a more sweeping charge. Socrates gets him to accuse him of being a complete atheist,[2] treating the sun as a stone and the moon as earth, and then, quite inconsistently, accusing him also of introducing new deities and spiritual agencies not recognised by the State.

An atheist is hardly the man to introduce new gods, and Socrates suggests that Meletus is merely having a bit of fun in this trial.[3]

In reference to the accusation of being a corrupter of youth, Socrates as in Xenophon's delineation appeals for any who have been corrupted to stand forth and accuse him; or let their relatives speak out,[4] many of whom are present in court. As matter of fact, declares Socrates, it will be found that they are ready to take his side, and stand by the man accused of corrupting their sons and brothers.[5]

But Plato also gives what is not found in Xenophon, a piece of reasoning to refute Meletus' charge, which at any rate is in the genuine Socratic manner.[6]

---

[1] He was in Asia from 401-399 B.C. Dakyns' Works, vol. i, pp. lxxxvii ff.; cp. Fouillée, *op. cit.*, i. 417.   [2] Apol., 26 c, d.
[3] Apol., 27 a.   [4] Apol., 33 d.
[5] Apol., 34 a, b.   [6] Apol., 25.

It is to the effect, firstly, that in human experience we find that it is always the few who are improvers. For example, in the case of horses, just a small minority, the trainers, act as improvers of them, and not the multitude, so that it is against all analogy of experience for Meletus to be right in the assertion to which Socrates manages to commit him that he alone should corrupt the youth while everybody else does them good. Secondly, it is only common-sense to admit that everybody likes to live with good neighbours, and nobody therefore would corrupt them intentionally, while if he does so unintentionally the fit procedure to apply is correction not accusation.[1]

We can imagine the sly irony of Socrates as he thus on his very trial gives a successful display of that argumentative ability which had been one cause of his being put there by the slower-witted, respectable Athenians.

Nor does he fail to tell the judges that the real cause of the general antipathy to himself is nothing worthier than the wounded pride and envy of those whose conceit of knowledge he has effectually stabbed.[2]

Having thus dealt with the counts of the indictment, he turns to discourse on his own position before his city's tribunal in a strain of lofty self-justification and admonition.

It is no part of a good man's business to scan the chances of life or death; one care alone is his, that of doing right. "Thou doest wrong to think that a man of any use at all is to weigh the risk of life or death, and not to consider one thing only, whether when he acts he does the right thing or the wrong, performs the deeds of a good man or a bad."[3]

He himself, who faced death at Potidæa, Amphipolis,

---

[1] Apol., § 26 a. [2] Apol., 20 d–23 E. [3] Apol., 28 B.

and Delium, in his city's cause, is not the man disgracefully to quit the search of truth and the life of a philosopher which God has laid upon him. It would be a tragic thing indeed if, having given his days to bring others to wisdom, he himself should be a castaway from its portals. And what else is the fear of death but a false appearance of wisdom? For who can tell whether death may not be the greatest good that can befall a mortal? Yet to fear it, is to assume that it is the greatest of ills.

"If I should be found to be wiser than the multitude, it would be in this, that having no adequate knowledge of the Beyond, I do not presume that I have it. But one thing I do know, and that is that to do injustice or turn my back on the better is alike an evil and a disgrace. And never shall I fear a possible good, rather than avoid a certain evil. . . . If you say to me, 'Socrates, Anytus fails to convince us, we let you go on condition that you no longer spend your life in this search, and that you give up philosophy. but if you are caught at it again you must die' —my reply is 'Men of Athens, I honour and love you, but I shall obey God rather than you, and while I breathe, and have the strength, I shall never turn from philosophy, nor from warning and admonishing any of you I come across not to disgrace your citizenship of a great city renowned for its wisdom and strength, by giving your thought to reaping the largest possible harvest of wealth and honour and glory, and giving neither thought nor care that you may reach the best in judgment, truth, and the soul.'"[1]

He warns them that he will go on with his mission of examining and criticising, and pointing out to young or old, native or foreigner, that they are reversing the true values of life, despising the things

[1] Apol., § 29.

of greatest import and exalting the things that matter little.

"So God bids, and I consider that never has a greater good been done you, than through my ministry in the city.[1] For it is my one business to go about to persuade young and old alike not to make their bodies and their riches their first and their engrossing care, but rather to give it to the perfecting of their soul. Virtue springs not from possessions, but from virtue springs possessions and all other human blessings, whether for the individual or for society. If that is to corrupt the youth, then it is mischievous. But that and nothing else is my offending, and he lies who says else. Further I would say, O Athenians, you can believe Anytus or not, you may acquit or not, but I shall not alter my conduct, no, not if I have to die a score of deaths."[2]

Uproar ensued on these words in court, but Socrates appealed for a hearing, and went on:

"You can assure yourselves of this that, being what I say, if you put me to death, you will not be doing greater injury to me than to yourselves. To do me wrong is beyond the power of a Meletus or an Anytus. Heaven permits not the better man to be wronged by the worse. Death, exile, disgrace—Anytus and the average man may count these great evils, not I. A far greater evil is it to do as he is now doing, trying to do away with a fellow-being unjustly.

"O Athenians, I am far from pleading, as one might expect, for myself; it is for you I plead lest you should err as concerning the gift of God given unto you, by condemning me. If you put me to death you will not easily find another of my sort, who, to use a metaphor that may cause some laughter, am attached by God to the state, as a kind of gadfly to a big generous

[1] Apol., 30 A.   [2] Apol., 30.

horse, rather slow because of its very bigness and in need of being waked up. As such and to that end God has attached me to the city, and all day long and everywhere I fasten on you, rousing and persuading and admonishing you." [1]

As proof that he has been engaged in a divinely imposed work he cites the fact that for it he has counted his own interests and concerns as nothing, always pursuing theirs, exhorting them to virtue, and that not for any earthly reward. " Of this you have one sufficient witness—my poverty. [2] . . . Be not angry with me speaking the truth, for no man will escape alive who honourably and sincerely opposes you or any other mob, and puts his foot down before the many unjust and unrighteous things that would otherwise happen in the city. The man who really fights for justice and right, even if he expects but a short career, untouched, must occupy a private not a public station." [3]

Socrates then proceeds to give examples of that unbending integrity of conduct, that regard for right, for which as it was he ran the risk of forfeiting his life, and to which had he been a public man he would most certainly have fallen a sacrifice.

But his life has been one of conversation and teaching at the call of God in oracles, dreams, and every way by which the divine appointment has ever been conveyed to any man.[4]

Has it been a life of corrupting influence? And Socrates sweeps his eye round the court and challenges those who have seen the effects of his teaching to speak out. He mentions Crito, Critobulus, Lysanus, Antiphon, Nicostratus, Paralus, Adeimantus, Plato, Æantodorus, who are there in court, and others too

---

[1] Plato, Apol., 30. [2] Apol., 31 C.
[3] Apol., 31 E, 32 A. [4] Ibid., 33 C.

he might name, whom Meletus ought to have as witnesses for the prosecution, if they admit the truth of the charges. But no! They are with Socrates.

Such is his defence. And now it is ended. Shall he, in order to influence his judges, bring in his wife and three children, to move them with prayers and entreaties? That would be to fall from the respect due to himself, to the court, and to the state. Let there be no limelight nor melodrama. His business is not to petition his judges, but to convince them; and their business not to grant justice as a gift, but as a right. They must abide by law.

"Clearly, if I tried to persuade you and overcame you by entreaty, when you have taken the oath of judge, I should be teaching you not to believe that there are gods, and my very defence would be a conviction that I do not pay them regard. But that is far from being so. I believe in them as no one of my accusers believes. And to you I commit my cause and to God, to judge me as seemeth best for me and for you." [1]

And so with a dignity of demeanour, the expression of an inward dignity of soul which would not brook that, for the sake of life and its affections, he should veer even a hair's breadth from the truth, or lead others so to do, Socrates closes his defence and calmly waits the verdict of the court.

We can feel the quiet nervous tension of his friends amid that bustle while the votes are recorded and counted.

Then the result is declared amid a strained hush —"Guilty."

Socrates again stands forth to speak.

All this may be familiar from Plato's "Apology" and from repetition ever since. But the same may be said

[1] Apol., 35 D.

of Jesus before Pilate. Yet one is never tired of it. It can never become commonplace. They are both of those great pictures which hang on the walls of Time, which we look at again and again, only to lose ourselves in deeper and deeper enthusiasm. The gold never tarnishes with handling. It may become as familiar as a sunset and remain as glorious.

"Men of Athens, many things keep me from being grieved that you have convicted me. What has happened was not unexpected by me. I am rather surprised at the number of votes on either side. I did not think the majority would be so little. As it is the transference of thirty votes would have acquitted me." [1]

The penalty proposed in the indictment was death. But according to Athenian usage the condemned had the privilege of naming a penalty himself, and in this situation Socrates cannot resist being gravely humorous.

He suggests that the only fitting penalty is to be maintained by the state in the Prytaneum as a reward for his services to Athens, like a victor in the races. Really if he is to estimate what he deserves he has no alternative but that proposition.

He may not suggest a fine, for he has no money to pay it with; nor exile, for if he can't be endured in Athens, it is hardly likely he will be tolerated elsewhere, and to alter his life is out of the question.

"A fine life it would be for one at my age always being driven out from one city and changing to another. For I know that whithersoever I go the young men will listen to my words, just as here. If I drive them away, they themselves will have me cast out, and if I don't drive them away their fathers and relatives will cast me out for their sakes." [2]

[1] 36 A.   [2] Apol., 37 D.

THE TRIAL

To the idea that he should give up his mission he can only reply that to do so would be to disobey God. "It is the greatest good for a man to converse daily of virtue and the other subjects which you hear me discussing, examining both myself and others, for the unexamined life is not worth living."[1]

So he proposes as alternative to death the fine of a mina, which is all he can see his way to pay, but at the hurried bidding of his friends Plato, Crito, Critobulus, and Apollodorus, he finally leaves it at 30 minæ (£122), on their security.

Again there is an anxious interval while the jurors decide between the penalties—30 minæ, or the death of Socrates.

When the decision is announced, the word is "Death." Socrates must die. The man who will not stoop to plead must bear the utmost punishment of law. He "who had never wronged another," and refused to wrong himself, is not for this earth. Athens prefers to be without her prophet. Let her sons nurse their illusions; leave them undisturbed in their conceit and pride; let them keep the semblance of knowledge rather than the sense of ignorance; sham before reality, convention before truth, dogma before revelation, rest rather than progress of the mind! The penalty is Death!

Again Socrates stands forth to say his last word, before the court which has condemned him departs to home or market place, to discuss the event which perhaps they think will meet with general approval and then soon be forgotten.

The innate dignity of the man is still about him. He reminds them that they must step out of that narrow court into another, the larger, juster court of Time, Truth, the World. They have taken but little

[1] 38 A.

from his life, but they have taken too much from their own reputation. He has scorned to appeal from their verdict to their sentiment in the usual way. Nor does he regret it.

"I would far rather choose to die with that demeanour than live by adopting the other.

"O men, hard it is not to avoid death, it is far harder to avoid wrongdoing. It runs faster than death. I being slow and stricken in years am caught by the slower, but my accusers, sharp and clever as they are, by the swifter wickedness. And now I go to pay the debt of death at your hands, but they to pay the debt of crime and unrighteousness at the hand of Truth. I for my part shall abide by the award; let them see to it also. Perhaps somehow these things were to be, and I think it is well." [1]

Then he tells them that men, before death, become clothed with a prophetic gift, and he too, about to die, prophesies with all the solemnity of a man done with this world.

He tells them that in vain have they attempted to escape censure on their ways and lives, others will spring up from the seed he has sown. If he scourged them with whips, these will scourge them with scorpions. The only honourable, the only possible escape from censure on their mistaken lives, is not by suppressing their censors but by taking thought to their own amendment. "With this prophecy I am free of you who have voted against me."

Then he turns to address those who voted for his acquittal: [2]

"Friends, who have acquitted me, I would like also to talk with you about this thing which has happened, while the magistrates are busy, and before I go to the place at which I must die. Stay then

[1] Apol., 39 A, B. [2] Apol., 39 E.

awhile, for we may as well talk with one another while there is time. You are my friends, and I should like to show you the meaning of this event which has happened to me. O my Judges—for you I may truly call judges—I should like to tell you of a wonderful circumstance. Hitherto the familiar oracle within me has constantly been in the habit of opposing me even about trifles, if I was going to make a slip of error in any matter; and now as you see there has come upon me that which may be thought, and is generally believed to be, the last and worst evil. But the oracle made no sign of opposition, either as I was leaving my house and going out in the morning, or when I was going up into this court, or while I was speaking, at anything which I was going to say; and yet I have often been stopped in the middle of a speech, but now in nothing I either said or did touching this matter has the oracle opposed me. What do I take to be the explanation of this? I will tell you. I regard this as a great proof that what has happened to me is a good, and that those of us who think that death is an evil are in error. For the customary sign would surely have opposed me had I been going to evil and not to good.

"Wherefore, O Judges, be of good cheer about death, and know of a certainty that no evil can happen to a good man, either in life or after death. He and his are not neglected by the gods, nor has my own approaching end happened by mere chance. But I see clearly that to die and be released was better for me; and therefore the oracle gave no sign. For which reason, also, I am not angry with my condemners, or with my accusers; they have done me no harm, although they did not mean to do me any good; and for this I may gently blame them.

"Still I have a favour to ask of them. When my

sons are grown up, I would ask you, O my friends, to punish them, and I would have you trouble them, as I have troubled you, if they seem to care about riches, or anything more than about virtue; or if they pretend to be something when they are really nothing, then reprove them, as I have reproved you, for not caring about that for which they ought to care, and thinking that they are something when they are really nothing. And if you do this, I and my sons will have received justice at your hands.

"The hour of departure has arrived, and we go our ways—I to die, and you to live. Which is better God only knows." [1]

The picture which in the "Apology" Socrates draws of himself as the prophet of the soul and of virtue, answering closely as it does to features of his life and labour as sketched by Xenophon, has been called in question by those who hold the opinion that the master's one interest and occupation was philosophical, concerning itself with the pursuit of concepts.

"Socrates, in the latter portion of the 'Apology' assumes the rôle of an exhorter and a preacher of virtue, one who addresses all he meets—followers and fellow-countrymen alike—and tries to persuade them to take thought of their highest interests. We need not dwell on the improbability that such a Socrates should have been the original of the Socrates of the comic stage. It is enough to point out that all we know of his positive ethical teaching is in contradiction with this account of him." [2]

Gomperz's explanation is that Plato substituted as the aim and endeavour of Socrates' activity what was just an incidental consequence of it, *i.e.* spiritual awakening and moral reformation.

On the other hand, we would argue that Plato was not

---

[1] Jowett's trans.   [2] Gomperz, Greek Thinkers, ii. p. 107.

THE TRIAL

the man to do so, either as the result of confusion or deliberation. He, too, was a member of the new school, and a critic of the old authorities in Athenian morality; we cannot conceive him throwing a sop like this to Cerberus, least of all when it was too late to be of any use in saving Socrates' life, and he had quitted this mortal stage.

Moreover, there is simply no reason for refusing to admit that there was nothing to prevent Socrates being, what in our chief authorities, Plato and Xenophon, he is represented as being, both a seeker for concepts and an examiner of lives, a prophet of individual and social morality. And if he had not been the latter as well as the former, how did he come to gain the enthusiastic discipleship of Xenophon, who, according to the class of critics we are dealing with, had no capacity to appreciate Socrates on his philosophical side at all?

How also did he become not only the inspirer of a school of thought like the Megarians, but of a discipline of life like the Cynic?

We still cling, then, to the all-round Socrates of the " Apology " of Plato, and not to the pedantic recluse of the " Clouds " of Aristophanes, to the great preacher and teacher and example of noble living, as well as to the discoverer of logical processes.

All sides are dear to us, and we shall not let them go, while we have a reason for holding them. He has the homage of our mind for his logical acumen, but he has the worship of our heart for his spiritual insight, his moral greatness, and his reforming zeal.

It would hardly be right to leave the condemnation of Socrates at this point, without some attempt to understand its significance and to appraise the conduct of the Athenians to whom it was due.

The future, which is on the side of a martyr, is too

apt to confuse the just and proper appreciation of its hero with the refusal to allow any sympathy with the motives, and any mitigation of the culpability and folly, of those who have done him to death.

Christian literature has amply furnished us with this one-sided method of historical criticism. The crucifixion of Jesus has never ceased to revolt the Christian conscience which he was the chief instrument in creating. The Church has never ceased to wonder how such a miscarriage of justice was possible, and has been forced back for explanation on two somewhat unnatural considerations, the implications of which it has not usually tried to reconcile, viz., the eternal purpose of the Supreme Power, God, in human salvation, and the unrelieved diabolical wickedness and malice of Jews and Romans.

If the former ground be taken seriously it must be followed by pity rather than indignation for those who had to be its mortal instruments—the same sort of pity as we have for Clytemnestra and Orestes and Œdipus. And as for the second explanation, a fairer research and a more discriminating temper are beginning to force on us the acceptance of the view that the Jews, particularly the Pharisees who were chiefly involved, acted from conscientious religious motives, rather than from personal hatred, while the Romans in all their Christian persecutions were instigated by a regard for political loyalty and the safety and integrity of their empire.

So also with the condemnation of Socrates. Whatever personal motives may have actuated those primarily responsible, in all probability there mingled with them reasons of religion and state, which would be the chief influence in the case of Athenian jurors generally.

As we have previously pointed out, in Socrates old

traditions and present institutions were brought into direct collision with new tendencies and ideas. Democracy was to be replaced by the aristocracy of mind; patriotic sentiments rooting themselves in, and clinging about, the little city republic were to be dissolved in the wider relationships of an intellectual brotherhood which knew no barriers of city walls. The kingdom of philosophy is a universal kingdom. Moreover, in the light of the new mentality of which Socrates was the incandescent focus, the old traditional religion of the city, the religion under which it had grown to greatness, was shown up as an idol with many cracks and fractures in it; its head was not 22-carat gold, and its feet were an admixture of clay.

The free criticism of the established religious order might easily bring on the city from its gods the dreaded Nemesis of impiety, with which their literature had so ingrained the Athenians, if indeed the disasters of the Peloponnesian War were not already signs of that Nemesis.

It isn't so very long ago since the English would have pretty generally found an explanation of national calamities in the irreligiousness and impiety of the population, or some section of it. Why, did we not quite recently hear the frightful fate of the Titanic spoken of as a judgment of Heaven on luxury and prodigality? Ill fortune cows and frightens people into superstitious ideas, and so may precipitate violent reaction.

To admit that such forces played on the Athenians is only to admit that they were human and no better than Christians in the bulk. But it is also to affirm that they were no worse.

If the limits of city life, or the narrow unities of national life are an ultimate and inviolable thing, then Socratic ideas and sentiments were against the order of things, and were dealt with accordingly.

Grievously hath he sinned, and grievously hath he answered for it, and no censure can be attached to the instruments of his fate. To them, indeed, these things *were* ultimate and inviolate, for they were just average patriots.

The tragedy is that the times demanded not average patriots, but pioneers—pioneers in thought and sentiment. As matter of fact there was a broad undercurrent of free thought in the age of Aristophanes and Euripides, which would account for the long immunity of Socrates from arrest, till the end of the Peloponnesian War, with its train of calamities, which introduced a period of reaction, during which Socrates was sacrificed. But in spite of temporary reaction, we can agree with Zeller that the deeper inevitability of the age was towards a broadening beyond the limits of merely national or city consciousness, and a departure from the religious orthodoxy with which the city's traditions were bound up. In the greatness of his own personality Socrates symbolised the break up of the age of authority and the rise of the age of reason and freedom.[1] And he is not the only one whom an age and people, panic-stricken at its own tendencies, has sacrificed to a passing moment of feverish penitence and superstition.

> "They grew too great
> For narrow creeds of right and wrong, which fade
> Before the unmeasured thirst for good."

And they paid the penalty.

[1] Cp. Zeller, Phil. der Griech., ii., 4th edit., 228–31.

CHAPTER XIV

(a) THE LAST SCENES

" It matters not how strait the gate,
How charged with punishment the scroll,
I am the master of my fate,
I am the captain of my soul."

W. E. HENLEY.

AND now we turn to lift the veil from the last scenes in the life of the master. In the twilight of the far past, it is but dimly we can discern just what happened. Plato has woven wonderful discourse into those last days—a discourse of a soul that already feels itself above time and time's sorrowful delusions, and sings the melody of the immortals.

The "Phædo" is one of the greatest books in literature. In it we have divine philosophy wedded to art by the imagination of a wizard mind and through it we look on Socrates as through "charmed magic casements" in a transfigured world of thought and faith and beauty. He moves in the witchery of starlight.

But if Socrates really did discourse like that in his narrow cell, discourse of the great wide world of diviner freer life beyond the prison-gates, it must all have come as a kind of revelation suddenly after the curtain fell on the scene of his trial.

There he left the future, unknown, entirely in the hands of God, with a quiet but adequate faith. Now in the "Phædo" wave after wave of argument for the immortality of the soul when it has shuffled off this mortal coil, flows out from his illumined mind upon the doubts and scepticism of his friends. It is great discourse if the world has ever heard such; but we for our part must assign these noble affirmations and proofs to the creative spirit of that superlative philosopher, and pupil of the master, Plato.

They are so rounded, so deep sounding, so bell-like in the clearness and wholeness of their ring, that they body forth a more certain conviction and assurance than we think Socrates ever attained. It is a grander oratorio of intellect than the inner ear of Socrates ever listened to; and yet we feel that it is not far away from his mood. His life trembled on the prelude of it, hesitatingly, and Plato takes up the theme, in his own full, bold strain, weaves chords and movements of his own inspiration about it, but ever and anon letting authentic notes of the departed and beloved master fall into the swell of the larger music, to mingle with it so that instinct alone, at times, can waveringly analyse out the original voice from the composer's.

It is not impossible for a man who assumes no certain knowledge of the fate of the soul after death to allay the pain and pang in the hearts of sorrowful friends, by dwelling on all the arguments for a good hope that death does not end all, that indeed " death " is but a covered way, " which opens into light." An agnostic is not a man who sees no arguments for a certain belief, but one who also sees arguments against it. And all the circumstances would induce Socrates, in that interval of farewell between doom and death, to bring forth all that he could say for the positive view.

It does not, however, seem to us that these considerations explain the triumphant, if interrupted, march of the reasoning in the "Phædo." And, moreover, part

THE LAST SCENES

of the argument rests upon a psychology and a metaphysic which were not beaten out on Socrates' anvil, but on Plato's own. The clean dualism of soul and body, nay the conflict between the two, as of an angel and a demon from different worlds, but temporarily thrown together, the theory of knowledge, and the philosophy of ideas, are, we still believe, distinctly Platonic. The lips are the lips of Socrates, but the voice is the voice of Plato.

It so happened that when Socrates was condemned to die, a period of thirty days had to intervene ere the sentence could be carried into effect, for the sacred embassy had just set out to Delos.

The story was that Athens had to pay a yearly tribute of fourteen youths to the Minotaur in Crete, but that Theseus had slain the monster, and freed the city from this terrible sacrifice. Athens at the time vowed to Apollo that if it were so freed it would send a yearly embassy to Delos, in the ship in which Theseus was supposed to have sailed. From the moment the priest of Apollo had crowned the ship till the time of its arrival back was a holy season, during which the city must not be polluted by any public executions.[1]

Thus Socrates lay in prison for a month. "During the whole of that time his life proceeded as usual. There was nothing to mark a difference between now and formerly in the even tenour of its courage: and it was a life which at all times had been a marvel of cheerfulness and calm content."[2]

Part of his time was spent in pious and pleasant exercise of composing a hymn to Apollo, and also of turning some fables of Æsop into verse.[3]

[1] See Phædo, § 58 ; Xen., Mem., iv. 8.
[2] Xen., Mem., iv. 8 ; Dakyns' trans., cp. Phædo, 63 a–c.
[3] Phædo, 61 ; cp. Diogenes Laertius, Life of Socrates, 22.

It was somewhat of a surprise to his friends that the practised philosopher, who knew himself and his limitations so well, should thus turn amateur poet; but the circumstance and explanation are indescribably human and childlike, and give a charming glimpse of his character. He explained this whim as due to a dream he had, in which he was told "that he should compose music." He had always taken this as referring to philosophy, "the noblest and best of music," but now he had a scruple on the matter, and so took to music in the more popular sense of poetry. There is something very innocent and comic in the wise, but essentially simple-minded dialectician tempting his poetical muse to flight on the fables of Æsop in this way.

The chief occupation, however, of his days was in the dearly loved discourse.

Prison regulations in Athens were apparently in some respects very humane, and Socrates could always have his friends with him. The names of the faithful group are given by Plato.[1] They used to gather near the place where his trial had occurred, which was near the prison, and there wait till the prison doors were opened, when they entered and generally passed the day with Socrates,[2] discoursing in the old way on the high themes of human thought and quest. The near approach of death made no alteration in the occupation of the sage. Death could not find him at a better occupation than that with which his life for the last thirty years had been filled. His ordinary life was the best preparation for death he could think of. It is a fine testimony to the ordered elevation of the work of these years.

Naturally the thoughts of the little group of friends turned to the question of whether nothing could be done to save the life of this man on the verge of seventy,

[1] Phædo, § 59. [2] *Ibid.*

who had won not only their mind's reverence but their heart's love.

They at anyrate, knowing him so intimately, and able justly to appreciate his worth, felt that the future would repeal the verdict of the Athenians, and that it would be demanded of them why they had done nothing to save so great and good a man from his own indifference to life and from the temporary passion and prejudice of the populace. Something must be devised to get Socrates saved. He must be asked to effect an escape from Athens that would be comparatively easy.

But who was to make the suggestion? It must come from the one among them who enjoyed the highest esteem and consideration, for it was a delicate business to suggest any hole and corner procedure to a man like Socrates.

The natural man for the task was, of course, Crito, the most honoured friend of the master. That is no artistic touch of Plato, as Jowett suggests, but the touch of a common instinct on the part of the group of friends. The dialogue Crito gives us is what passed between the two on this matter.

At once Socrates felt it to be shady and beneath his dignity. He run away in disguise? But he knew it was suggested out of love and grief, and it gave him a fine opportunity for argument.

It is the last[1] opportunity of persuading Socrates. There are rare touches behind Plato's description. Crito is at the prison long before there is any chance of the doors being open. He can't rest. Only two days before the fatal day! It is still dark, with the sentinel stars above, and Crito is already there. He manages to get access, and we can imagine his doubt and excitement, conscious of his purpose.

He enters the cell of Socrates. All is dark, not a

[1] Crito, 44, suggests it was not the first time of advising flight.

movement. Socrates is lying on his couch asleep. Only the measured heaving of slumber is to be heard. And the man is due to die within forty-eight hours!

Crito has not the heart to disturb that rest. So he sits down to watch and wait and think.

At length the dawn is just about to break outside, and the sleeping figure moves and wakes.

"Soc. Why, what are you doing here at this hour, Crito? It must be very early.

"Crito. Yes, it's just daybreak.

"Soc. Have you just come?

"Crito. No, I came some time ago.

"Soc. Why did you not waken me at once then, instead of sitting there in silence?

"Crito. Socrates, I would not like myself to have such watch and sorrow. But I've been amazed at seeing you sleep so peacefully. And I did not wake you at once to steal away that peace. Often before in your life I have thought you happy in your disposition, but never half as much as now, that with fate so close you should take it so quietly and easily." [1]

Socrates notices in Crito's demeanour there is something on his mind, and asks him bluntly what has brought him so early.

Then Crito tells him how near the fatal day is, and pleads with him to consider his friends, and their grief at the prospect of his loss, to consider what people will say of his own (Crito's) apparent indifference to secure his friend's escape from death. Yes, he and others besides are ready to put anything he has at Socrates' disposal.[2]

He pleads with him through his sense of duty "to wife and children"—the hardest argument against a good man.

But Socrates waves all such considerations aside.

[1] Crito, 43.   [2] Ibid., 45.

How his conduct will appear to superficial crowds matters nothing to him. How would a wise man judge it? To do what the crowd approves and does was never his way.

Is it right or is it wrong, that's the question. Consequences, aye though they be death, don't count.

And so Socrates weighs the alternatives in the strict balance of conscience. The Athenians may have done him wrong; their law may be unjust to him, but " no man may render evil for evil, or retaliate."[1] " Never is it right to ward off wrong with wrong."

It has always been his principle to be obedient to the laws, to treat them as sacred: to them he owes that order and society which alone makes a man's own life and personality worth anything. His residence in Athens was a contract to be loyal to the laws of Athens. Besides, what is the good of him at his age uprooting the practice and profession and good name of a lifetime? And what has any other town or city to offer him, when Athens has refused him?

All through this argument the " Laws of Athens " are personified, and it is their voice which speaks and suggests these considerations, their last word being:

" ' Listen, Socrates, to us who have brought you up. Think not of life and children first, and of justice afterwards, but of justice first, that you may be justified before the princes of the world below. For neither will you nor any that belong to you be happier or holier or juster in this life, or happier in another, if you do as Crito bids. Now you depart in innocence, a sufferer and not a doer of evil; a victim not of the laws but of men. But if you go forth, returning evil for evil, and injury for injury, breaking the covenants and agreements which you have made with us, and wronging those whom you ought least to wrong, that is to say,

[1] Crito, 49.

yourself, your friends, your country, and us, we shall be angry with you while you live, and our brethren the laws in the world below, will receive you as an enemy; for they will know that you have done your best to destroy us. Listen, then, to us and not to Crito.'

"This is the voice which I seem to hear murmuring in my ears. Like the sound of the flute in the ears of the mystic; that voice, I say, is humming in my ears, and prevents me from hearing any other. And I know that anything more which you may say will be vain. Yet speak, if you have anything to say.

"CRITO. I have nothing to say, Socrates.

"SOC. Leave me then to follow whithersoever God leads." [1]

So ends the "Crito."

Socrates then deliberately prefers to die, and his associates probably spoke no more on the subject of flight.

The next scene Plato gives us [2] is on the morning of the day of his deliverance from earth.

A number of his associates, Athenians, and from other cities, have as usual come early to the prison. When they arrive the jailer tells them to wait, for the Eleven are with Socrates, "taking off his chains and giving orders that he is to die to-day."

When they are allowed to go in, they find Socrates with the chains off, and Xanthippe, his wife, sitting beside him, with their child in her arms. She had been a shrew, and had given him many a scolding, but we doubt not, though rather coarse of grain, she had loved him deeply in her own way. Diogenes Laertius relates that when she had heard the news of his condemnation, she said "You will die unjustly"; to which, with his usual humour, he only replied, "Would you rather have me die justly." [3]

---

[1] Jowett's translation.   [2] Phædo, § 59 ff.
[3] Diogen., ii. 5, § 35.

When the friends entered whom perhaps she had never regarded as much else than a set of idlers with a bee in their bonnet, a melting emotion coursed through her, and she turned to her husband, " O Socrates, this is the last time you will speak with your friends or they with you."

Socrates looked over to Crito and said : " Crito, let someone lead her away home."

Some of them then led her away crying and beating her breast.

Then Socrates, sitting up on his couch, bent his leg up and began to rub it, delivering himself the while of some reflections on the psychology of pain and pleasure. Still the philosopher!

And now we pass to the last solemn events of the tragedy, lightened up only by the unquenchable cheerfulness and good humour of the central figure.

And one or two little traits we must not miss ; they are so truly of the man, and doubtless fond reflection recalled them and dwelt on them again and again. We would feign believe them historical, though if anyone chooses to regard them as only the fineness of Plato's realistic art, we must even let him think so.

Crito who, as already said, holds a special place and relation to Socrates, having been under his guardianship, and acting for him in all personal affairs requiring delicacy and confidence, a sort of paternal relationship to this great man, who at fully seventy is still the absentminded philosopher, the child—Crito, seeing he is going to fling himself into an argument with the wellknown alacrity and zeal of the tireless hunter of concepts, gets restless and fidgety, and when he has got Socrates' attention, tells him that the attendant has said that if he gets heated with debate it will interfere with the action of the poison he has later to drink, in which case he may have to take it twice or three times. The officer has been rather insistent to Crito on the point, being doubtless a bit excited by the stern duty which lies before him. But Socrates dismisses the warning abruptly as rather a nuisance. "Give him my compliments, and tell him to be ready for his duties, which is to administer it twice, or, if that won't do, three times." And then on he goes with his lofty reflections on the philosopher's life and death.

Another incident reveals the man.

Socrates has been moving along in the debate with great *éclat*, a sort of triumphal procession of intellect, the disciples looking on as usual with profound admiration. Then comes a point when Simmias and Cebes seem to shiver all his fine constructions, and a feeling of compassion and unpleasantness seizes on the little group.

Socrates, too, is feeling the shock of the argument, and apparently needs time to marshal his broken forces again. There he sits on his couch, with Phædo a little lower, on a stool just down at his right hand, and he is playing with his young and enthusiastic admirer's hair, stroking it down against his head and neck. "He had a way of playing with my hair," says Phædo. It's a fine little natural touch. Then he looks down at the lad, and says, in a few simple words in which pathos meets jest hiddenly.

"To-morrow, perhaps, Phædo, you will cut off this beautiful hair."

"It seems so, Socrates," I said.

"Not if you listen to me," said he.

And Socrates goes on to advise him to cut off the glory of his hair in sorrow for the slain argument, unless it can be brought back to life. If it cannot, Socrates too will cut off his hair along with Phædo on the morrow.

The delicate play of pain-touching humour in this

little episode is perfectly exquisite; it is a smile Socrates casts through the "lachrymæ rerum" in Phædo's heart to lighten them for a little. It is exquisite.

Then he proceeds to warn the young men against the temptation to become sceptics in regard to reason, because they may be called on sometimes to admit they have come to wrong conclusions. Pessimism and cynicism may come from pitching one's expectations too high in regard to men and things. Disappointment of our trusts, miscarriage of our efforts, must not lead us to give up the search for truth and reality. It was this frame of mind at a difficult moment that raised Phædo's admiration to enthusiasm.[1]

The high discourse came to an end, and Socrates rose and went into the bath-chamber, Crito with him.

When he had taken his bath, his three sons and women-folk were brought to him, and he spoke with them for a little, and gave them some directions, in Crito's presence. Then they went away, and Socrates returned to where his friends awaited him.

While he had been absent at the bath the sense of the greatness of their loss came upon his faithful friends more than ever. "He was like a father of whom we were being bereaved, and we were to pass the rest of life as orphans."

Sunset was drawing near, and little was said. Each sat with his thoughts.

The jailer entered, the man from whose hands Socrates was to receive the hemlock cup, one who, perhaps, had done that stern duty often enough before, and who was not to be easily touched with emotion. But now the callousness of officialdom for once was broken,

[1] Phædo, § 89.

and this rough jailer became a man again, at the contact with one supremely great soul.

"Socrates," he said, "I shall not have to complain of you as I have of others, that they vent their anger and curses on me when I give them the poison at the command of my superiors. I have found you in your time here the noblest and gentlest and best man that has ever been in this place, and I know you will not be angry at me, but at those who are the cause of this. And now you know my errand, good-bye, and try to bear as lightly as you can what must be."

And with that he burst into tears and turned to go away.

And Socrates, looking up at him, said: "And you, good-bye; I'll do as you bid."

And then addressing his friends: "What a gentleman he is. All the time we've been here he would come to me, and sometimes he conversed, and was the best of fellows, and how fine of him to weep for me. But now, Crito, the poison, if it is prepared. If not, let him get it ready."

The rest had better be told in the words of Plato, translated by Jowett:

It was the hour when the sun was just resting on the western sea, the hour of richest colour, when the glow is on the world, and ere the grey of twilight wraps all things in its still melancholy.

Socrates had asked that the cup be given to him; he is done with the world and there is no call to delay further his exit from its little stage. He will away to the land beyond the river.

"Crito made a sign to the servant, who was standing by, and he went out, and having been absent for some time, returned with the jailer carrying the cup of poison. Socrates said: 'You, my good friend, who are experienced in these matters, shall give me directions how I am to proceed.' The man answered: 'You have only to walk about until your legs are heavy, and then to lie down and the poison will act. At the same time he handed the cup to Socrates, who, in the easiest and gentlest manner, without the least fear or change of colour or feature, looking at the man with all his eyes, Echecrates, as his manner was, took the cup and said: 'What do you say about making a libation out of this cup to any god? May I, or not?' The man answered: 'We only prepare, Socrates, just as much as we deem enough.' 'I understand,' he said, 'but I may and must ask the gods to prosper my journey from this to that other world—even so—and so be it according to my prayer.' Then holding the cup to his lips, quite readily and cheerfully he drank the poison. And hitherto most of us had been able to control our sorrow, but now when we saw him drinking, and saw, too, that he had finished the draught, we could no longer forbear, and, in spite of myself, my own tears were flowing fast, so that I covered my face and wept over myself, for certainly I was not weeping over him, but at the thought of my own calamity in having lost such a friend. Nor was I the first, for Crito, when he found himself unable to restrain his tears, had got up and walked away, and I followed; and at that moment, Apollodorus, who had been weeping all the time, broke out in a loud and passionate cry which made cowards of us all. Socrates alone retained his calmness: 'What is this strange outcry?' he said. 'I sent away the women mainly in order that they might not offend in this way, for I have heard that a man should die in peace. Be quiet then, and have patience.' When we heard that we were ashamed, and refrained our tears; and he walked about until, as he said, his legs began to fail, and then he lay on his back, according to the directions, and the man who gave him the poison now and then looked at his feet and legs, and after a while he pressed his foot hard, and asked him if he could feel; and he said 'No'; and then his leg, and so upwards and upwards, and showed us that he was cold and stiff. And he felt them himself, and said: 'When the poison reaches the heart that will be the end.' He was beginning to grow cold about the groin, when he uncovered his face, for he had covered himself up, and said (they were his last words)—he said: 'Crito, I owe a cock to Asclepius, will you remember to pay the debt?' 'The debt shall be paid,' said Crito; 'is there anything else?' There was no answer to this question; but in a minute or two a movement was heard, and the attendants uncovered him; his eyes were set, and Crito closed his eyes and mouth.

"Such was the end, Echecrates, of our friend, whom I may truly call the wisest, and justest, and best of all the men whom I have ever known." [1]

Diogenes tells that when he was about to drink the poison, Apollodorus offered him his own finer mantle to die in. "Why," he replied, "is my own cloak fit to live in and not to die in?" [2] True or not, it gives the spirit of the man.

We have followed till its close the life of Athens' sage. He drank the poison and awaited its fatal action with the hopeful dignity and quiet which he felt befitted death and himself. He rebuked his grief-stricken friends for bursting into tears and weeping. Even Crito had not been able to restrain himself, but with that perfect feeling which existed between them and the philosopher, he had moved away a little, to give vent to his sorrow apart.

He knew Socrates' exquisite delicacy of feeling for just the fitting thing, a feeling which had led him to cover himself over when he drank the hemlock.

[1] Jowett's trans. [2] Diogenes Laertius, ii, 5, 35.

THE LAST SCENES

Touches like these draw us to Crito; all who love Socrates must love his lover, him who would have given anything to save him, and whose hands performed the last affectionate office of closing his eyes and mouth. Blessed indeed the heart which felt that love, and the hands which did that act. So long as the name of Socrates shall be reverenced, so long will this deed be spoken of as a memorial to him. On him, the great heart, broken for its greatness, leaned for the fulfilment of whatever earthly duties were due by it. Crito was the confidential friend and agent. To him Socrates was "beloved Socrates."[1] It was he who sat and watched and wondered while the great man, with death hanging over him, slept, as a child sleeps. What *he* thought of Socrates and felt towards him was not for words or comments. They were of the deep things for which there is no speech.

(*b*) And now, in conclusion, we wish to gather a few of the tributes of reverence and appreciation, which others who were inspired by his influence and touched by his lordliness and goodness, have paid to him.

First comes Plato, with the noble gift of the grandest works of human thought within our ken. The glorious creations of his superlative mind he gives as his tribute to Socrates, at whose feet he had sat—who had first opened to him the doors of the infinite world of thought.

No sentence of appreciation even his great art could have coined can equal in impressiveness the fact that in all his dialogues the chief figure is Socrates.

To have won that distinction, and the admiration out of which it sprang, is colossal proof of the real greatness of Socrates' mind, and the no less real admiration of his greatest pupil.

It is to Plato we owe also the testimony put into

[1] Crito, § 44.

the mouth of the brilliantly gifted but loose-principled and erratic Alcibiades, in whose heart there seems to have gone on a tussle between the better and the worse, the ideal and the sinful, such as later tore the inner life of young Augustine for many years in Carthage, the pull of an ardent enthusiasm for the pursuit of knowledge and wisdom against the perilous lust of the flesh and the evil pride of life. In the case of Augustine the good won, in that of Alcibiades the worse prevailed, and he left the company of Socrates to pursue the path of worldly ambitions.

Agathon was celebrating with friends his victory in the competition with tragedies, and the company were extemporising speeches on love, when in burst Alcibiades, drunk, and roystering, his head decked with ribands, which he brings to transfer to the head of Agathon.[1]

Suddenly he sees Socrates, and asks for some of the ribbons back wherewith to "crown the marvellous head of this universal despot . . . who in conversation is the conqueror of all mankind."[2]

And then he launches into an eulogy of the "universal despot," which, drunk as he is, he yet declares to be only the sober truth.

"I shall praise[3] Socrates in a figure which will appear to him to be a caricature, and yet I do not mean to laugh at him, but only to speak the truth. I say, then, that he is exactly like the masks of Silenus, which may be seen in the statuaries' shops, sitting with pipes and flutes in their mouths; and they are made to open in the middle and have images of gods inside them.

"When we hear any other speaker, even a very good one, his words produce absolutely no effect upon us in comparison, whereas the very fragments of you and your words, even at second hand, and however imper-

[1] § 212.   [2] § 213.   [3] § 215.

fectly repeated, amaze and possess the souls of every man, woman, and child who comes within hearing of them. I have heard Pericles and other great orators, but though I thought they spoke well, I never had any similar feeling; my soul was not stirred by them, nor was I angry at the thought of my own slavish state. But this Marsyas has often brought me to such a pass that I have felt as if I could hardly endure the life which I was leading; and I am conscious that if I did not shut my ears against him, and fly from the voice of the siren, he would detain me until I grew old sitting at his feet. For he makes me confess that I ought not to live as I do, neglecting the wants of my own soul, and busying myself with the concerns of the Athenians; therefore I hold my ears and bear myself away from him. And he is the only person who ever made me ashamed, which you might think not to be in my nature, and there is no one else who does the same. For I know that I cannot answer him or say that I ought not to do as he bids, but when I leave his presence the love of popularity gets the better of me. And therefore I run away and fly from him, and when I see him I am ashamed of what I have confessed to him. Many a time have I wished that he were dead, and yet I know that I should be much more sorry than glad if he were to die: so that I am at my wit's end."[1]

The close of the "Memorabilia" sums up Xenophon's appreciation:

"Amongst those who knew Socrates and recognised what manner of man he was, all who make virtue and perfection their pursuit still to this day cease not to lament his lot with bitterest regret, as for one who helped them in the pursuit of virtue as none else could.

"To me, personally, he was what I have myself

[1] Jowett's translation.

endeavoured to describe: so pious and devoutly religious that he would take no step apart from the will of heaven; so just and upright that he never did even a trifling injury to any living soul; so self-controlled, so temperate, that he never at any time chose the sweeter in place of the better; so sensible, and wise, and prudent, that in distinguishing the better from the worse he never erred; nor had he need of any helper, but for the knowledge of these matters, his judgment was at once infallible and self-sufficing. Capable of reasonably setting forth and defining moral questions, he was also able to test others, and where they erred, to cross-examine and convict them, and so to impel and guide them in the path of virtue and noble manhood. With these characteristics, he seemed to be the very impersonation of human perfection and happiness."[1]

We may also quote the concluding words of the "Apology," which has come down to us as from his pen:

"For myself, indeed, as I lay to mind the wisdom of the man and his nobility, and can neither forget him nor, remembering him, forbear to praise him. But if any of those who make virtue their pursuit have ever met a more helpful friend than Socrates, I tender such an one my congratulations as a most enviable man."[2]

And further, this fine testimony:

"He never hurt a single soul either by deprivation of good or infliction of evil, and never lay under the imputation of any such wrong-doing."

Phædo, in the dialogue of Plato of that name, gives us what he may be taken to have felt about Socrates while the latter was lying in prison waiting his end.

"I was affected in a wonderful way in his company.

---

[1] Dakyns' Works, vol. iii. pp. 181, 182.
[2] Dakyns, iii. 195.

No feeling of pity entered my mind as one would expect, being present at the death of a friend, Echecrates. He seemed to me happy in his mien and in his conversation, and he died so fearlessly and nobly, that I could not but believe that the divine hand was in it leading him to the gates of the Beyond, and that his lot would be blessed when he arrived there if ever man's was. And so no regret seized me as one would have expected at such an extremity." [1]

Here we too, with joy at the gift of such a man and such a life, take our leave of Socrates.

[1] Phædo, 58 e.

INDEX

"ACHARNIANS, THE," of Aristophanes, 10, 283, 291 *n.*
Adam, 235; on Socrates' prayers, 240
Æschines, 275, 294
Æschylus, "Agamemnon," 92; 214, 215
Agathon, 334
Alcibiades, 40, 295, 334
Alopece, parish of, 9
Amphipolis, Socrates at, 103, 305
Anaxagoras: studied by Socrates, 22, 30; Mind in the Universe, 30; fails to apply the principle, 33, 281; 299
Anaximander, 28
Anaximenes, 28, 281
Antisthenes: Socrates on, 58; on work, 148
Anytus, 299
Apollodorus, 311, 331, 332
"Apology" of Plato, its historical value, 300; tribute to Socrates, 336
Apuleius, "De Deo Socratis," 216, 250
Archelaos, a teacher of Socrates, 22, 86
Aristarchus, Socrates' conversation with, 143
Aristippus, 86, 196
Aristocracy of Talent, 163
Aristodemus, 208
Aristophanes, *see* "Clouds"; on the Gods, 225–227; corruptions of sacrificial system, 237; on contemporary prayer, 238, 239
Aristotle, 7, 38, 127, 155, 176, 180
Aristoxenos, 41
Asceticism and Socrates, 49 f.
Asclepius, 332

Aspasia, 23, 291
Athenians, the: their conduct to Socrates, 316, 317; Freethought among, 225, 318; superstitious element, 317; compared with Christians, 317
Audition, 250
Authorities, for Socrates, 5–8; their incompleteness, 6; its causes, 7; their comparative worth, 8

BECKER's "Charicles," 11, 47, 63, 65; 84; 291
Bennett, Arnold, quoted, 142, 190
"Birds" of Aristophanes: on Socrates' personal habits, 46, 47; 65, 226, 227
Body, the, Socrates' care for, 52
Boeckh, "Public Economy of Athens," on Socrates' circumstances, 61, 62; cost of living in Athens, 67
Bury, "History of Greece," quoted, 102; on Xenophon as historian, 133

CAMPBELL, Lewis, "Religion in Greek Literature," 215, 228
Carlyle, quoted, 1; Socrates compared with, 116; on work, 146, 200
Chærecrates, 151
Chærephon, 111, 285, 295
Charicles, 297
Chesterton, G. K., quoted, 171, 172
"Clouds" of Aristophanes, 8; on Socrates' appearance, 38; personal habits, 48; view of woman indicated, 74; Socrates and science, 127, 128; Socrates' religion in, 221; 264;

INDEX

273 ff.; interpretation of, 277, 286–288; its treatment of Socrates, 277, 278; value of its portraiture, 278 ff.
Common-weal as motive, 201, 202
Connus, tutor of Socrates, 148
Couat's " Aristophane " quoted, on cost of living at Athens, 67; Greek houses, 63; 103, 227, 273
Courage defined, 181, 182
Criterion, the, in Morality, 204, 205
Critias, 294, 297
Crito, 295, 308, 311, 323, 327, 329, 331, 332, 333
Critobulus, Socrates' conversation with, 152, 241, 308, 311
Cross-examination, Socratic, 112; example of, 175

DÆMON, the, (Divine-sign) of Socrates, 110, 250; a constant monitor, 251, 313; a peculiar experience, 251; its negative function, 251; not the voice of Conscience, 251; represents a special communication of God, 252; its interpretation, 253 ff.; its general significance, 262
Damon, a tutor of Socrates, 23
Definition, Socratic, 176; its influence on Plato, 177
Delium, Socrates' conduct at, 102, 306
Delphic Oracle on Socrates, 111
Demetrius of Phalerum quoted, on Socrates' circumstances, 61
Democracy of Athens: its character, 108, 109; Socrates on, 120; Aristotle, Aristophanes, Socrates, and Plato's view of, 290, 297
Democritus, 29
Demosthenes quoted on marriage, 71
Design in the World, 209; Design and Modern Science, 209, 210
Diogenes Laertius, 6
Diopeithes, 299

Domestic Economy in Athens: houses, 63, 64; meals, 65, 66; cost of living, 66, 67; wages, 67
Döring, 7, 189, 200, 242

ECHECRATES, 331, 332
Education in Athens: elementary, 14 ff.; advanced, 17 ff.
" Electra " of Euripides, 74
Emerson quoted, 159
Empedocles of Acragas: his teaching, 29; 281
Enemies, treatment of, 150 ff.
Equality, Socrates' view of, 116 ff.
Erasmus: quoted on Socrates, 2
Ethics, his sole interest in manhood: Plato on, 125; Xenophon on, 127; Aristotle on, 127, 174, 176. *See also* under Teaching
Eupolis, "Fragments," 279 *n*.
Euripides, "Electra" quoted, 74; on theology, 228; Socrates' influence on, 101

FARNELL, " The Cults of Greece," 214, 215
Fouillée: on the Dæmon of Socrates, 257, 267; 278; on Plato's " Apology," 300
Fox, George, Inner Light, Trances and Voices, 249, 261
Friendship: Socrates' passion for, 88 ff.; his philosophy of, 90 ff.; 154
"Frogs" of Aristophanes, 66, 227
Fustel de Coulanges, 17

GOD, Designer of Nature, 209; His beneficence, 209, 212, 230; All-seeing, 211; Omniscient, 211; Omnipresent, 212; His righteousness, 212, 213; a Spiritual Being, the Mind of the Universe, 209, 211, 212; His Moral Goodness, 213; monotheism or polytheism comparatively unimportant to Socrates' trust in God, 239; reveals His Will in Visions and Signs, 248, 249, 250; Special Revelation, 252
Gomperz, 40, 71, 75, 93, 185, 187

Good, the, 194 ff.; variations in Men's ideas of, 194; the Good and pleasure, 194; relative Goods, 198; the criterion of, 204, 205
Grote, "History of Greece," 41, 54, 297.; his "Plato," 71, 92

HAPPINESS, 200 ff.; Happiness an activity, 203; of Socrates, 301
Hereafter, the, 267 ff.; Agnostic attitude, 267, 306, 314; not an evil, 268, 313; Socrates' optimism and trust, 269, 313
Hermogenes and special intercourse with the gods, 264, 301
Hesiod, 16, 49, 147
Hieronymus the Rhodian, 68, 69
Holm, "History of Greece," 105
Homer, 16, 293

IDEAS, relation of Socrates to Platonic Theory of, 177, 178, 179
Individual and State, 163 ff.; Joël quoted, 165; Socrates no anarchist, 166; his social sense, 167; his individualism, 166, 171, 172

JAMES, William, 190, 216, 259
Joël, 120; on Socrates as Rationalist, 133, 141; Cynic influence on Xenophon, 148; 153; 240; on the Dæmon, 253
Judicial procedure at Athens, 298, 299
Jury at Socrates' trial, 298
Justice defined, 182, 183

KANT, his maxim of conduct, 151
"Knights," the, of Aristophanes, 103, 226, 284, 290
Knowledge and Virtue, 179 ff.; supremacy of, in conduct, 192
Knowledge of Self, 33, 113, 122

LAMPROCLES, Socrates' son, 68
Legends of the gods, Socrates' distaste for, 223, 224
Leucippus, 29

Love, Socrates' philosophy of, 96–99; dangers of carnal love, 93 ff.; Socrates, the apostle of a pure love, 99, 100, 295; his love of all men, 293
Lycus, 299
Lysias, 295

MACAULAY, Lord, quoted, 37, 39, 87, 135, 247, 291
Mahaffy, "Social Life in Greece," 291 *n*.
Market-place of Athens, 84, 85
Marriage in Athens, 71 ff.; Demosthenes on, 71; Xenophon on, 71
Marsyas, 335
Martineau, 210
Materialism of pre-Socratic philosophy, 30; Socrates' dissatisfaction with, 30, 281
Meletus, 299
"Memorabilia" of Xenophon, date of, and value, 6
Minotaur, annual tribute to, 321
Monotheism, tendency to, in Greek literature, 214 ff.; Homer, 214; Æschylus, 215; Aristotle, 215; survival of lesser cults, 216; Socrates' position, 216, 230; compared with modern Christians, 231
Murray, Gilbert, quoted, 19, 101, 225
Myrto, daughter of Aristides, 68, 69
Mysticism of Socrates, 113–115, 244–246
Mythology, the Greek, Aristophanes' treatment of, 225–227; Plato's, 228; Socrates', 229

NOTE-BOOKS in Greece, 7

OPTIMISM, religious, of Socrates, 211; as to death, 269, 270, 301, 312, 313

PANÆTIUS, quoted by Plutarch on Socrates and Myrto, 69
Parmenides, 21; his teaching, 29
Passion in Socratic ethics, 187 ff.
Pausanias, 19

INDEX

Peloponnesian War, 9, 10; introduction of Asiatic cults during, 292
Pericles, 10, 14, 23, 292
Phædo, the; Socrates and science, 25 ff.; the philosophic life, 50; value of the "Phædo" on Socrates, 50, 51, 319, 320
Phænareté, mother of Socrates, 9; her character, 9
Philosophy and common life in Socrates, 144
Piety of Socrates, 219–221, 231 ff.; current ideas of, criticised by Socrates, 232, 233; it must be based on knowledge, 234; Döring quoted, 242
Plato, 7; his theory of Ideas, 177, 178
Pleasure and virtue, 186 ff.; pleasure and The Good, 194 ff.; Socrates not a Hedonist, 195, 197; qualities of pleasure, 197
Plutarch, "Lives" of, 6; on Socrates' looks, 39; on Socrates' circumstances, 61; Socrates and Xanthippe, 77; 296; "Moralia" of, 247, 251
"Plutus," the, of Aristophanes, 13 n., 237, 238
Potidæa, Socrates' conduct at, 102, 305
Prayer, 238 ff.; contemporary forms of, satirised by Aristophanes, 238, 239; prayers of Socrates, simplicity of, 239; his faith and trust in God, 240
Prison: Socrates' demeanour in, 321; his occupations in, 321, 322; free conditions of, 322
Prodicus of Ceos, a tutor of Socrates, 24; "Choice of Heracles," 49
Protagoras, on Socrates' gifts, 24
Pythagoras, on sacrifice, 235

"REFLECTORY," the (or Notionden), 282
Reformer, Socrates as, (1) in morals, 93–99; Zeller and Sorel's views, 99; (2) in politics, Joël's and Döring's views, 120; Xenophon cited, 121
Relativism in morals rejected, 204–207
Religion: in Greek home life, 12–14; the foundation of Socrates' character, 208; Socrates' sympathy with established cults, 217; comparative unimportance of rites and doctrines, 217, 218; Socrates a conformist, 219; inner experience, 244, 247, 252
Revelation of God, its modes, 248–250, 252, 308; special revelation, 252, 264
Revenge: Xenophon's testimony, 152; reasons for doubting it, 152, 153; Socrates opposed to, 155 ff. "Apology" and "Crito" quoted, 156; "Gorgias" quoted, 157; "Clitophon" quoted, 158; conclusion from, 159
Reverence for Laws, 168
Robertson, F. W., 242
Rousseau, "Emile" of, 51
Rulers, need of Science in, 164

SACRIFICE: Socrates' teaching on, 234 ff.; its meaning, 234; its value lies in the right spirit, 234, 235; Pythagoras cited, 235; sacrifice and forgiveness, 236; corruptions of the system, 236, 237; the value of Socrates' teaching, 237
Saint-Beuve, 148
Scepticism, contemporary with Socrates, 225 ff.
School: in Athens, 14; elementary curriculum, 15, 16; objects of education, 17; advanced curriculum, 17 ff.
Science: Socrates' passion for, in youth, 21, 26; need of Science in public officers, 117 ff.; need of Science for conduct, 124; Physical Science given up by Socrates for ethical, 125–129

Self-discipline, necessity of, to virtue, 188 ff.; *self-reverence* of Socrates, 307
Silenus, 334
Sin, doctrine of, 184 ff.; Plato and Aristotle quoted on, 185; possibility of sin, 191
Smith, Sydney, 51
Society, its basis, 162. *See under* Teaching
Socrates—
 advanced education, 20 ff.
 Anaxagoras studied, 30 ff.
 anecdote of Crito, 21
 appearance of, 36 ff.; Aristophanes on, 38; Xenophon's "Banquet" on, 39; Alcibiades in the "Symposium" of Plato on, 40; "Phædo" on, 40
 compared with Robert Burns, 24
 date and place of birth, 9
 dissatisfaction with Contemporary Science, 26, 30
 enthusiasm of, for Science, 21, 26; for knowledge, 22, 112, 130
 home training, 12–14
 Humanism of, 33
 knowledge of our ignorance, 33; knowledge of Self, 33, 113, 122, 123
 mental powers, 24
 parentage, 9
 parents' circumstances, 9, 10, 11
 philosophy, his vocation, 34
 school-life, 14 ff.
 teachers, 21, 22
 teleology, 32
 testimony of Protagoras, 24
His character—
 attention to the body, 51, 52
 Christian spirit, 153, 336
 courage in battle, 102, 103; in public life, 104, 105, 106, 107, 108
 geniality and humour of, 39, 40, 42, 56, 57
 happiness of his life, 53, 54, 336
 humility, 112, 131
 irony of, 112, 118, 119, 131
 love of all mankind, 293
 loyalty of, to Athens, 104, 167, 168
 personal habits, 46, 47, 48, 55, 56
 religious optimism and trust in God, 211, 269, 270, 301, 312, 313
 self-mastery of, 42, 49; its purpose, 54; 93 ff., 102
 self-reverence of, 307
 Socrates and Asceticism, 49 ff.
 unselfishness of motive, 42, 43, 45
Domestic Circumstances, 61 ff.; Boeckh on, 61, 62; Demetrius of Phalerum on, 61; Plutarch on, 61; Xenophon on, 61
 abstinence from Politics and its causes, 108–110
 apostle of a pure Love, 99, 100
 apostle, the, of Reality, 116, 132, 134, 135
 Club-life, 95, 96
 compared with Johnson, 86
 death of, 330–333
 Equality, view of, 116
 ethical mission, 136 ff., 273, 306, 314, 315
 haunts of, 83, 84
 home, 65
 influence of, and its causes, 2–4
 intellectual mission, 112, 115
 love of city, 86, 167
 love of men and books, 87
 mysticism in Socrates, 113–115
 oligarchy, regarded as sympathetic with, 292, 293 ff.
 on the vice of carnal love, 93 ff., 96
 Passion for friendship, 88, 89
 philosophy of Love, 96–99; Zeller on, 99; Sorel on, 99
 Prison, 3, 319 ff.; his demeanour in, 321, 324; occupations in, 321, 322; refuses to escape, 325, 326
 prophet of the Inward Life of Reason, 133, 142, 150

INDEX

Socrates (continued)—
  rationalist, as, Gomperz and Joël referred to, 133
  relations with Myrto, 68, 69
  sense of natural beauty, 87
  significance of, 1, 2, 318
  Socrates as social reformer, Joël's and Döring's views, 120; Xenophon cited, 121
  Sophists, Socrates regarded as one, 275; his respect for, 275; similarities of, with Socrates, 276
  view of the family, 80, 152
  Xanthippe, his wife, 76 ff.
  Trial, the—
    dignity of demeanour, 309, 311
    its causes, 289 ff.
    optimism, 313
    reply to charges, 302, 303, 304
    Socrates' frame of mind, 301, 302
    the process, 298, 299
  Tributes to—
    by Alcibiades in "Plato," 334
    by Phædo in "Plato," 336
    by Plato, 333
    by Xenophon, 335-336
Sophist, Socrates regarded as, 275, 291; similarities of, to Socrates, 276; 17
Sophroniscus, 9
Sorel, quoted, 99, 128, 264, 275, 278
Soul, the, its value, 266; its Divine nature, 266; its functions, 267; immortality of, 267 ff.
Spencer, Herbert, 17
Stevenson, Robert Louis, 146
Subliminal self and Dæmon of Socrates, 259, 260
" Supernatural," the, 258, 260

TAYLOR, A. E., 7; Socrates and dying to live, 55; 69; 124, 128 on Socrates' relation to Physical Science; 152, 264, 275, 300
Tauler, mystic, on work, 149

TEACHING: (*a*) *Ethics*
  Conflict of popular judgments, 173
  Good, the, 194 ff.
    The Good, its criterion, 204, 205
    The Good and Happiness, 200 ff.
    The Good, and Pleasure, 194; Socrates not a Hedonist, 195, 197; qualities of pleasure, 197
    Rejection of Relativism in Morals, 204–207
    Subordinate and relative Goods, 198
    The Good and Utility, 198 ff.
    The Good, and Well-doing, 200; common-weal, 201, 202
  Passion in Socratic Ethics, 187 ff.
  Search for Universals by cross-examination and definition, 174-176
  Self-discipline, necessity of, 188 ff.
  Sin, involuntary, 184; its possibility, 191
  The *Virtues:* Courage, 181, 182; Justice, 182, 183; Piety, 234
  Virtue is knowledge (or wisdom), 180; Virtue and Pleasure, 186 ff.
(*b*) *Religion:* Design in the World, 209; God, His nature and perfections, 211–213; monotheism and polytheism in Socrates, 216; belief in minor deities and spirits, 222; distaste for legends of gods, 223, 224; purification of theology, 229; on sacrifice, 234 ff., see under Sacrifice; prayer, 238 ff., and under Prayer; revelations of the gods, 248–250, 252; the Dæmon, 250 ff.; views as to its interpretation, 253 ff.; not the leader of a cult, 264, 265

TEACHING: (c) *Society*: Mutual service its basis, 162; aristocracy of talent, 163; individual and State, 163 ff.; Socrates' social sense, 167; reverence for Laws, 168; unwritten Laws, 169 ff.; his individualism, 166, 171, 172
(d) *The Soul*, doctrine of, 266 ff.
(e) *The Treatment of Enemies*, 150 ff.; his Humanitarian principle, 151; family quarrels, 151; Christian spirit, 153, 159–161; Joël referred to, 153; 155 ff.; revenge: Xenophon quoted, 152; reasons for doubting him, 152, 153; *Revenge*: Socrates opposed to: "Apology," "Crito," "Gorgias," "Clitophon" on, 156–158; conclusion, 159
(f) *On Work*, 143 ff.
Athenian view of work, 145 conversation with Aristarchus on women's work, 143, 144
nobility of work, 146, 148, 149
Teleology, need of, 32, 209
Thales, 28
Theology, Aristophanes' treatment of, 225–227; Socrates' influence on, 229
Theseus, 321
Thoreau, 44
Thucydides, 10, 102, 103
Trance-like absorption of Socrates, 244–246
Trial, its causes: Socrates' speculation, 289; offence of cross-examination, 290; identification with Sophists, 291; circle of Aspasia, 291; political causes, 292 ff.; Critias and Alcibiades, 294, 295; justification by Xenophon on last point, 296, 297

Trial, the: the charge against Socrates, 300; the Authorities, 300; Socrates' reply, 302, 303, 304; the procedure, 298, 299
Tributes to Socrates, 333 ff.
Tucker's "Life in Ancient Athens," quoted, 63, 64, 299

UNDERHILL, Evelyn, quoted, 114
Unjust argument, the, 282
Utility and The Good, 198 ff.

VIRTUE, definition of, 180, 181
Visions sent by the God as signs, 248, 249; Tertullian and Paul quoted, 248; George Fox, 249

WELL-DOING, the Good, 200
Whibley's "Companion to Greek Studies," quoted, 64, 65, 89, 299
Wise man as moral standard, 205, 206
Woman in Athens, 69 ff.; Xenophon's views on ideal wife, 71, 75; woman's position, 73; Aristophanes' "Clouds" referred to, 74; Euripides' "Electra," 74; Themistocles quoted, 75
Work, *see under* "Teaching of"

XANTHIPPE, Socrates' wife, 60, 76, 77, 326, 327
Xenophanes of Colophon, 29
Xenophon: dates of Life, 6; his "Memorabilia," 6; his "Banquet," 7, 56, 57; a disciple of Socrates, 101; tribute of, to Socrates, 335, 336; Prof. Bury on, 133

ZELLER, 54, 99, 163; on the Dæmon, 255; on Plato's "Apology," 300; 318
Zeno, 21
Zimmern's "Greek Commonwealth" quoted, 63
Zopyrus, 40

Printed by BALLANTYNE, HANSON & Co.
at Paul's Work, Edinburgh